CONSTANT
BATTLES

St. Martin's Press New York

CONSTANT
BATTLES

The Myth of the Peaceful,
Noble Savage

Steven A. LeBlanc
with Katherine E. Register

www.stmartins.com

ISBN 0-312-31089-7

First Edition: April 2003

10 9 8 7 6 5 4 3 2 1

To Laura Lee Stearns
for her long and valued support

CONTENTS

ACKNOWLEDGMENTS   ix

PROLOGUE: Finding Warfare in All the "Wrong" Places   xi

chapter one
Warfare and Ecology: Myth and Reality   I

chapter two
Was There Ever an Eden?   23

chapter three
Enter Conflict   55

chapter four
Our Earliest Past   77

chapter five
Warfare Among Foragers   100

chapter six
Conflict and Growth Among Tribal Farmers   128

chapter seven
Complex Societies   157

chapter eight
War or Peace for the Future?   199

NOTES   231
LIST OF ILLUSTRATIONS   245
REFERENCES   247
INDEX   265

ACKNOWLEDGMENTS

Long before this book had come together in my mind, while my thoughts on warfare and ecology were evolving and not yet fully formed, I was teaching archaeology at UCLA and then came to the Peabody Museum of Archaeology and Ethnology at Harvard. At both universities I have had the good fortune to interact with several scholars who not only gave me important insights into relevant issues but forced me to think more carefully about my own ideas.

Fortunately, there are some very politically "noncorrect" biological anthropologists at Harvard. In fact, some might even call them "fanatical sociobiologists." Among these, Richard Wrangham and his students, especially Michael Wilcox, stand out. They and the milieu they have created for discussion have been very helpful. At UCLA, Dwight Read, a mathematically oriented anthropologist, had been wrestling with some of the same issues I was grappling with but was approaching them from a very intriguing perspective. He and I spent considerable time trying to understand the implications of a more realistic approach to human competition and population growth. His questioning of my thoughts and the ideas of others did more than anything else to focus my own thinking. And finally, it was Lawrence Keeley's important book *War Before Civilization* that made me aware I was not alone in refusing to ignore the reality of warfare in the past and its significance in the lives of ancient people.

This effort has been a collaboration with my wife, Kathy Register, who not only made my original writing readable but whose constant questioning enabled me to convert my academic jargon and orientation into a book that will, I hope, be accessible to a wider audience. She, as well as our sons Bryan and Nathan and my sister Grace, was willing to cope with me for several years while I was researching and writing.

We both would also like to thank Fred Register for his valuable critique of early drafts of this manuscript, and I also appreciate the help of Christine Hastorf, Jeff Carr, Tom Cummins, Irv and Nancy DeVore, Gregory Finnegan, David Frayer, Martin Muller, Robert Gardner, Robert Ganong, William Iseminger, Marshall Weisler, Patty Jo Watson (who directed or codirected many of the field projects I worked on), and Richard Watson.

My thanks also go to Gene Stokes, who over the years has accompanied me on some of my explorations and provided insight into matters of warfare. The staff of the Peabody Museum of Archaeology and Ethnology and the Tozzer Library at Harvard have been exceedingly helpful in a variety of ways. And, finally, I most especially thank my editor, Diane Reverand, who encouraged me to undertake this endeavor.

PROLOGUE

FINDING WARFARE IN ALL THE

"WRONG" PLACES

*W*ar today and in the last century seems unprecedented in intensity, ferocity, and the numbers of lives claimed. With this ominous cloud hanging over our heads, it's easy to believe that humans have somehow abandoned the benign behavior that characterized our earliest history. What happened to those "noble savages" of old who were content to live in peace and harmony and were not out to colonize and exploit the undeveloped world? The ecological catastrophes occurring all around us present another modern maelstrom—and no ecosystem is immune, from the oceans to the tropical rain forest, from the pristine Arctic to the ozone layer. Humankind today seems to have abandoned a reverence for nature and lost long-held abilities to live in ecological balance. Has "progress"—that escalating desire to be bigger, better, faster, stronger—totally extinguished our ancestral instincts to grow everything we consume and hunt only what we need to sustain us? Many view the march of civilization not as a blessing but as a curse, bringing with it escalating warfare and spiraling environmental destruction unlike anything in our human past.

Contrary to exceedingly popular opinion, and as bad as our problems may be today, none of this is true. The common notion of humankind's blissful past, populated with noble savages living in a pristine and peaceful world, is held by those who do not understand our past and who have failed to see the course of human history for what it is.

I am an archaeologist. I have spent my career attempting to make sense of the past, and I find a world completely at odds with popular misconceptions. Not only is the past I observe not peaceful and pristine, but, cruel and ugly as it may be, it provides great insight into the present. The warfare and ecological destruction we find today fit into patterns of human behavior that have gone on for millions of years. Humans have been destroying their environments for a long time and continue to do so for the same reasons they did in the past. Much of today's warfare reads just like the warfare of tens of thousands of years ago—the same causes, the same tactics, and the same attitudes. Careful study of the past can provide us with a much more clear understanding of the causes of and reasons for modern warfare and ecological imbalance not evident simply by trying to make sense of the present without a context. As such, this proper grasp of the past has invaluable benefits for humankind today. We are far better off understanding the past than ignoring it, or believing a mythical version of history that bears little resemblance to what actually took place.

A myth, due to its very nature, is not grounded in any reality, so is susceptible to total manipulation. Though we can manipulate reality, it is subject to objective questioning, because we presume there is an objective basis to it. Once we accept a myth as truth without any consideration of its reality, how do we question its implications or manipulation on objective grounds? Myths are dangerous, and we are better off without them. My purpose here is to debunk some of the most prevalent myths my profession and the general public have about human history. My hope is that we can look objectively at these intensely emotional issues and their implications.

If I am right, then why have archaeologists and historians not been telling us of these truths? I believe it is not just the general public that misunderstands the past, but also most scholars who study it. While my purpose here is not to rail against my colleagues, it is impossible to ignore the fact that academia has missed what I consider to be some of the essence of human history. The past has been sanitized, and the recorders of history have often cast humans as having lived in ecological and peaceful bliss. This is simply not true, but why do I see what so many of my colleagues have missed? For one thing, the past is elusive and not always easy to observe.

I have undertaken archaeological fieldwork in many different locations on several continents, on sites from very different time periods. During the last thirty-odd years, I have worked on digs as a student, as a regular member of the crew, or as the director of multiyear projects. After all this time as an archaeologist, I have only recently come to realize that wherever I have dug, regardless of the time period or place, I have discovered evidence of warfare. I have excavated sites in the eastern United States, the Middle East, Peru, and two areas of the American Southwest, and each of these projects yielded evidence of warfare—once I bothered to look for it. These observations have been directly bolstered by visits to dozens of other ongoing excavations.

I never chose to join these projects or selected the sites to excavate with the purpose of finding warfare. The evidence just turned out to be there—or at least *I* think the evidence was there. Most of my archaeological colleagues don't see warfare as often as I do. Some never see it anywhere, and others see it only occasionally—and usually not on the sites or time periods with which they are working. Other archaeologists see the evidence for warfare but dismiss it as not being of any real interest. Their attitude seems to be, "Sure, there was some warfare in the past, but it was incidental and inconsequential, and had virtually no impact on human history." How do I square these attitudes and assessments of some very good archaeologists with my own observations? This prevalence of warfare—is it my perception, or is it reality?

Even though my theories have been met by a fair amount of scholarly resistance over the years (and that's putting it nicely), I have been compelled to ponder the question, Just how common was warfare in the past? I have finally concluded that warfare was *quite* common in the past, and that my findings on three continents and within multiple time periods were not a fluke but the norm. This led me to reason that if conflict *was* common, then it must have been an important occurrence in the course of human history. In short, I decided that I wasn't seeing things that did *not* exist; instead, my colleagues were ignoring things that *did*.

From this confluence of ideas came the realization that not only was I dealing with a major misunderstanding about human conflict in the past, but that there had been surprisingly little scholarly effort devoted to trying to understand *why* there was so much warfare throughout human history. Part of this may well be because these scholars simply don't know how much warfare existed in the past, but it is also because they have chosen to ignore most of the warfare they do know about. As I began to work through these ideas, I realized that if we misunderstand the past, then we also misunderstand the present, because humans automatically compare the present with how we think things were in the past—be it the weather, taxes, or what constitutes a "basic" education. Yet misunderstandings between the past and the present can be dangerous. My hope is that this book—with its sometimes harsh and cruel implications—will clear up some of these misconceptions.

We are much better off understanding the reality concerning warfare and human ecology, and getting this right is very relevant to understanding how humans became humans and how we function as humans. A thorough comprehension of this history must in some way enable us to better understand ourselves today. Could warfare in the distant past have ever been worse than it has been the last century? At this very moment, we are destroying the rain forest, depleting the seas, and possibly changing the world's climate. Does this mean we no longer know how to live in harmony with nature? The answer to both these questions is, not necessarily. Only history can tell us if we are getting more warlike or more peaceful, and whether we are becoming more or less ecologically in balance. And history provides a surprising answer.

Since the beginning of time, humans have been unable to live in ecological balance. No matter where we happen to live on Earth, we eventually outstrip the environment. This has always led to competition as a means of survival, and warfare has been the inevitable consequence of our ecological-demographic propensities. The question that remains is whether humans are genetically programmed to be this way. Or do we have the ability to change the fundamental human-environmental relationship that not only has been with us for millions of years but in many ways has made us who we are today? I hope to show that though our history has been far less peaceful and pleasant than most of us are comfortable hearing about, our past does not doom our future. We humans are doing better than we realize. This may come as cold comfort to a world filled with warfare and plagued by ecological disasters, but I believe that a careful reading of human history—our real and very long history—shows that the opportunity for positive change is great.

What I present here combines archaeology, ethnology, ecology, history, and primatology. All these disciplines require subtle and detailed analysis and interpretation, and by necessity I do not go into all the nuances and alternative interpretations they warrant. I hope the reader will appreciate not getting bogged down in such arguments, and I will suffer the criticisms of the experts.

I was hard-pressed to present these theories in both a historical and sociological framework that the general reader could follow. I decided to lay out a broad scheme of human history, using chimpanzees as an analogue for our very early human history. This analogue is imperfect but extremely revealing about our past. I then focus on the million-plus years that humans lived without farming—the majority of our history—under the social organizational concept of *foragers*. And finally, I break up the remaining era of human history—which began with agriculture—into three concepts: *tribes, chiefdoms,* and *states.* This formulation, which is hardly original and admittedly oversimplified, enables me to combine archaeological and ethnographic examples from around the world and provide some insights into how human ecology, human demography, and warfare have evolved in tandem. It also provides a means to bridge the past with today. As the reader will see, much of the modern world continues to live more like the tribes and chiefdoms of the past than contemporary city dwellers. And much of the warfare today is more like past tribe- and chiefdom-level warfare than the high-tech wars of the modern era.

I try throughout to provide enough archaeological and ethnographic detail to allow a real feeling for these ancient societies to come through. In the span of about a century and a half, modern scholars have learned a great deal about the human past, a surprising amount, given how hard it can be to figure some of this stuff out. I believe that learning about our long and exceedingly complicated human past satisfies far more than just idle curiosity, and I hope I have been able to apply to today's world the knowledge of the ancient world that only the earth can reveal.

STEVEN A. LEBLANC
CAMBRIDGE, MASSACHUSETTS
AUGUST 2002

chapter one

WARFARE AND ECOLOGY:
MYTH AND REALITY

*N*ew Mexico's El Morro Valley, like the entire American Southwest, is one fantastic archaeology lab. The dry climate of Arizona, New Mexico, and the southern parts of Utah and Colorado leads to unusually good preservation, allowing archaeologists to trace the path of early humans in the region back thousands of years. El Morro, situated at an altitude of seven thousand feet along the Continental Divide, is a vast, semiarid series of sandy plains broken up by huge rocky outcrops, called mesas, that periodically erupt out of the landscape and dominate the horizon. Today, this is Zuni country, but in the ancient past it was home to the Anasazi ancestors of such present-day pueblo people as the Hopi, Zuni, and Acoma.

Some of the largest Anasazi archaeological sites in the Southwest are located on top of El Morro's mesas. Ponderosa pines now cover the slopes and sagebrush dots the valley bottoms but, as the archaeology shows, corn, beans, and squash once grew on the valley floor. Life as a farmer would have been possible in El Morro in the past, but precarious. Winters were (and are) cold; an early frost or a heavy summer hailstorm could destroy an entire year's crops. When the Anasazi lived in the valley, it may have been a bit more hospitable, but today no one could survive as a corn farmer there.

In the early 1970s, my colleagues and I began doing archaeological field-work in the El Morro Valley and discovered seven very large prehistoric pueblos, all dating from around A.D. 1275 to 1325 and housing upward of one thousand people each. Two of these communities were located on mesa tops that were not easy to reach. Surrounded by two-story-high unbroken outer walls, the villages were perched on steep-sided mesas. Both the way the villages were laid out and where they were located suggested that military defense most certainly was an aspect of their construction. This defensive posture was impossible to miss—they could have seen an enemy coming from miles away. Even a sneak attack would have been almost impossible on a village situated four hundred feet up on an isolated outcrop. Other communities we uncovered within the valley were fortresslike constructions with equally high outer walls.

That warfare, or some sort of intergroup conflict, was a possibility among the Anasazi that we mentioned in our National Science Foundation grant proposal, but it was neither of much interest to myself or my colleagues nor was it deemed important by academia at that time. NSF had given us funding to figure out what these seven-hundred-year-old communities farmed and hunted, the impact of climate change, and the nature of their social systems—not to look for warfare.

Within a few days of beginning our fieldwork, we discovered a site that was burned to the ground and from which the people had clearly fled for their lives. Pottery and valuables were left in place on the floors, and bushels of corn still lay in the storerooms. As our research progressed through that summer, we eventually determined that this site was burned and abandoned, and that immediately afterward a large, much more defensive site was built in its place nearby. The building stones had been removed from the earlier site and used rapidly to construct its replacement. The earlier site comprised individual, single-story houses somewhat spread out around the area. The replacement site consisted of apartmentlike rooms with adjoining walls that formed a solid rectangle one hundred yards across with unbroken outer walls two stories high—in other words, a fortress. The evidence indicated that something catastrophic had occurred at this ancient Anasazi settlement, and that the survivors had almost immediately, and at great speed, set about to prevent it from happening again.

As we continued our fieldwork, the role warfare played in the lives of El Morro's early inhabitants slowly percolated into our awareness. Several other villages we excavated also had abandoned their nondefensible houses and built "forts," including the ones on the mesa tops. We began to consider how the inhabitants of one village may have attacked another village. One group, which had built its community against a cliff for protection, had cut a hole through the cliff wall in order to see potential attackers coming. Our research team still continued to think along the traditional anthropological ideologies of the day: that the explanations for the *really* significant events in the valley would be found in the form of new social organizations, or in the effects of drought or other climate changes.

Thirty years ago, we archaeologists thought warfare may have existed, but we considered it almost irrelevant—and certainly not central—to our understanding of past events and people. Today, scholars are coming to realize that the evidence my colleagues and I uncovered in the El Morro Valley was part of a process that led to warfare throughout the entire Southwest, with attendant massacres, population decline, and areal abandonments that forever changed the way of life in the region.[1]

It took more than twenty-five years, and a great deal of additional fieldwork and library research, for me finally to change my initial naive view of the past and of humans in general. My take on warfare is now very different from what it was. Though these new ideas about conflict seem exceedingly obvious to me, I arrived at these conclusions not by means of abstract theory, but by being forced to look at warfare based on conclusive evidence I found in the ground. The central importance of warfare throughout human history came to me slowly, prompted by archaeological fieldwork in a number of different regions and reinforced as I tried to reconcile theoretical positions that became increasingly impossible to accept.

Why couldn't I—or any of my colleagues—see the magnitude and the implications of the warfare that was displayed before our eyes at El Morro? We were simply not conditioned to see it. The idea that all was peaceful long before writing in the ancient past was, and is, how most archaeologists and anthropologists see the world. The prevailing scholarly view is that warfare was of little social consequence in the past and is relatively unimportant in understanding the human condition. Though in the last three decades more archaeologists are prepared to see warfare for what it is, there continues to be an institutional reluctance within anthropology and archaeology to ignore or discount evidence for conflict among past societies. And that reluctance goes back to the eighteenth century.

Academics are not the only ones with these views. For a variety of reasons, almost everybody seems to be preoccupied with the idea that all was peaceful in the hundreds of millennia of the human past.

Why don't all archaeologists see the clear evidence for warfare? When I ask archaeologists if they think warfare occurred in the prehistoric past, they always say, Yes. When I ask if it was a major component of the lives of the people they are studying, they almost always say, No. The reluctance among archaeologists to see warfare occurs because they have an important human trait: empathy. If you spend years in the desert in a dig camp where, even with all our modern technology, keeping the camp functioning is a major effort, you cannot help being impressed with the ingenuity, skills, and determination of the ancient people you are studying. Hacking your way through the jungle to reach the remains of a great city with beautiful murals and inscribed stela leaves you with a sense of awe and amazement of the accomplishments of these long-gone people. They become *your* people.

As the archaeologists begin to understand those ancients, they become attached to them. "My People" could not have had warfare. The reluctance to see warfare for what it is also derives being politically correctness. Archaeologists and ethnologists have an audience. The audience wants to hear about peace and not about warfare. When most archaeologists find evidence for warfare, "their people" must have been defending themselves against some nasty people from somewhere else. Defensive warfare yes, never offensive warfare. This natural and admirable human propensity to see the achievements of the peoples whose history archaeologists recover results in a false and incomplete history and a major misunderstanding of our past.

A very recent example of this reluctance to accept evidence of past conflict can be found with Ötzi, the Ice Man. In 1991, hikers in the Alps came across the frozen body of a man more than five thousand years old. Nicknamed Ötzi, this individual caught the fancy of the world, most especially Europeans, and his miraculously preserved tools and clothes—even the contents of his stomach—were subject to intense scrutiny by scientists. Ötzi carried a variety of items with him, including a bow, a quiver of arrows, a stone dagger or knife and, most unexpectedly, a hatchet with a copper blade. Prior to this find, scholars had thought such copper tools had not been used in this part of Europe until many hundreds of years later. Among anthropologists, much speculation was given to how Ötzi had died. The most popular explanation was that he was a shepherd and had fallen asleep and frozen to death in a snowstorm. Another possibility put forth was that Ötzi was a trader and was crossing the Alps "on business," so to speak. Either way, a sad but peaceful scenario for his death was assumed by scholars and was broadly accepted.

Little was made of such details as the fact that the hatchet Ötzi carried lacked wear marks, indicating that it had never been used to chop a tree, and that the copper from which it was fashioned was probably too soft for chopping. Everything changed in the summer of 2001, when new X rays revealed that Ötzi had a fatal arrowhead still in his chest. According to the Ötzi Web site, the earlier explanations for the Ice Man's demise were wrong.

It seems obvious to me that Ötzi had been shot in the back and died from warfare, like many of his contemporaries in the late Neolithic period of Europe. His "hatchet" was most likely a battleaxe, and he was armed to the teeth. It needn't take an arrowhead embedded in bone to suggest the obvious. For one thing, anthropologists and historians know that the battleaxe was a preferred weapon for hand-to-hand combat in Europe from 6000 B.C. to A.D. 1000. In fact, many of Europe's social groups—the

Franks, Saxons, and Lombards, for example—were named after the distinctive close-combat weapons they traditionally carried.

In spite of a growing willingness among many anthropologists in recent years to accept the idea that the past was not peaceful, a lingering desire to sanitize and ignore warfare still exists within the field. Naturally, the public absorbs this scholarly bias, and the myth of a peaceful past continues. If one analyzes popular culture, such views seem to dominate our outlook of the past. For example, it was the "cowboys" who decimated the Indians. (True, but the Indians fought fiercely among themselves long before the encroaching Euro-Americans arrived.) Or it was the "white man," including North African traders, who terrorized the native Africans. (This is also true, but the Africans, too, had previously warred for millennia.) The Chinese desire for exotic woods and spices from the tropics changed traditional relationships among the people of Southeast Asia, leading to intense conflict in places like the Philippines. (Yes, but the region was far from peaceful in earlier times.)

Just how pervasive is this idea that peace prevailed in the past, or that scholars ignore the warfare before their eyes? Think about some of the most cherished and popular "wonders" of the world. Such famous tourist attractions as China's magnificent Great Wall or Greece's beautiful Acropolis are actually evidence of warfare.[2] China's wall was obviously constructed for defense, but consider the frequency and intensity of the warfare threatened by Mongol and Manchu horsemen to have compelled the Chinese to devote so much human labor and sacrifice to create a fifteen-hundred-mile-long wall of such massive proportions. The Acropolis was originally occupied as a walled Mycenaean fortress town. Only many hundreds of years later did it became a temple area. The view is certainly fine and the breezes delightfully cool at the top of that steep hill, but again, constructing a fortified town with walls built of massive multi-ton stone blocks at the top of such a promontory was no mean feat—nor was it an easy or convenient place to live. What tourist comes away from the Acropolis with the idea that in fact, the Mycenaeans (the pre–Classic Greek contemporaries of fabled Troy) fortified almost all their palace towns, and warfare was, in reality, as commonplace and intense as the *Iliad* portrays?

Even more evidence of warfare is found among the paintings at Lascaux and other caves in France and Spain.[3] These earliest known human artworks feature magnificent renditions of bison, mammoth, and deer but also include sticklike human figures with spears projecting into their bodies. Somehow, descriptions of these less-than-harmonious sides of the world's wonders don't often make it into the travel brochures. There is a failure to

This photo of the Dani people of Highland New Guinea, taken in the early 1960s, shows what seems to be a chaotic melee characteristic of tribal farmer warfare, and even a minor rain shower can cause this warfare to cease for a day. This has led many to not consider this to be "true war," yet the proportional death rate exceeded that of either World War.

look for or see evidence of warfare because of a myth and the preoccupation with the idea that the past was peaceful.

In its simplest form, this misconception portrays humans as peaceful by nature and considers them to have been so for millions of years. This notion assumes that for much of human history people lived in nonviolent societies and maintained pleasant, helpful, symbiotic relationships with their neighbors. While there surely were bellicose periods, war was not the norm or a constant threat. Popular belief also holds that only after the development of "civilization," or highly complex societies, did things begin to change. The common assumption is that only when these increasingly more complex societies spread, and in particular when European civilization came to dominate much of the world through colonizing, was warfare introduced (and induced) to the far corners of Earth. This is the impression one comes away with when reading many books on how we became human and who wound up where on Earth. Such an impression misses the essence of human history.

Most people today would admit that, of course, there was *some* conflict in the past, but the presumption is that it was occasional. Many still believe that only if the impact of civilization is minimal or nonexistent can examples of the peaceful life way that had existed for millennia be found. Warfare in popular culture and much of academia is perceived as a plague spreading and infecting innocent, "primitive" peoples who had previously been spared the scourge of intergroup conflict.

Even when this myth of a peaceful past can be overwhelmingly dispelled, as it can be for recent prehistory (that is, the last ten thousand years or so), popular assumption remains that things were generally peaceful during the *previous* several million years. The discovery by Jane Goodall and her coworkers that our closest relatives, the chimpanzees, are *not* peaceful came as a surprise to most scholars, rather than a predictable expectation.

Now, it's one thing for me to claim that warfare was heavily represented in the sites and places in which I have done fieldwork, but just because I have seen warfare in my own work does not automatically mean it was common everywhere. If a peaceful past is a myth, warfare should be in evidence in almost all times and places. Obtaining a clear picture of the real prevalence of early warfare often requires intense research because of the confounding effect of European impact on traditional societies before they were well studied. The sciences of anthropology and archaeology rely on three main evidentiary sources. The archaeological record includes artifacts, architectural plans, and environmental information, such as ancient pollen or animal bones from meals, derived from digging. Or it can simply be a matter of locating the prehistoric sites where people lived and studying the patterns of these sites over the landscape.

Anthropologists look for evidence by using information found in historical documents, including written accounts by early explorers or visitors to a particular region. Or they turn to the accounts of ethnographers, professionals, usually anthropologists, who study a community or culture by living among them for a period of time. Generally, archaeological evidence is all scholars have from ancient people who left no written records; thus they are "prehistoric." Of course, such people had oral histories (that is, histories that are usually not available to us), and some even had writing, for example the Indus Valley civilization, which is still lost because the writing is not yet deciphered.

Looking for evidence of early warfare usually focuses on the archaeological record and the very first written accounts of societies. These early accounts almost always show evidence of warfare, even when anthropologists often a hundred or more years later found peace. When there is a good archaeological picture of any society on Earth, there is almost always also evidence of warfare. It does not seem to matter whether people live on islands: The small islands of Micronesia, such as Palau, are covered with forts. Or lived in harsh climates: Both the Australian Aborigines of the desert and the Eskimo of the Arctic had lots of war. Or the lush climate of Hawaii, where warfare was endemic from soon after it was settled. Some of this conclusion has been summarized by Lawrence Keeley, author of *War Before Civilization*, who makes this very point.

Keeley's most telling observation is that in many traditional societies from which such information could be obtained by ethnographers—the people of highland New Guinea or the Yanomama of the Venezuelan rain forest, for example—25 percent of adult males died from warfare well into the middle of the twentieth century. Such a high fatality rate from warfare is found archaeologically as well, although it is harder to get similar estimates. I have visited excavations in the presumed peaceful Southwest where men had been scalped, the heads of enemies taken as trophies, and entire villages massacred with the bodies left unburied. Twenty-five percent of deaths due to warfare may be a conservative estimate. Prehistoric warfare was common and deadly, and no time span or geographical region seems to have been immune.

We need to recognize and accept the idea of a nonpeaceful past for the entire time of human existence. Though there were certainly times and places during which peace prevailed, overall, such interludes seem to have been short-lived and infrequent. People in the past were in conflict and competition most of the time. Which groups prevailed and survived, and how people interacted with their neighbors, had great impact on the way we humans organized our societies, how we spread over Earth, and why people settled where they did. Today in parts of the world, things are much the same—war is a constant and critical part of their lives. These wars are not an aberration, but a continuation of behavior stretching back deep into the past. To understand much of today's war, we must see it as a common and almost universal human behavior that has been with us as we went from ape to human.

If, as I see from the overwhelming evidence, warfare has indeed shaped human history so profoundly, then the obvious question is, Why? For a long time I focused on trying to figure out why there was past warfare in the Southwest. Once I realized that *everyone* had warfare in *all* time periods, then the question changed markedly. Many scholars have asked why some societies have warfare. They ask why a *particular* society, or even a bunch of societies, has warfare. They believe, whether they realize it or not, that a unique set of circumstances caused the warfare—revenge, bloodlust, greed, and the like. It's as if a doctor had entered a room filled with predominantly healthy people and began asking why a few people were sick. Each was probably sick for a different reason.

If essentially every social group on the globe has experienced conflict in practically every time period, then the cause must be general. The likelihood that a number of randomly different causes would result in ubiquitous warfare for millennia is very remote. Finding the solution to this slightly different problem is more akin to the doctor who, upon entering the room and realizing that everyone in it has the same disease, begins to look for a single risk factor. Scholars need to be looking for a general cause for the presence of warfare over the course of human history. Of course particular circumstances were involved in wars. In some few time periods there were exceptions and peace prevailed. (Someone in the doctor's room may have an illness different from all the rest, or may even have two illnesses at once.) But the broad, general reason for warfare is of primary importance. This puzzle was different from the one I had originally anticipated.

In attempting to answer the much more fascinating question of *why* warfare was so prevalent in the past, I kept coming back to the idea that people had to be fighting for real reasons. Reasons like revenge or to gain prestige just did not seem important or universal enough to account for so much warfare over such great spans of time and space. In the process of my research, the one theme that kept recurring as I looked at particular cases was that the subjects were fighting over something, whether it was land, food, or even access to women for wives. Or to put it more broadly, people seemed to fight over scarce resources. For most of the time in the past, the most scarce and valuable resource was the most basic: food.

If prehistoric warfare was a result of food being scarce, the question that arises is, Was food hard to come by most of the time in the past? This question led me square up against another popular misconception. Not only was it commonly assumed that the past had been peaceful, but there was a very strong belief that it had also once been a land of plenty, a veritable Garden of Eden. This pristine past world is believed to have been peopled with inherent conservationists, inhabitants who carefully managed and took care of their environment and made sure they never misused or overexploited any precious resource.

As I began to question this premise, I came to the revelation that I, and most other people (scholar or not), was under the spell of a second myth: the myth of the inherent conservationist. The reality is that not only do humans not have hardwired ability to act in an environmentally benign manner today, but they rarely, if ever, had such an ability in the past. Humans have not been able to control their population growth, nor have they been able to avoid overexploiting their environments. I am not referring just to modern humans, but to all humans, as far back in time as one wants to look.

Of the two myths, misunderstanding the human ecological situation is probably more profound. This second general misperception of the prehistoric world is perhaps even more ingrained in current thinking than the myth of a peaceful past and, as a consequence, is much harder to dispel. Once again, academics are not immune. Just as with the evidence for warfare uncovered with the Ice Man or in the El Morro Valley, scholars can and have missed evidence of past ecological events or conditions that might later seem obvious. Archaeology is a key tool in addressing these issues in the past, for it is only archaeology that provides a great time depth and worldwide perspective on these issues.

Archaeology may seem to an outsider to be a romantic and eventful scholarly field, but results can sometimes be slow in coming. Digging, if done right, is a meticulous process. Once a field season is complete (typically after a few months), all the artifacts must be carefully analyzed: The animal bones, charred remains of plants, and ancient pollen preserved in the soil must be identified and studied; pottery must be glued back together and materials carbon-dated. All this can take years. And each archaeologist's work is published independently, so it can take even longer to consolidate information from many different projects. Combining all this information is exciting, but it requires patience. This is equally true for ethnographers, who try to provide a complementary line of evidence by studying living cultures in the field. A generation may go by before a picture of an entire region emerges. Figuring out what happened in the past or around the world is a slow, painstaking process, and it is very easy to miss the forest for the trees.

For example, scholars are now generally in agreement about the location of the site of ancient Troy. Known today as Hisarlik, it is located in western Turkey near the entrance of the Dardanelles strait, which connects the Aegean Sea to the Black Sea by way of the Sea of Marmara. With respect to water, Homer's description of the bay and the location of Troy doesn't fit. Studies have shown that the bay fronting Troy has almost completely silted in since the circa 1300 B.C. Trojan War. What happened? The best explanation is that overgrazing, and perhaps hillside farming, denuded the uplands, resulting in enough erosion to fill in the bay during the intervening three thousand-plus years. This pattern of overgrazing and hillside-farm erosion

In prehistoric times, the El Morro Valley in New Mexico had seven large defensive towns. One was perched on the mesa top in the distance. In A.D. 1250 the residents lived in dispersed houses, but after a series of attacks, these were abandoned and the large fort-like towns were built. This was the beginning of a wave of warfare that engulfed the American Southwest as the climate deteriorated.

is seen all over the Aegean and suggests neither conservationist behavior nor ecological balance. Changes in local plants seen in ancient pollen and charcoal recovered by archaeologists are indicators of past overexploitation, in places as diverse as Madagascar or the American Southwest.

It is not that archaeologists did not see the warfare at Troy; obviously they did. Nor is it that they did not see evidence for environmental degradation; again, that is clear. Rather, the implications of these findings were missed. I always remember the reaction of newlywed friends upon returning from their honeymoon cruise through the Greek islands. Without realizing that they had embarked on their trip with any preconceived notions of the Aegean landscape, they were shocked at the barren, desolate, rocky islands they encountered. The few goats that called many of the Greek islands home could barely gnaw off much in the way of food, they said. My friends hadn't realized that the Mediterranean islands—settled for millennia by early farmer-herders from Southwest Asia—have been deforested and overgrazed for centuries. What is left, essentially, is a denuded landscape. Only the presence of such domesticated plants as olives and grapes that can grow in this transformed environment, and the proximity of nearby lands where such crops can be marketed, allows a significant number of people to live on the Greek islands.

That human-induced environmental change is universal is increasingly clear. After witnessing and reading about environmental degradation in other areas and eras, I considered that perhaps this, too, was not just a disconnected, localized phenomenon. Scholars have been so preoccupied with the evidence for specific examples of environmental degradation in the past that we haven't been asking the right questions. The issue isn't why the ancient people who lived in the Aegean overgrazed their land and silted up their bays, but why this process seemed to repeat itself again and again, in all time periods around the world. Environmental degradation was not a unique and rare accident; it was inevitable. I would expect farmers always to cause such problems. The consequences of environmental stress will be scarce resources, and the consequences of scarce resources will be warfare.

Why was this so hard for me to accept for so long? Why had I not seen what the fundamental questions about humanity were? If a peaceful, ecologically balanced past is bunk, why do people living in the twenty-first century cling to the idea that at some point in our past there was peace and ecological perfection? This belief is undoubtedly the result of a universal desire to know that things *must* have been better in the past. Living in a time of warfare and environmental degradation, modern humans have an overpowering longing to believe that the past wasn't at all like the present. The problem is that things were not better in the past. We have not fallen into a unique period of warfare, and we need to understand this if we are to cope successfully with today's war. Warfare in the past was pervasive and deadly. Humans and war have always gone hand in hand. Sanitizing the past causes us to ignore important lessons from it. Or worse, to badly misconstrue the present, to our detriment.

The unwillingness to understand the nature of human behavior with respect to the environment has been reinforced by "the myth of the noble savage." This romantic notion, which can be traced to the eighteenth century, combines the two myths I've outlined. In the last few centuries, a need to believe that humans have lived in peace and balance with nature was compelling. In the mid–eighteenth century, at the height of the colonial period, when new, exotic lands were being explored by Western Europeans for the first time, a growing awareness of "noncivilized" people from around the world provided a sharp contrast to European society, which was beginning the transformation of the Industrial Revolution. Jean-Jacques Rousseau is closely associated with the concept of the "noble savage."[4]

Rousseau and his followers captivated the scholarly and general populations of the 1750s with the idea that "nothing could be more gentle" than humans when living in their natural state. Rousseau believed that humans had lived in such a state of nature for most of our history.

At the time Rousseau first formed his concept (1750–1754), he looked to societies from around the world to support his argument. Over time, it seems that the native people of North America, along with a few other social groups like the Australian Aborigines, have become the poster children of the "noble savage" concept today. The fact that this popular myth is embodied by the North American Indians has its origins in Western Europe.

Although two hundred years old, the myth that humans remained in ecological balance throughout our entire history and have only recently "lost" this ability to exist in balance with our natural surroundings is very much with us today. There is an overwhelming belief that food was generally plentiful in the past, that our ancient ancestors ingeniously made productive use of all parts of the animals they killed, wasting nothing, and knew the ways of all the animals and the values of all the plants, and so wanted for nothing. People in the past are believed to have learned to put vast numbers of plants to productive use, cleverly resorted to nontraditional foods in the occasional time of scarcity, moved to new locales unaffected by the troubles, or otherwise escaped the consequences of daily provisioning problems. The presumption, among scholars and laypeople alike, is that for most of human history food shortages were a rare or an inconsequential problem. Such periods occurred, of course, but they were not a major determinant of human behavior.[5] The few examples of peace come when people first arrived in new lands, be they the Americas or islands like Hawaii, where the resources were plentiful and people sparse. Leaders can temporarily impose peace, as in parts of the Roman Empire or the Inca after their conquest. In spite of the paucity of such peaceful times, most people have held on to the notion that, in one form or another, a real Garden of Eden existed in our collective past.

As for the notion that "indigenous" people of the past lived in ecological harmony and were, in some fashion, inherent conservationists, the record disproves this. It's certainly true that many traditional people lived directly off the land and were very much tied to the natural world and their immediate surroundings. Many traditional cultures have religions that were and still are centered on their main food source. Corn figures very prominently in Hopi religious ceremonies, for instance. Being aware and worshipful of one's natural resources is a far cry from actually practicing ecological conservation.

One common myth asserts that Native Americans "killed only what they needed."[6] As we know, many Plains Indians were spiritually linked to, and celebrated, the buffalo, which was their main food source. Long before the Spanish arrived and brought horses, steel knives, and arrow points (and later guns) to North America, the Plains Indians had a difficult time hunting buffalo. Sneaking up on a herd and killing a few of these huge creatures was very difficult. The Plains Indians, like other traditional people in other parts of the world, sometimes used the ingenious method of stampeding a herd over a cliff in order to kill them.

If you've just run a herd—or even part of a herd—of buffalo over a cliff, how can it be said you've killed "only what you needed"? You're hungry, your family's hungry, everything you need to survive out on the harsh North American plains is linked to this magnificent yet elusive creature, so you kill them any way you can. If that involves running a hundred animals off a cliff, you use as much as you can from among the pile of dead at the bottom of the drop-off—probably the top fifty or sixty animals—and leave the rest. Archaeologists have found many sites on the Great Plains where buffalo had been run off cliffs, and we know that only the top layers of animals were usually processed. The rest of the animals underneath were untouched. There was no other way to do things prior to about three hundred years ago.[7]

I use this example not to propose the idea that the Plains Indians were trashing the environment—far from it. They were certainly much more respectful and aware of their natural surroundings than most current societies, especially most of modern-day America. However, the idea that Native Americans, as well as other early humans the world over, lived in ecological harmony is pure fantasy. Just as with early warfare, "civilization" is perceived as the culprit that disengaged humans from being intimately knowing and attuned to the environment. As the myth goes, this loss of sensitivity results in the environmental problems and food shortages that are known from written history and from the twentieth century.

Humans in the past did learn to extract food from plants that are poisonous or initially inedible, they learned to hunt almost all species of large mammals, and they evolved clever ways to try to avoid overexploiting certain resources. As ingenious and impressive as many of these behaviors and skills were, they do not at all ensure that humans remain in ecological balance—in the past or present.

Coming to grips with these two myths is hard, which is undoubtedly why they survive. We all would prefer to believe that living in peace and in harmony with nature is the natural order of things. It's hard to accept the idea that constant battles and heedless gobbling up of the nearest natural resources occurred in the distant past. Warfare, especially, presents a very emotional and seemingly illogical situation. People get killed in warfare, and many "innocent" victims, who were in no way involved in deciding to fight, are often killed and maimed in it. This aspect of modern war is the most paradoxical and horrible. But the question remains whether all war is so seemingly senseless. The First World War was horrific. The British had fifty-seven thousand casualties in a single day on the Somme; when the battle of Verdun was over, eight hundred thousand men were dead. The Second World War was worse. More than twenty million Russian casualties and almost ten million German are just a few of the incomprehensible numbers. Having recently confronted war on a scale and consequence unique in human history, are both scholars and the general public perhaps so biased that we cannot look at war as humans did in much of the past?

Much of war today is more like human warfare in the distant past than it is the First or Second World War. These are "little" or local wars, fought over local issues. We have been relatively immune to these wars, except having to avoid them as tourists. But they are real and deadly to millions, and to these people they are not senseless—they are necessary for their very survival. Fighting in Afghanistan, Central Africa, or even the Balkans is a continuation of patterns and reasons for war that have been with us since we were humans. We have only recently learned that we ignore these "tribal" wars at our peril, because they can arrive at our doorstep with today's technology. We must not dismiss modern wars as bizarre and senseless; we must learn to see them for what they are—an unpleasant but real part of the human existence.

We also need to see wars and war deaths in the scale of the participants. While a million war deaths sounds, and is, terrible, if it is out of a population of hundreds of millions, it is no more terrible than a battle in which four or five people are killed in a society of a few hundred. In one month alone after September 11, 2001, more Israelis and several times more Palestinians died, as a proportion of their total populations, than did Americans in the World Trade Center. If war kills people you know, or members of your family, or severely affects your daily life, the absolute numbers killed are not the point. War and peace are relative, not absolute.

Though this myth of a peaceful past is present in the minds of many scholars and laypeople, it does not seem to be actively reinforced by a strong political agenda. There is no serious attempt to promote the myth. This is not the case with the myth of the ecologically balanced human, uncorrupted by civilization.

The interaction of the Native North Americans and their environment is, of course, complex.[8] Moreover, the idea that all these Indians were the same, in this or any other regard, is nonsense. There has been far too much generalization and simplification of the issue of how the Native North Americans were adapted and ecologically situated. In particular, the role of Native North Americans and the environment is twisted up in today's ecology movement and in ideas about Native Americans in general.

Some of the "facts" about the ecology and Native Americans are little more than deliberate political propaganda, while other "facts" are deeply and truly held beliefs—although these latter "facts" are not necessarily true, either. Unfortunately, mainstream Americans tend to use Native Americans as surrogates for all "native" peoples, "innocent savages" or those not debased by Western civilization. Not only does the tremendous variability in behavior, subsistence, and social organization of traditional or indigenous people vary far too much to use them *as a group* as a surrogate or archetype for anything, but such an approach also misses a critical factor about the histories of these societies. Lumping them together so stereotypes them that they are portrayed in some way as less than real people.

There is an important kernel of truth in the idea that the early inhabitants of North America were living in balance with nature. In fact, by the time most of these groups were studied or even recorded by Europeans or Euro-Americans, they had suffered such population decline and had obtained enough new technology—including horses, sheep, and other animals, metal tools such as arrowheads, knives, and axes, textiles, guns, and new crops and fruit—that they were able to live comfortably with the resources available to them. A similar situation prevailed in Europe for a couple of centuries after the Black Death. If the population rapidly declines substantially, there will be plenty of food and land to go around for several generations, and a false impression of actual long-term ecological balance can result.

The early chroniclers and anthropologists who described or studied the North American Indians did not portray the real, long-term situation—because they didn't see it. The provisioning problems of most humans are not daily or even annual concerns. They are, in fact, much more periodic. There can be a number of good years, and only occasionally a few bad years. A couple of bad years in succession will result in a crisis. Seven years of good followed by seven years of bad may be biblical, but long before the seventh bad year there will be a crisis. Much of the time, even groups teetering on the verge of starvation will not appear to be in such a tenuous position to an outside observer. The early European explorers, settlers, and recorders of North American life had little understanding of these factors and, consequently, often saw only people living in ecological bliss.

The tenuous balancing act of eking out a long-term living within one's

This astonishing pile of bones, the remains of about 1,000 warriors, is from an Iron Age (ca. 200 B.C.) fortified town in France. The excavators believe the bodies of killed enemies were racked up outside the defensive walls, much like the Aztecs had racks of tens of thousands of skulls of sacrificed victims. The display of human trophies is found worldwide and is evidence of how serious warfare was in the past.

environment is still difficult to observe. Take, for example, the real story of *Nanook of the North*. The first, and still perhaps one of the most engaging documentary films about indigenous people, *Nanook* was made by filmmaker Robert Flaherty and first shown in 1922 to great fanfare and acclaim in places like New York City. Nanook and his family and relatives, Itivimuit Eskimos living in northern Canada, were shown building an igloo, harpooning a walrus, and otherwise displaying an impressive set of Arctic survival skills—as well as a surprising amount of good nature in the face of such a difficult environment. After watching this powerful film, the observer is struck by just how ingenious and intrepid humans can be. However, the viewer is not told that two years after the film was made, Nanook was caught in a storm while hunting, ran out of food, and starved to death. In spite of new technologies such as steel knives and guns, and a greater ability to communicate and obtain outside help, Nanook did not live in a land of plenty.[9]

Another classic example of a popular misperception involves America's own Pilgrim beginning. As all American schoolchildren know, in 1620 the

Mayflower contingent occupied an "abandoned" Wampanoag Indian village on the coast of Massachusetts, just south of present-day Boston. The history books neglect to point out that the previous inhabitants of this village were not on vacation in Florida—they were dead. Disease, fighting with Europeans, and slave-raiding by Europeans had already taken a heavy toll on the Wampanoag people well before the Pilgrims landed on "virgin" lands. The newly arrived Pilgrims were not a threat to the surviving Wampanoag's resource base. On the contrary, the English were the potential source of very valuable technology—namely, iron and steel, weapons, and cloth.

The Wampanoag were viewed as peaceful, friendly, helpful, and living in ecological balance, because they were all those things in 1620. This does not mean they had lived this way a hundred years earlier. There is ample archaeological evidence for considerable warfare all over the eastern United States, including New England, prior to 1492. Only sixty years after the Pilgrim landing, things changed dramatically. In spite of further population declines among the native people of New England, the Indians of eastern New England were in ecological crisis by the late 1600s. The English colonists had expanded so rapidly that the Native Americans were not able to exist on their resources and resorted to warfare to fight for survival. The so-called King Philip's War was the result.[10]

What has occurred over the centuries is that the blending of the original misunderstanding of the actual ecological situation of the people of North America with the eighteenth-century European desire to fabricate "noble savages" for heuristic purposes has resulted in a well-developed myth that has become widely believed in many camps. This myth has been embraced by the environmental movement and by Native Americans as well.

If I am correct and it's just a myth that humans were ever truly conservationists, then the problem is not that we have lost some magical insight that enables us to live in ecological balance. I cannot stress too strongly that my argument is not a justification for our present behavior.[11] It's easy to cite just how insensitive modern people can be. The destruction of the American buffalo, the current destruction of the tropical rain forest, the extinction of species at a record rate, and the near extinction of many others are all well known and all too real. Americans *do* use far more energy per capita than any other people on Earth. It is very likely that modern people are less "ecological" than people in the past. Due to extraordinary advances in technology, we inhabitants of modern societies are less affected by our individual behaviors and have become more cavalier and unwilling to face the consequences—at least for a while.

When all is said and done, the reason there are not millions of buffalo roaming the Great Plains today is not that they were hunted to their near extinction a century ago. They are not there because the Great Plains have become "the breadbasket of the world" and are filled with wheat and corn farms. There is no longer room for the buffalo to roam!

Though all people around the world and in all time periods have had trouble maintaining ecological balance, and though many of the effects humans have made on the environment are understandable—as are episodes of past warfare—one must be careful not to use behavior in the past as an excuse for behavior today. Just because humans have fought wars throughout history, and because humans have been unable to live comfortably within the constraints of the environment, does not mean we cannot today live without warfare and should not strive to attain an ecological balance. If we do not strive to understand what we have done in the past and why, it will only make it harder to get it right in the future. Much of the world today has the same survival problems virtually all humans had in the ancient past. Land and food are in short supply, and there is continuous competition for such resources today, just as in the past. People do starve to death, and their neighbors will kill them and take their land if they get a chance. Ecological balance is much more important and critical than protecting an endangered species in North America or Europe. Not recognizing that the social organization and the ecological situation of much of the world are a far cry from ours keeps us from seeing how ecology and warfare are intertwined today, just as they have been for millions of years.

Studying ourselves and our past is certainly one of the most compelling subjects for humankind, but it is also one of the most problematic. Finding out things about ourselves or our past societies that we would prefer not to know—or having strong preconceived beliefs about humans or the past—can create a thick cloud of misinformation that obscures this process. Penetrating that cloud can be just as hard as pulling the actual information from the earth. In spite of what seemed to be the impossible task of reconstructing human behaviors of five thousand, one hundred thousand, or even a million years ago, great progress has been made. Thanks to advancements in the fields of anthropology (archaeology and paleoanthropology) and biology (human ecology and primatology), scholars have reached a point in our combined knowledge of the past in which some fairly clear patterns are emerging. Yet these two myths—that the past was a land of perpetual peace and perfectly balanced ecological harmony—have obscured our scholarly ability to appreciate the universal aspects of the human past and delayed our understanding of the fundamental nature of human behavior.

Looking at these topics through the course of human history does more than just clarify the past; it enables us to look at the future from a new perspective. I will examine more closely the two myths of a peaceful and ecologically benign past—and explain the evidence that proves they are, in fact, myths. At our disposal are archaeological data from many regions and many time periods, and ethnographic information from cultural anthropologists working in the last century all over the world. We can turn to historical data—humankind's earliest written documents and accounts of the first explorers and visitors to a region. All this information provides a full and often surprisingly clear image of the past.

In tackling these issues, trying to begin at the beginning is not so easy. Humans have not always been human; we have a prehuman past as well. Even fully modern humans—that is, people who were every bit as intelligent as and behaviorally complex as people today—lived and functioned in many different ways. Humans have not always lived in societies that were organized the same way. While anthropologists have constructed a number of schemes to deal with these differences, the most useful is a four-type taxonomy: forager bands, tribal farmers, chiefdoms, and states. Forager bands and tribal farmers are roughly egalitarian societies, in contrast to chiefdoms and states, which have important status differences incorporated into them and are much more socially complex.

Humans live in many different types of places, from small, isolated islands to large cities. We have survived by many different means, for more than a million years as nomadic foragers, then about ten thousand years ago as village-dwelling farmers. More recently, most people have lived as members of societies with complex trade, markets, and monarchs. All humans cannot be lumped together; understanding the past is harder than that. This variability in how and where people have lived is a great boon, because it provides the opportunity to see how humans have reacted in different situations.

The first step in this tour of the past is to look more closely at what I mean by warfare and ecological balance. Then the focus is on our ape relatives in order to paint a picture of what has made us human and what that tells us about being human—and about human warfare. Next, I explore the very distant past and turn to the ethnographically known foragers of more recent times to see how warfare and ecology played out over most of human history. I will turn to more recent times (as an archaeologist, I consider the last ten thousand years or so as "recent") and the beginnings of

The highland peoples of New Guinea were engaged in almost continuous warfare when encountered by European gold seekers in the 1930s. No-man's-lands separated competing social groups, and lookout towers like that shown here had to be manned to guard against surprise raids. Some anthropologists believed this warfare was "ritual" with few deaths and was of little consequence, yet about 25 percent of the men died from such "inconsequential" warfare.

farming. Then I will examine the development of more complex human societies to see how population growth and warfare have shaped the human cultural traditions we find ourselves in today. Finally, I look to the future to see what these changes portend. Throughout this process, I'll explore what type of war is found in these situations and whether something important happens to human warfare when our social organizations and other situations change.

My goal is not simply to recount the human past, but to address a particularly nagging question: Are we doomed by our past to fight constant battles, now and forevermore? After all, if warfare has been with us for millions of years, could humans have been genetically selected for a propensity toward conflict? Warfare could be as much a part of us as our ability to learn to speak. In attempting to answer this question—and others—the journey leads through six million years of history and to many different societies, past and present. A deeper understanding of past warfare will enable us to better understand the future of warfare. Just because a peaceful past and a time of a Garden of Eden are myths does not mean that they cannot be attained in the future. The ultimate question remains: Are the myths within our grasp?

chapter two

WAS THERE EVER AN EDEN?

During the 1960s, I lived in Western Samoa as a Peace Corps volunteer on what seemed to be an idyllic South Pacific island—exactly like those painted by Paul Gauguin. Breadfruit and coconut groves grew all around my village, and I resided in a thatched-roof "house" with no walls beneath a giant mango tree. If ever there was a Garden of Eden with food all around just for the taking, this was it. I lived with a family headed by an extremely intelligent elderly chief, named Sila, and he and I spent long hours talking about a wide range of topics. The first landings on the moon were then being planned, and space exploration was a particularly engaging subject.

One day, Sila happened to mention that the island's trees did not bear fruit as they had when he was a child. He attributed the decline to the possibility that the presence of radio transmissions had affected production, since Western Samoa (now known as Samoa) had its own radio station by then. I stood beneath a mango tree, which was loaded with fruit, and asked how it could possibly produce more than what I saw and suggested that what had changed was not less fruit, but more mouths to feed. Upon reflection, Sila decided I was probably right. Being an astute manager, he was already taking the precaution of expanding his farm plots into some of the last remaining arable land on the island, at considerable cost and effort, to ensure adequate food for his growing family in the future. On the one hand, Sila was cognizant of his escalating provisioning problem, but on the other hand, he was not quite able to grasp the overall demographic situation. Why was this?

The simple answer is that the rate of population change in our small Samoan village was so gradual that during an adult life span, growth was not dramatic enough to comprehend fully. The same thing happens to us all the time. Communities grow and change composition, and often only after the process is well advanced do we recognize just how significant the changes have been—and we have the benefit of historical documents, old photographs, long life spans, and government census surveys.

Demographic changes are not perceived on a daily basis, and the consequences usually become evident only when there is a crisis. The same can be said for environmental changes. The forests of Central America were being denuded and encroached upon for many years, but it took Hurricane Mitch, which ravaged most of the region in late October 1998, to produce the dramatic flooding and devastation that fully demonstrated the magnitude of the problem. Alterations in the environment can occur so gradually that the differences seem to "sneak up" on us. Conversely, outside forces, like weather or natural disasters, can produce immediate drastic changes that have profound effects, but they are not felt until some time in the future. The natural environment is resilient, and at the same time delicate, as modern society keeps finding out. And it was just so in the past.

These observations about Mother Nature are intertwined with the two popular myths of peace and ecological balance in the past. A peaceful past is possible if people lived in ecological balance. If you live in a Garden of Eden–like setting surrounded by plenty, why fight? What warfare that might have existed in such a scenario would be minor, incidental, or even aberrant. It could not be the norm, because conflict would have been neither necessary nor beneficial to anyone. By this logic, warfare comes about as a result of being out of balance with nature. If someone as smart as Sila couldn't perceive population growth, and if humans all over Earth today degrade their environments, could people living in the past be expected to be any different? The answer to that question, and the many others that follow, can be answered with the help of human ecologists.

The word *ecology* conjures up images of biologists studying how plants and animals interrelate in the rain forest or in a stagnant pond. The field of human ecology bridges the gap between traditional anthropology, with its emphasis on social behavior, and ecology, which emphasizes the world without humans. Human ecology deals with the same interlocking aspects of nature but with the focus on how humans interact with their environments.[1] The role of human-ecological studies is to test ideas of how humans relate to the overall environment, rather than simply assuming how humans must behave.

What evidence is there that humans were ever able to live for an extended time in ecological balance? If there was true ecological balance in the past, just what would it look like? This turns out to be a difficult question to answer. Part of the difficulty is definitional. Humans do survive, and the world's ecology has not been completely destroyed. Ecological balance does not mean simply survival. The concept evokes the popular notion of the inherent conservationist. Many scholars as well as much of the general public still believe there are "traditional" or "indigenous" people around the world who have a spiritual connection with their surroundings that somehow guarantees they will live in ecological balance. Often, these traditional societies' primary staple became the focus of religious and ceremonial activity, whether it be the buffalo of the Plains Indians, the corn of Mesoamerica, or the cattle of Southwest Asia and Europe. Delegating this religious aspect to the food chain is seen to ensure proper behavior and long-term ecological balance.

There is little, if any, evidence that ideal ecological behavior ever existed for long. How such social mechanisms—religious or otherwise—could have been developed or worked in theory, much less in practice, has never been determined. Religion or custom does not guarantee that an individual, much less an entire group, will do the right thing. Some social behaviors, like not collecting honey from beehives that face to the north, may help to reduce overexploitation because bees in 25 percent of the hives would be left alone to propagate new hives. But this benefit is more likely accidental than by design. Other rules, like not hunting pregnant female animals, may have been deliberately chosen to enforce conservationist behavior. How could such belief systems or social practices have been set up, either by luck or design, to work perfectly? They would need to work to ensure there would be no environmental degradation, overexploitation, or excess population.

Careful research shows that none of the proposed social behaviors that would naturally regulate human populations actually do so. Some scholars have suggested that the Maring of highland New Guinea had a wonderfully balanced system in which a rising number of domestic pigs triggered mechanisms, such as big feasts for which many animals were slaughtered to reduce the herds and bring things back into balance. (The entire model is much more elegant and complex than this.) In anthropological terms, this supposedly was an example of a self-regulating process that had evolved and was perpetuated by custom. Closer examination by researchers has shown that though such cycles existed, they did not eliminate unsustainable human population growth, environmental deterioration, or warfare. There were self-regulating mechanisms among the Maring, but no such customs solved their fundamental environmental, conservationist problems.[2]

There is always the chance that societies did exist in the past that *had* developed effective social mechanisms to prevent the degradation of their environment, but such groups have not been studied. Perhaps what these groups were doing was sustainable over the long run without bouts of starvation, disease, and warfare. For the sake of argument, let us assume that inherent conservationism existed. Such an ecologically balanced attitude would have to meet certain criteria. One is sustainability: The human population should be stable, or at least rise and decline gently. Population size should be regulated by social rules of birth spacing, abstinence, and the like, and not by warfare, famine, or disease. The other need is the ability to accommodate alterations in climate and technology. Since climate and technology do change frequently, in order to remain in ecological balance over time these alterations must be accommodated. If the society was plunged into warfare, famine, or disease with every significant change, this would hardly be a group in sustained balance.

One criterion an ideal society would *not* have to meet is that of preserving nature exactly as it was. A group can remain in ecological balance and still cause mass extinctions and greatly change the local vegetation. Most people today would consider the notion that nature can be altered as not being ecological or conservationist in attitude. In truth, it is possible to eliminate all predators, change the forest composition, and then live in harmony with the environment that is left.

These considerations illustrate just how difficult it is to agree on what a society made up of inherent conservationists would be like. Human impact on the environment seems to be more prevalent and significant than generally realized. Extinctions and changes in plant and animal composition have been ubiquitous throughout our history. Nevertheless, such powerful impacts do not necessarily prevent sustainability. Humans can modify their environment substantially and, in theory, still be in sustainable situations. The real concern here is with ecological sustainability.

There is a question of what exactly is a "natural" environment. There are no "natural" environments left on Earth. If, by natural, one means environments that have not been affected or modified by humans, they have all been long gone for many thousands of years. The last great uninhabited landmasses—those of Australia and America—were colonized more than ten to fifty thousand years ago. Even the harshest part of Siberia was occupied more than twenty thousand years ago. Everywhere in the world, fire and hunting were the first human factors to have an impact on the environment, but farming and tree clearing had a major, if not far greater, role. How much of the desertification in Africa and Asia is a result of human impact, especially overgrazing? Did humans replace the saber-toothed tigers

The Samoan chief Sila and his wife with a few of their grandchildren. Even lush tropical islands have only limited food supplies, and the population can outgrow the resources. Yet it is hard for someone, even as astute as Sila, to recognize the degree and consequences of population growth in their lifetime.

and other large predators that preyed on elephants? Humans are now part of elephant ecology because we eventually became their only predators. In the New World, humans arrived just as the Ice Age was waning, more than twelve thousand years ago. Though humans have been in the New World for less time than in the Old World, we have populated the Americas long enough to have had a hand in the present ecology. Humans have changed the ecological "mix" for our own benefit. The use of fire increased the diversity of human habitats and made the plants and animals useful to us more plentiful, while it reduced the range of unuseful species. If we take *natural* or *pristine* to mean "not affected by humans," then much of what we think of as natural is not.[3] Taking all that into consideration, it makes no sense to talk about humans as inherent conservationists if one means by that people who do not impact their environment. No humans leave their environment as they find it, and they have not for the last fifty thousand years or so.

The word *conservation* is often used simply to mean "nonwasteful." Just because you don't waste something doesn't guarantee there will be enough of it. If groups of inherent conservationists exist, the behaviors of the members of those societies are such that species do not become extinct, biodiversity is maintained, and the plant and animal populations, the land, and the water are not being degraded over time. Just because past societies did not cause extinctions, did not degrade the environment, and did not radically alter the landscape does not mean that such groups had some special ability to live in harmony with nature. A society could wreak havoc on the environment but have such a small population that the overall impact on its resource balance would be negligible. Pregnant female animals can be hunted and still not severely reduce the species numbers, if the number of human hunters is too small to matter.

The harsh Arctic provides a good example of this situation. Humans are common in these frozen environments only in locations where animals—whales or caribou, for example—regularly pass through in migration. In order to survive, Arctic people must kill and store a lot of food from these migration points, and such an existence will support only a limited population. Consequently, the overall number of humans living in Arctic regions is low, and the overall impact they have on the environment is slight. This harsh reality does not make the Arctic hunters conservationists. The Arctic people did not undertake a population count of the caribou or whales before they hunted them. They possibly could judge whether the animals' numbers were lower or higher from one season to the next, but when the numbers were low, the Arctic people did not hunt less until the numbers rebounded. Some Arctic people may have starved because there were fewer caribou, and so the total amount of hunting was reduced, but this is not conservation.

A society can believe it is being sensitive to nature and can be having a minimal impact on the environment, but the group might simply be conducting itself in an efficient or practical manner. Why kill what you cannot eat? Why destroy birds' nests for the fun of it? Either from social or religious rules—or simply because there was no reason to waste effort—such "pseudo-conservationist" behaviors were common in much of the world.

In order to have true conservation, the resource—whatever it might be: wild game or plants, honey, water, farmland—must be utilized so that it does not become depleted, regardless of need. Even though one's family or village is hungry, that field won't be planted, that animal killed, or that beehive destroyed because of the realization that the long-term ecological balance will be altered for the worse. This is no easy task—now or in the past. A group may deplete the resources around its camp and then pack up and move, giving the environment in that particular area ample time to recover. Similarly, a forest can be cut down in the tropics and crops planted, then the plot can be abandoned and the forest will rejuvenate. As long as camp is moved frequently enough, an area is vacated long enough, or the proper length of time is allowed before a plot is refarmed, the resources will not be depleted overall.

Such behaviors are often associated with what many ecologists and anthropologists call "optimal foraging." This concept revolves around the idea that humans are highly rational and hunt or collect only those species that give the greatest return for the time and effort expended. For example, the farther a hunter is from camp, the larger an animal will be hunted, because it is a waste of effort to carry a small animal all that way back to camp, but if the hunter begins to run out of arrows, he will take a less desirable animal rather than go home empty-handed. Ethnographic studies of modern foragers show that their hunting and foraging behavior closely mimics the optimal-foraging model. This means they will not start out to hunt particularly rare species because it's not an efficient use of their time and effort, since such animals are few and far between. As hunting reduces the numbers of some species, the foragers shift their aim toward other, more common animals because the cost, in time, of getting the rare ones is too high.[4]

But this is not conservationist behavior. It is behavior that is focused on the short term. Deciding to stop hunting a species that has become rare differs from consciously hunting that animal so lightly that it *does not become* rare. The true conservationist will not kill a rare species, even when it is easy to do so. The forager who is optimizing is not wasteful but is preoccupied only with the short term. The conservationist will sometimes need to forgo short-term needs in order to assure ample resources for the long-term future.

Consider the old stories of the American Plains Indians using every part of the buffalo—and I use this example only because it is so commonly repeated. In fact, Native Americans were no more or less conservationist than many other peoples around the world. Just because there was a use for

all parts of a buffalo does not mean that all parts were used from every animal that was taken. The major need among the Plains people was for buffalo hides and meat. It has never been shown—either archaeologically or
ethnographically—that if only hides were needed, then hunting did not
take place, or the reverse. The hoofs were used for glue, the sinew for making bows, and even the tails were used for fly whisks. Nonetheless, the Indians did not need as many fly whisks as they did buffalo hides.

Conservationist behavior is not simply a matter of using all the game
that is captured. It is not just a matter of refraining from hunting for sport,
nor is it optimizing social behavior. Conservationist behavior requires
avoiding overhunting, regardless of one's needs—as well as maintaining a
small enough human population that the society's needs remain within the
reproductive potential of the animal species involved.

To find evidence of conservationist behavior in the past, scholars must
be able to observe whether human populations were being controlled so
that overhunting, overfarming, or overcollecting of wild plants, shellfish,
and other foods did not take place. Archaeologists can sometimes judge
this by the size of the animals being taken. If the remains of the tortoises or
the shellfish found on a coastal California site become smaller over time, we
can assume that the animals are being overexploited and fewer and fewer
are allowed to reach full size.[5] Similarly, if crop yields fall and more and
more land is being cleared for farmland in Guatemala or Central Africa,
resulting in more and more erosion on the hillsides, we can assume that the
farmland is being overused and not being allowed to regenerate, or that the
domestic herds are overgrazing. Archaeologically, it is easier to see the *absence*
of conservationist behavior than its presence.

The analysis of soils, erosion, and other changes to the physical landscape can also yield clear signs of whether the plants and animals used by
past societies show evidence of overexploitation. Did plants and animals
become extinct, like the giant moa among the Maori of New Zealand about
five hundred years ago? Even local extinctions are relevant, such as sandal-
wood in Southeast Asia, which was exploited by the Chinese beginning in
the sixth century and then overharvested for the Chinese market by Europeans in the 1800s.

If true ecological balance exists, then human populations should be stable. They would not grow rapidly for long, nor would they crash. When
there is good archaeological information, we very often find periods of
rapid growth followed by severe declines. In the Americas, scholars have
observed this in the Maya area, in the American Southwest, and in the eastern United States. It is also found in the Levant, including present-day

Israel and Lebanon, where the population in the latter Neolithic (around 5500 B.C.) suddenly dropped precipitously, after having been one of the most densely settled parts of the region.[6] All such evidence suggests a lack of ecological balance.

Even more subtle types of evidence of ecological stress are available. By means of chemical analysis of teeth and bones, physical anthropologists can assess levels of nutrition among people who lived in the past. In the American Southwest, for example, by studying ancient human remains, we know that in the late A.D. 1200s there was an increase in anemia, poor teeth, periods of no growth in children, and other evidence of nutritional stress, soon followed by a dramatic population decline. Analysis of skeletal stature can be used in the same way. After analyzing the skeletal remains of the Maya elite as compared to nonelite burials, considerable differences in physical stature between the two classes are evident. Such differences would make sense if resources were scarce—the elite members of Maya society were consistently getting more to eat and grew taller, while the non-elites had less food and perhaps less nutritious diets. The apparent poorer health of the non-elites does not compute if there was ecological balance and all the Mayas were adequately provisioned. Exactly the same type of disparity in physical statures is found among the European classes before the Industrial Revolution, differences that have been shown to be associated with considerable variations in nutrition.

As with archaeological information, it is easier to see evidence for non-conservationist behavior and a lack of ecological balance in the historic and ethnographic record than it is to demonstrate that such balance took place. Overexploitation of the ocean fisheries is a growing concern today, as it should be, but in the 1500s and 1600s, one of the main interests the people of northern Europe had in New England was access to new fishing grounds, as well as new sources of timber and the like, because such resources were in short supply in Europe after centuries of exploitation. Similarly, history books often portray the American fur trade revolving around Kit Carson and other mountain men trapping the beaver of the Rocky Mountains. In reality, there had been plenty of beaver in New England and across much of the continent at one time. These animals were trapped to near extinction in the more eastern regions very early on after the Europeans arrived. This overexploitation was practiced by Native Americans and Europeans alike.

The intense hunting of African elephants to feed the ivory trade had long historical roots. Only after the trade in ivory became linked to the world economy did the slaughter of elephants escalate to such high levels

Prior to the horse, hunting buffalo was not easy. One of the best methods was the buffalo jump, depicted here by Alfred Jacob Miller in 1867. Used for thousands of years by the Plains Indians, a jump could result in hundreds of buffalo being killed, often far more than could be consumed. The Plains Indians, like everyone else on earth, had no mechanisms to avoid affecting their environment or preventing depletion of their resources.

that it resulted in a great reduction in the animals' range. The endless search for spices, exotic woods, and marine animals instigated by the Chinese had a huge impact on the ecology of much of Southeast Asia. The Chinese quest resulted in overexploitation and with the replacing of native vegetation with nutmeg and clove trees for trade spices.

Such examples are legion, and one can get into ceaseless debate about why indigenous people often took part in such overexploitation. Of course, their economies had been turned upside down by the introduction of new tools, cloth, decorations, and other things the indigenous cultures wanted. Much of their land was taken, and people were being swept up into European power politics. For example, Indians were pulled into the struggle between France and England for Canada. Even if a traditional society could not be conservationist in such a milieu and survive, that does not mean groups were not conserving their resources before such impact by a dominating culture. Conversely, though a lack of conservation ethic under the circumstances is understandable, there is no guarantee that any group was truly conservationist before impact. Recounting such events does not reveal a complete picture, and so the historical accounts of ecological balance or imbalance are much less informative than the archaeological information.

There are far fewer ethnographic and historical accounts of social groups and their ecology in which there had *not* been such impact by the world economy, and these are very hard to interpret. There is ample historical documentation of the impact the Vikings had on such places as Iceland, which was colonized in the Middle Ages. It's known that the Icelandic forest was quickly destroyed and the population rapidly outstripped the island's resources, which is why Eric the Red went on to colonize Greenland and his son tried to colonize North America. They needed the land and the trees. One can argue that the Vikings were Europeans, and everyone knows *they* have never been conservationists.[7]

Well, then, how about South America? There, as shown by ethnographic studies conducted in the early 1960s, the Yanomama would build a village in the tropical forest of Venezuela, plant some crops, and begin to hunt the animals in the vicinity. After a few years the animals would be hunted out to such a degree that the group was forced to move its village. One can argue that the Yanomama overexploit the game and should hunt less in order to sustain the wild population. Conversely, one can argue that they are not actually hunting any game to extinction, just overexploiting it locally. When they move, the wild population recovers. So over the region—and the long haul—their existence in this environment is a sustainable process. With this interpretation, the Yanomama are not necessarily conservationists in their day-to-day behavior, but it all works out just fine. But ethnographic studies reveal that the Yanomama are always hungry for meat (protein), usually have to fight to find a new place to build their new village, and live in constant fear of attack from people trying to take their land.

Similarly, from ethnographic studies first conducted in the 1950s and 1960s, we know that valleys in the New Guinea highlands had been turned into wall-to-wall farming villages with tens of thousands of people farming very small plots and raising pigs for protein. The forest cover and wild animals had been exterminated for miles. The hills on the edges of the valleys, accessible to only a small portion of the population, contained the same species of plants and animals as before. The New Guineans had not extincted entire species, they had just radically changed the ecology of the valleys. They had been doing this for a long time, and as a system, it was sustainable. Though the system was sustainable, there was no real balance at all. The real mechanism to maintain balance was the occasional slaughter of people. Ethnographic studies have shown that warfare was constant and endemic in the New Guinea highlands.

Previously uninhabited islands are an even better place to examine human impact on the environment. Island ecological situations tend to be less complex, and the absence of other social groups makes the situation clear. Our information about the colonization of islands derives from archaeology, historical accounts, and modern studies of island fauna and flora. Dating the charcoal from ancient forest fires makes it possible to record changes in the frequency and intensity of the fires. Paleontologists determine which animal species were extincted, and geomorphologists can find cycles of soil erosion. If humans were really capable of conservationist behavior, one would think they should be particularly so on islands, because there is nowhere else to go if they get it wrong. Just the opposite usually happens. Madagascar, for instance, was initially settled by a small group of people from Southeast Asia around A.D. I. The first settlers were living along the coast of this very large island off Africa, but in about seven hundred years they had spread across the entire island and in the process extincted almost all large game, including hippos, tortoises, giant lemurs—some two dozen species in all.

An almost identical story can be told for the Caribbean islands, including Haiti, Jamaica, Puerto Rico, and Cuba. The initial settlers reached the islands by boat between 3000 and 2000 B.C. Modern studies have shown that some twenty-one genera, including ground sloths and giant rodents, were extincted on the islands, and all show evidence of the use of fire for clearing vegetation. When Columbus reached these islands, the people were far from being in ecological balance, as evidenced by ample warfare and cannibalism. The word *cannibal* derives from Carib, one of the linguistic groups then occupying some of the islands.

The Hawaiian Islands, initially occupied around A.D. 300, provide a repeat of the same story. Researchers have shown that thirty-five species of birds were extincted—more from habitat transformation than as food sources. In addition, large flightless waterfowl and ibis, which were very useful food sources, were wiped out. By the time of Captain Cook's arrival in the 1700s, there was considerable food stress and warfare among the Hawaiians. The same thing happened on the islands of the Mediterranean, but initial settlement occurred so early on those islands that the cases are not as clear-cut.[8] On all these islands, the human impact was probably slow enough that no single generation would have perceived what was taking place.

The evidence from such island colonizations is quite damning. What better place to be a successful conservationist? One would assume that the initial colonizers were few in number, so social rules could be easily

Climate changes more rapidly than most people realize. During the Little Ice Age the weather rapidly turned cold, and glaciers grew and descended into Alpine valleys. Towns had been built with no idea that glaciers could threaten them, as seen in this 19th-century print, which was drawn after the glacier had begun to retreat. Such climate shifts often led to increased warfare over resources as the food supply was reduced.

enforced; the island landmasses are small enough that the inhabitants should be able to see what overexploitation was causing; and there was no reason to grow the human population rapidly to be able to defend against human competitors. Examples of similar island colonizations by Europeans, Asians, and American Indians are available, and the pattern is worldwide— and always the same: A few people occupy the new land, they exterminate many species, they heavily modify the landscape, and their numbers grow. They never remain in anything approaching ecological balance.

Mainland studies give a similar result. The Hadza, for example, are a small group of hunter-gatherers who live near Lake Eyasi in Tanzania. They exist by collecting a number of different roots and by hunting both large and small game in a rather sparse and unpromising environment. Unrelated to the Bantu-speaking farmers and herders that populate much of Africa, the Hadza are similar to, but culturally and linguistically distinct from, the more famous Bushmen or !Kung of southern Africa. Living in such a harsh environment, the Hadza people would be expected to be careful conservationists. Yet, ethnographic studies reveal that the Hadza give little attention to conservation of their food resources. When women dig up roots, they do not attempt to replace any portion of the plant to grow again. When they gather berries, heavily laden branches are often torn from the trees and carried back to camp. When a woman is building the framework of her grass hut, she is as likely to use branches from berry trees as from any other type of tree.... When a nest of wild bees is found and raided for its honey, no portion of the comb is left to encourage the bees to stay on. Moreover, little effort is made to leave the nest suitable for reoccupation.... In hunting, no attempt is made at systematic cropping.... There are no inhibitions about shooting females (even pregnant females) or immature animals.... If two animals are killed on the same day, the more distant one may be abandoned.[9]

This account is hardly the stuff of a deeply ingrained conservation ethic critical to survival. The Hadza are not alone in this behavior; researchers see it throughout the world in many time periods and places. Irven DeVore relates once watching !Kung women collecting tubers. The women found a nice patch and dug up all the tubers. Then they selected only the largest specimens to carry back to camp. They did not replant the smaller ones to grow larger but left them to dry out and die.

Another point to consider is that just because conservationist behavior is well intended and deliberate does not mean it's successful. Some traditional societies, the Paiute of Nevada and Utah, for example, conducted group hunts in which they drove such game as jackrabbits from an entire valley into nets and dispatched them. But if the hunters were starving and the animal numbers were not fully recovered, would they not hunt to keep from starving in the short term?

Having found these examples, and others, I wondered whether I hadn't just happened upon a few dramatic cases of societies having failed to live in ecobalance. I systematically went through the last thirty years of studies published in the journal *Human Ecology*, the obvious place for such work to be reported. There are no clear examples of conservationist behavior in any traditional societies reported during the last three decades. There are good examples of short-term maximization, and even a couple of cases that might possibly be interpreted as conservationist behavior, but it is not the common, widespread norm many would expect to find if traditional peoples were inherently capable of creating their own Edens.

In spite of all the studies and all the lines of evidence that can be brought to bear on the issue, actual evidence for conservationist behavior that works well enough to result in ecological balance does not seem to exist. Most people—including traditional societies—simply do not expend more effort than is immediately needed even though a long-term gain in overall effort would result, nor do they avoid consuming what is immediately available in order to ensure that more of that particular resource will be available in the future. Such a sweeping statement is very hard to demonstrate because it must be based on negative evidence. I can only conclude that the difficulty of finding any evidence of ecobalanced conservationist behavior strongly suggests that, even if such behavior ever existed in the past, it was exceedingly rare and is not an inherent human behavior. Humans are not blessed with a conservation ethic to keep them in ecological balance. Though one might wish this to be the case, unfortunately, it appears otherwise. This lack of conservationist behavior is only one part of the human–resource balance equation. Without such behavior, what is the relationship between us and the environment really like?

"Food was Plentiful." Thus reads the opening text for the Smithsonian Museum of Natural History's exhibition on California Indians. Such rosy statements are typical of many, if not most, museum exhibits and introductory texts about Indians and other indigenous peoples around the world. Most visitors—even most anthropologists—probably do not perceive there is anything wrong with such a statement. Nonetheless, the phrase "food was plentiful" totally misrepresents the most fundamental aspect of human existence. I am not asserting that there was some sort of evil intent on the part of people living in the past to use up their resources faster than they could be replaced. The real problem is my friend Sila's problem—population growth. If you outgrow your environment, you're going to use up your natural resources and be out of ecological balance. The fundamental ecological relationship of humans to the environment— and even more important, to each other—is exactly the opposite of the Smithsonian's exhibition text: Food was scarce.

Now, this does not mean that food was *always* scarce throughout the year, or even that food was scarce at some time *every* year. Such a view of food availability misunderstands the nature of the problem. Almost everywhere in the world, changes in seasons affect the availability of food for humans. A very lean period of only a few weeks is a very severe problem for humans. Not only do adults have to get through this time of scarcity, so do infants. A nursing mother must be able to stay alive and produce enough milk for her child to survive. Virtually everywhere on Earth each year is not like every other year. A drier year, a year with a hurricane, a year with a swarm of locusts—all will affect the food situation. If the impact comes when food is plentiful, there may be no significant long-term consequence. On the other hand, if the problem coincides with the low point in the annual food cycle, then the consequences could be severe. It isn't a question of whether food was *sometimes* plentiful, it's a question of whether it was *always* plentiful. Scholars know much less about that question than might be imagined.

Finding a balance between resources and population growth can be best observed by looking at one of the most benign places on Earth, the Polynesian Islands. Coconuts, breadfruit, taro, and other plants grow plentifully there. Changes between seasons are minor, plants grow year-round, and some bear fruit or mature throughout the seasons. It is hard to imagine how anyone could be hungry, much less starve to death, in an environment like this, but starvation is not at all uncommon in Polynesia. Most of the islands are so small that when something goes wrong, it goes wrong for everyone. What often unbalances the delicate ecological island environments is a hurricane, known as a typhoon in the Pacific.

When I was living in Samoa, the eye of a typhoon went directly over my house. Our village had absolutely no warning; it simply started raining, by night it was raining torrentially, and in the middle of the night we were in the midst of the typhoon. By morning, it was all over. Fortunately, this was a small typhoon and damage was minimal. Hundreds of trees were blown down and a few houses were destroyed, but that was about it—nothing like the really powerful tropical storm it could have been. The problem was that this typhoon hit our island just as the breadfruit was ripening. These amazing trees produce great quantities of a fruit about the size of your head that becomes ripe and edible for about two months each year. The wind thrashed the fruit so hard the stems broke and the fruit began to rot. There was plenty of breadfruit for a week, and then none. Essentially, the same thing happened to the banana crop, and a month or so later people in our village were actually hungry. Luckily for us, the typhoon was a minor one, not everything was lost, and Samoa was connected to the larger world food supply. In addition, some families, like mine, had fortunately overplanted taro and had excess to share. A few of my neighbors were hungry, but no one starved. Yet it was all too easy to see what could have happened in the past. When scholars look back through the early accounts of life in Polynesia, we find many instances of famine, starvation, and the drastic social consequences of food shortages. Even this "tropical paradise" was no Eden.

Many biologists and anthropologists use the concept of carrying capacity to describe the limitations of the local environment to support a popu-

Complex societies can amass labor to build terraces, like those seen here on Bali, and otherwise increase farm productivity and the carrying capacity. Soon, however, population grows to consume the new output, and the society is once again under food stress.

lation of animals, including people.[10] The idea in its simplest form is that the territory or region available to any group contains only a finite amount of usable food for that group. Different environments can carry or support different numbers of people: deserts can support fewer people than woodlands, the Arctic can support very few, and so on. Of course, for humans in particular, the carrying capacity can be changed in a number of ways. One can choose to eat what was previously not considered food—for example, worms, bugs, and the like. Or an animal that was considered sacred by some people could become food to others. New foods can be discovered. Such "discovery" of the "new" often has taken the form of learning how to prepare a previously known potential food that was bitter or even poisonous. Acorns, manioc, and the trunks of various palm trees are foods that are edible only after being carefully and laboriously processed. Discovering how to store or preserve food well also changes the carrying capacity, as it is the availability of food during the leanest times that is critical. Storage is not easy. In the Middle Ages about a third of the grain crops were lost to rot or rodents.

Another way to change the carry capacity is to produce more crop yield from the same patch of land. The most common, but not the only, way to do this is to farm. By expending a lot of effort, farmers get more calories from the same space than foragers do. Most farmers combine these last two methods of increasing the carrying capacity by farming and storing the "new" food they grow—and by staying in one place to protect the stored food and the right to their farmland. Farmland can be improved by building terraces like those of Bali, the Levant, or the Andes, or irrigation canals like those of Mesopotamia or coastal Peru, or dams and reservoirs like those in prehistoric Mexico and the American Southwest. There are many other kinds of water control systems, especially from the New World, including raised fields, sunken fields, and stone mulch gardens.[11] However, the same principle applies. More effort is expended to make the same plot of land even more productive.[12]

Of particular interest are changes brought about by maritime innovations that linked the world, beginning in the fifteenth century. When the Spaniards brought horses to the New World, they changed the Plains Indians' way of life. Before horses, the Indians were corn farmers who settled along the river edges and followed the buffalo herds on foot, with dogs to carry their gear and food. These same people, beginning in the 1600s with the arrival of the Spanish, were transformed into the famous horse-based societies the Sioux, Cheyenne, Pawnee, and others of the Great Plains. The introduction of metal tools, knives and guns, for example, was also extremely important in this transformation. All these advancements enabled the Sioux and others to move farther and faster, and carry much more gear and processed food. They were able to hunt more efficiently and to better process the meat they obtained.

The exchange of crops also had a dramatic impact on carrying capacities. The South American sweet potato transformed the agriculture and demographic situation in the New Guinea highlands as it moved across the Pacific after Columbus. The potato did the same thing in parts of Europe—Ireland being the best-known example. These dramatic changes, which occurred in the last few centuries, make it very difficult to assess the original carrying capacity–population relationships in many places. What may appear to be a situation of a social group living in ecological plenty in the very recent past is often a group whose numbers were depleted and whose technology improved just before they were studied. Such societies do not provide evidence for long-term ecological stability.

On the reverse side, the more a resource is used, the less productive it becomes. This is obvious today in fishing stocks, which in many places around the world have been so depleted by overfishing that yields are a fraction of former levels. Such behavior also occurred in the past: Lewis and

Clark encountered areas along their famous journey where the game had been hunted out and their party went hungry. Farmers too, can overexploit the land by overirrigating (which causes salt buildup), allowing erosion, and reducing fertility by failing to rotate crops or allow for sufficient fallow seasons. Herding almost invariably causes overgrazing and a reduction in plant productivity. Humans often degrade their environment with the effect of decreasing the overall carrying capacity.

All these factors suggest that the carrying capacity of any area is not fixed and can be altered by changes in human behavior—new technology, a willingness to work harder, new crops, overexploitation, or new attitudes toward food and lifestyle. This seeming *plasticity* of the carrying capacity has led some scholars to believe that any long-team shortages in food can be met by humans simply by changing their behaviors, thereby changing their area's carrying capacity. In practice, though, this is not correct, except in a few exceptional times and places. What researchers have discovered is often quite the opposite: Rather than being able quickly to change behaviors and change their region's carrying capacity, groups that have been using a particular landscape for a long time have been found to have worked out most of the useful technologies and discovered most of the usable plants and animals. What often strikes researchers when they study peoples all over the world, in the present and the past, is human ingenuity and how much they know about the plants and animals in their domains.

Almost all the dramatic changes in the land's carrying capacity either occurred slowly—as the result of agriculture, for instance—or were the result of the introduction of new plants, animals, or technologies from outside. The potato in Europe, cattle on the American plains, steel tools in many tropical areas all had almost immediate effects on the carrying capacity of these areas. Yet the places from which these same wonderful new technologies originated had long before been altered by these innovations and were no longer able to use these same plants, animals, or technologies to increase their own carrying capacities any further. Most of the time, it is hard for any population to increase its area's carrying capacity very much in the short term, especially in the face of changing climate or other factors affecting this capacity. For the potential to be greatest—for changes in lifestyle or attitude to have a big effect—often requires behavior changes by the entire society, not just some individuals. It is unlikely that every time a society needs to increase its community's carrying capacity, the inhabitants can domesticate a new plant or animal, discover a wild plant that is both common and nutritious, or devise a major new technology.[13] Regardless of how well any society utilizes its resources, regardless of how much it conserves them, if there are too many people for those resources to support, the resources will become depleted or inadequate. Consequently, no society can have an ecological conservation ethic that works unless that society somehow addresses this population–resource balance issue.

Another way the carrying capacity could be altered is by changes in climate. The world's climate is less constant than scholars used to think.[14] For years, much of the premise of geology and biology was that change on Earth occurs gradually—and not just climate change, but all sorts of other changes in the world's ecosystem in general. Almost every relevant scientific discipline is now beginning to recognize that change can be much more rapid and more dramatic than previously acknowledged. This does not make the fundamental conclusions of geology or biology inaccurate, but it does greatly affect how events play out and how these phenomena must be studied. For example, climatologists now know from studying ice cores and ocean- and lake-bottom sediments that the Ice Age ended about 14,500 years ago and the world warmed up for one thousand years. Then in a few decades it plunged back into the Ice Age again, only to warm suddenly once again thirteen hundred years later.

Given this new evidence, researchers must now conclude that the world's long-term climate patterns can change rapidly. The Dust Bowl is America's best-known example of such rapid, radical environmental change, but changes in England in the early 1800s were probably more profound. At that time, England's climate became significantly milder in the space of a generation or two. Changes of a similar magnitude have occurred, including a cooling trend at about the time the Romans abandoned England (around A.D. 400). Rapid climate change has become a focus of research because of contemporary concern with global warming. One possible explanation for global warming is simply that it's a natural climatic variation. The world can rapidly warm in a generation or two, and it has happened in the past. Dramatic but short-lived changes in climate cam be caused by volcanic eruptions spewing dust into the atmosphere, blocking out the sunlight and cooling Earth for a few years, such as the eruption of the Tambora volcano in 1815. It produced so much dust in the atmosphere that the sunlight was blocked and the following frigid year became known as "the year without summer." Crops failed to mature in the cold and an estimated eighty-two thousand people died from starvation, far more than were killed in the eruption.[15]

Such changes need not be as dramatic as the Ice Ages of twenty thousand to forty thousand years ago to be significant. One of these relatively minor changes is known as the Medieval Warm Period, followed by the Little Ice Age. [16] The Medieval Warm Period began in the A.D. 800s and ended in the 1200s. During this period, much of the world was warm and moist, a warmth that exceeded even that of today. The climate was good for crops in most places around the world. From the archaeological and historical records we can see that the population soared in some places, Scandinavia and the southwestern United States among them, and resource abundance helped launch the construction of Gothic cathedrals, the colonization of Iceland (ca. 874) and Greenland (ca. 985), as well as the Shetland and Faeroe islands, and briefly, Vinland (North America) by the Scandinavian Vikings.

Then the warmth waned, and by 1250 to the 1300s the world began to cool—and it cooled very rapidly. The so-called Little Ice Age had arrived. By 1317, famines caused by failure of crops to mature caused thousands of deaths in England and other parts of Europe. The cold grew in intensity and reached its peak between 1500 and 1700, when glaciers in the Alps surged, destroying farmland and flattening villages in their wake. No one would construct a substantial house if a glacier threatened to destroy it. The buildup and movement of the ice must have been fast enough that the Swiss and other Alpine people must not have anticipated it. The Little Ice Age did not fully end until the 1800s. The English winters Charles Dickens describes in *A Christmas Carol* and George Washington's bitter winter at Valley Forge, Pennsylvania, remind us just how much colder it was, and not all that long ago. The cold may have been just an inconvenience for Ebenezer Scrooge, but for regions of the world, it reduced crop yields and even made places unfarmable. [17]

What happens to societies when the climate gets worse or better for a few centuries, or even for a generation or two? Is there enough extra food to get through a multiyear change for the worse? Usually not. And, equally important, what happens when the food supply suddenly improves? Do humans respond to the increased plenty by increasing their population? If so, what happens when the benign climate gets bad again? If the human populations in the past had food aplenty, then perhaps these changes would not matter much. If they were using only half or two-thirds of the available food, and the climate deteriorated, the new lesser food supply still might have been adequate. But if food was rarely in great excess, then even minor climate change held the potential for disaster.

Populations do exceed their area's carrying capacity on occasion, but just what does exceeding the carrying capacity mean? It's not a question of hav-

Manioc root was widely eaten in much of lowland South America. Poisonous, it requires great effort to process. Here a woman is laboriously squeezing out the poison by twisting a fiber "tube" containing ground manioc flour. People would never depend on such a poor food as a staple unless food was chronically in short supply. Today we use manioc as tapioca.

ing plenty of food, then running out of food. As the group nears the limits of its region's carrying capacity, the lean times of the year become *very* lean—there can be chronic hunger but not actual starvation. Remember, the Yanomama are constantly hungry. There are plenty of Yanomama, so they are not all dying of starvation, though they are close to the carrying capacity of their rain forest environment. Being near carrying capacity means that there are chronic shortages and that a person's health, reproductive success, and general well-being are affected by the availability of food on an annual basis. Just how bad is "bad" is partially subjective and a function of the alternatives. Can more work bring some relief? Can eating less desirable foods help? Is an individual hungry enough to attempt taking land that would provide more food from someone else? The carrying capacity is being pressed when such decisions need to be made on a regular basis.

Even if no outside factors result in carrying capacity stress, the human ability to reproduce always comes into play. Humans can grow their populations with amazing speed. The Hutterites, a religious sect that migrated from Europe to South Dakota in the 1870s, are a classic example. In the nineteenth and early twentieth centuries, Hutterite women bore an average of 9.8 children each. One segment of the group grew from 443 individuals in 1880 to 8,542 people in 1950, a staggering twentyfold increase in only seventy years.[18] To put this rate into perspective, if the world's present population of 6 billion grew that fast for one hundred years, there would be 400 billion people on Earth in the year 2100.

An average of slightly more than two children per woman is all that is needed to maintain the status quo, yet almost nowhere in the world, until very recently, did women have so few. Neither was it considered the appropriate cultural behavior to have only two children. Typical farm families had many times this number. Humans have almost always produced more off-spring than are needed to keep the population constant. In some foraging societies, mothers nurse each child for a very long time, spacing children about four years apart. Such very long birth-spacing intervals result in few births per woman, sometimes dipping as low as four or so children per mother, but this still results in significant growth potential. Only in some recent urban societies do birth rates ever fall into the circa two-children-per-woman range, on average.[19]

Although many factors affect the human ability to reproduce—from the amount of fat in the diet to the types of food available for newly weaned children—what matters is that humans, like all other animals, are capable of producing children at a much higher rate than necessary to replace themselves. Charles Darwin observed that animals that breed very slowly, elephants and some whales, for example, are fully capable of increasing their numbers exponentially. As most of us have learned from television nature programs, elephant herds living in Africa's national parks increase their numbers until they destroy their reserve environments, and the wardens must then cull the herds. Yet the parks are not that old, and the herds have not been protected for very long. Similarly, the California gray whales were hunted almost to extinction. When they were first protected in 1946, it was estimated there were no more than one thousand gray whales left. By 1992 there were more than twenty thousand. When predators are eliminated and food is available, elephants and whales, despite having gestation periods even longer than humans (although they mature faster), can reproduce rapidly.

Now, one might think that humans do not reproduce rapidly because they simply don't want to. When women in traditional societies all over the world are asked how many children they want, the answer seems to be "as many as possible, as long as it's not too many." The desire for lots of children is very strong in just about all traditional societies. Though it is true that infant survival in most societies is low and half the children can die before reaching adulthood, when a child dies, there is motivation to replace him or her if possible. If the child dies at an early age, the mother is no longer nursing and can soon get pregnant again.

The anthropological record demonstrates repeatedly that when resources are ample and people are not crowded into unsanitary cities, infant mortality is not nearly 50 percent, and far more than two children per woman survive to reproduce.[20] Given the right conditions, human growth can be explosive, as was seen with the Hutterites. We see similar rapid growth rates among colonizers of land that has recently been depopulated, for example, areas of the Americas after European diseases decimated the native people. When a new, efficient technology becomes available—such as the steel plow introduced by the European pioneers on the Great Plains, the potato in Ireland, and iron tools in sub-Saharan Africa—population growth takes off.[21] Virtually every society on Earth is capable of rapid population growth.

The human reproductive process depends to an extent on food availability and the need to acquire it. When women are poorly nourished, they conceive less often and their infants are less likely to survive. When food is scarce, women must spend much more time trying to find or grow food, thereby limiting their ability to reproduce. When food is plentiful, the reproductive rate goes up; when it is scarce, the rate falls. Though this concept may seem simple, don't forget that any abundance of edibles is accompanied by consequences. If food was plentiful at any time and place in the past, the reproductive rate would have gone up. The subsequent increase in population would increase the number of mouths to feed. What was once plentiful would soon become scarce. The cycle is ages old: It is true for our foraging ancestors, our early farming ancestors, and the first civilizations. Reproductive rates will almost always be constrained by nutrition, and food will almost always be scarce.

The adult population is obviously affected by food shortages as well. If an adult happens to get sick when malnourished, he or she is less likely to survive. All individuals become much more susceptible to diseases like tuberculosis when suffering from a lack of food. Populations one might otherwise think were immune are extremely sensitive to such food stress.

Some of the most relevant examples of this food availability–reproductive rate phenomenon come from England during the last few hundred years.[22] As early as the 1600s, English parish records accurately recorded births and deaths, and we have good information about grain prices during the same time periods. The cost of grain was closely related to its scarcity—in times of poor crops, the price went up—and the correlation between the cost of grain and the number of deaths in many parishes is very close. From this information, research has shown that in English farming communities—areas one would have considered well buffered from the annual fluctuations of the harvest—the death rate was significantly influenced by the grain supply. When grain was scarce and expensive, the death rate sometimes doubled that of good harvest years. People may not have starved in the classic sense of not eating at all but they certainly died from want of food when they succumbed to disease in their weakened condition.

These seventeenth-, eighteenth-, and nineteenth-century English farmers could do little to mitigate the consequences of the food shortages. The death rates recorded are dramatic enough for us to believe that people must have realized they were at risk. Certainly they knew when a crop was bad and what was going to happen. Had they been able to do something about this—move to new and better places—they would have. They did when they could. Had they been able to take food from their neighbors, they no doubt would have seized the opportunity. Can it have been otherwise over much of the rest of the world?

If carrying capacity is relatively fixed and the human population can grow rapidly, reproductive rates are a key issue. One might ask, why don't people simply regulate their numbers to avoid the carrying capacity problem altogether? If population was way below the carrying capacity and could be kept there, then there would be no problem. Perhaps the most obvious "solution" to the population–resource balance challenge is the attempt to regulate population growth by social rules and traditions. Though humans are the most social of all creatures and many societies have rules that tend to reduce the number of children, the question is, do those rules work well enough to solve the problem?

Humans regulate population growth in many ways, including increased birth spacing by nursing infants for a long time, raising the age of marriage, preventing a portion of the population from marrying, promoting taboos against intercourse during certain times and circumstances. Prolonging

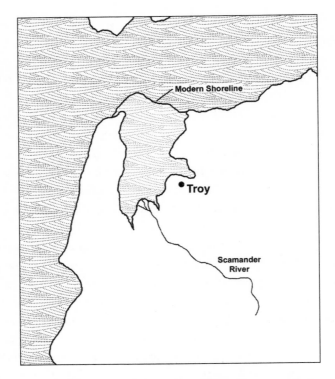

Homer's descriptions of the setting of Troy do not match the present environment, because the bay in front of the city has silted up from tree cutting, overgrazing, and over-farming since the Greeks destroyed the city more than 3,000 years ago. Farmers especially degrade their environments, and the Middle East has the longest history of farming in the world, hence some of the most degraded land on earth.

breast-feeding is particularly effective. The harder it is to obtain food, the less likely the mother will be able to tend two small children; by continuing to nurse one, she will not have another. The less food available, the fewer children. Similarly, if one needs to pay a bride-price, or accumulate a prescribed level of wealth to set up a separate household, marriages will be postponed when times are difficult, reducing the population most when the problems are greatest. The extreme form of this custom is having social requirements so difficult to meet that many members of the society never marry at all. This was the case in England in the 1700s and 1800s when considerable numbers of women went into domestic service, never to marry. There was also the almost universal practice of infanticide.

One of the most important methods of population control has been infanticide, the intentional killing of infants. The fact that infanticide was such a common practice in the past can come as a shock to many people today. Anthropologists have found that the practice occurred in a variety of forms, some direct and some indirect. We are concerned with the demographic consequences of infanticide, not with how it was accomplished. Male and female babies are born in almost equal numbers. When there are far more young boys than girls in a society, we can assume that some type of infanticide was being practiced, even if it was only selected neglect. Since in the past abortion was much more dangerous for the mother than was childbirth, infanticide was a less risky approach—and one that selectively allowed a baby of a particular sex (usually a boy) to survive.

In some societies—Eskimos (Inuit), for example—the couple would make a very public decision and simply place the baby outside. If another couple wanted the baby, they took it in. If not, the infant died. In the 1700s and 1800s, Europeans developed institutions to give this practice the appearance of propriety. Foundling hospitals were established, after the leadership became upset at the sight of so many abandoned babies along streets and roads. These hospitals had special doors designed to allow an adult to leave a baby anonymously. Allegedly orphanages, these institutions spelled death for the majority of infants that crossed their thresholds. Most scholars believe that about 90 percent of all babies soon died. Hundreds of thousands of infants were admitted to foundling hospitals; one estimate has seventy-five thousand babies per year in France alone.[23]

In addition, most babies still slept with their mothers in eighteenth- and nineteenth-century Europe, and some were accidentally suffocated when parents rolled over on them in their sleep. This became a common event, and most scholars believe that many of the "overlaying" accidents recorded were in fact deliberate acts of infanticide.[24] When European missionaries reached Melanesia and Polynesia in the 1700s and early 1800s, they attempted to stop the common practice of infanticide, while the very same thing was taking place at home. Infanticide was practiced in Japan and elsewhere in Asia, in the ancient states of Southwest Asia, and by peoples of the Amazon. In addition to the Inuit (Eskimo) foragers, the Australian Aborigines practiced infanticide, with one scholar estimating that perhaps 50 percent of all births ended that way.[25]

The real question is whether a society—by whatever means—can adjust its behavior to result in population stability at the requisite level. If population numbers go up, can groups decide to use social mechanisms to raise the marriage age, increase infanticide, proclaim that long periods of nursing are healthier for babies, or that convents are appropriate places for more women? As compelling as this scenario sounds, it does not work. In order

for these mechanisms to be successful, everyone in the society must cooperate with the new "plan" (whatever it is), which is not easily accomplished.
China's present efforts to limit families to one child is another form of
population control and has had a very significant impact on the growth
rate, but the population is still growing.[26] In addition, the response must be
very fine-tuned. If the plan works and the population does decline, social
rules must be changed again to enable the group to grow once more, or else
it will become extinct. Ultimately, the population must stabilize at well
below its location's average annual carrying capacity to avoid changes in
productivity that occur from year to year.

The group must recognize that a single good harvest year, or even a few
good years, does not really mean anything. The population cannot be
allowed to grow. Even with ample supplies of food, people still must practice infanticide, or not get married, or delay having another child. If the climate changes for the better, eventually it will be perceived as the new norm
and the population will grow to a new appropriate level. A sharp downturn
and a bad year or two will not support the expanded population, but the
mechanisms to control the numbers are slow acting. Postponing getting
married has an impact on the population only many, many years later.

If controlling population at a sustainable level by social methods is a
challenge, we can consider whether unforeseen events, like disease and natural disasters, which occurred throughout the ages might have been automatic means to control growth. At some times and places, epidemics have
devastated populations, the most notable cases being the bubonic plague
that afflicted Europe and Asia beginning in the 1340s, and the cataclysmic
impact of European diseases, such as smallpox and measles, in the New
World after 1492.[27] As with the arguments just made for weather-related
catastrophes, the timing of epidemics would have to be perfect to result in
keeping populations in proper balance. Epidemics did have an impact on
population growth in the past, but they could not have regulated it.

For most of human history, populations were too small and too spread
out to enable epidemics to take hold. Studies of major epidemics—cholera
in China or India, bubonic plague in the same regions as well as Europe—
show that populations have been slow to recover in a few instances, and vast
areas were left empty in some cases. What appears to be a demographic
catastrophe must be put into a proper time scale. In Europe and the New
World, in the cases of such epidemics as the plague, for which we have good
records, it took the population somewhere between one hundred and two
hundred years to recover. Even in the most catastrophic epidemics known,
populations eventually recovered and went on to grow. There is no reason

to believe that over the long haul, repetitive occasional epidemics just happen to occur at the proper frequency to control population growth.

The same logic applies to natural disasters. Surely catastrophes did occur in the past and had an impact on populations. This is not to say that such events would keep populations in proper balance. For example, suppose a flood, hurricane, earthquake, or the like occurred once every ten years and 11 percent of the people died each time, but between disasters the population grew 10 percent. In that case, every ten years the population would get smaller until, finally, in a few centuries, it would be extinct. If between catastrophes the population grew 12 percent, then the population would slowly grow. After a few generations, the population would exceed the carrying capacity in spite of the regular catastrophes. It would be a miracle if the natural disasters and birth rates perfectly balanced.[28]

Tikopia, a small island in the South Pacific, provides a good illustration of just how these issues of ecological balance, carrying capacity, and population control can affect a society. Once again, if there is any place in the world where people must be aware that they should keep their population in check, and where resources are in relative abundance, it is a Pacific island.

When Europeans first arrived on Tikopia in the early 1800s, they found a tropical paradise. The island consists of only six square miles of lowland surrounding a small lagoon. It was settled by Polynesian voyagers, probably around 900 B.C., and lies some two hundred miles from its nearest neighbors, the Melanesian Islands (except for the speck of an island of Arunta). Tikopia's population probably never exceeded one thousand two hundred people until the last few decades.[29] The Tikopians, being few and isolated, are so culturally similar that one would think the island the perfect place to use social rules, either by threat or social pressure, to keep the population under control. According to early ethnographers who studied Tikopia in the late 1800s and early 1900s, that indeed was the case.

For hundreds of years, the islanders had a number of communally encouraged mechanisms to control population, including celibacy, coitus interruptus, a cultural norm of two children, as well as abortion and infanticide. These mechanisms were actively and publicly encouraged by the ruling chiefs, and the community recognized and publicly acknowledged that the danger from population growth posed a real threat of starvation. The resources of the island and the sea were not boundless, and it was far too easy to grow beyond the carrying capacity. As land was limited, there was room for only so many trees, even though a breadfruit or coconut tree can be very productive. A lagoon can be overexploited and its yield drop dramatically. The open ocean can vary considerably in its productivity over the

Moa and other large flightless birds were extincted by the Maori soon after they colonized New Zealand, around A.D. 1000. If humans were able to live in sustainable balance, they would be careful not to eradicate large mammals, thereby reducing their food supply. The Maori must have been aware that they were diminishing the numbers of such a large animal, yet they did not stop hunting them. This staged scene was created in 1899 by Peter Buck, the great Maori anthropologist, by using a museum recreation of a moa based on an excavated skeleton.

year, and years. The ability to fish successfully on a consistent and regular basis was probably lower than one might expect. And, again, there's the weather. A typhoon can come near enough to an island to destroy the tree fruit before it matures, leading to a sudden loss of expected resources. A drought could cause the same type of problem. In short, it was possible to starve in "paradise," and the Tikopians knew it. In fact, as late as 1950, a drought caused such problems that the population was saved from starvation only by shipments of food from outside, something that had not been possible in the past. Inevitably environmental changes in the island's ecology must have occurred in the past, and any degradation of such a small ecosystem must have accentuated food stress.

Ethnographic studies indicate that in the past abortion and infanticide—not rules of celibacy, late marriages, or the like—were the mainstays of population control. And the degree to which population control was practiced was substantial. When pressure from missionaries and other outsiders caused infanticide and abortion to be outlawed in the early part of the twentieth century, the Tikopian population began a rapid growth. It grew from 1,281 people in 1929 to 1,750 by 1952, or 37 percent in only twenty-three years.[30] Clearly, such a rate of increase could not have existed for long in the past and with a population density of over 300 people per square mile was only possible by importing food. Although the other social constraints on demographic growth may have been partially effective, infanticide and abortion were critical to population control. Even when these measures were practiced, along with many other social-behavior mechanisms to control growth, nothing worked. All the good intentions were insufficient to keep the population from increasing,

Tikopian oral traditions describe past populations growing to the point that people simply had to leave. A large contingent of people would sail off on outrigger canoes to find a new place to live. Who chose or was chosen to leave is not clear, but most likely it was the most marginalized, lowest status people who had the least to lose. Since there are not colonies of Tikopians all over Oceania, we must assume that most of these voyages failed. Either the pilgrims never found landfall before they starved, or they drowned in storms. If they did land, they could have been considered a new food source rather than welcome colonists, cannibalism being a regular practice among their nearest neighbors on the Melanesian Islands. The ultimate and final solution to the Tikopians' growing numbers was for some segment of the society to play a Russian roulette–type population control. During past centuries, a portion of the island's population was forced to depart, with only a small chance of surviving.

Even on the relative "Eden" of an Oceanic island, living a conservationist lifestyle is difficult, if not impossible. In order to live in ecological balance, human societies must do several things. They must not degrade their environment over time. Even if they do find the means for sustained conservationist behavior, they must keep their population far enough below the carrying capacity so the annual variation in food supplies does not create provisioning crises. Even if both these requirements are met, the society must also be able to adapt to changes in the climate or technology that threaten this balance. Finally, they must be able to respond to true long-term changes in the environment while ignoring short-term variability. Accomplishing all this is a tall order, and there is no evidence—not in the archaeological, ethnographic, or historical records—that humans have ever attained this balance for more than a couple of centuries anywhere on Earth. All humans grow, impact their environment, and, sooner or later, exceed the carrying capacity.

Being resourceful creatures, humans have developed various coping mechanisms in order to stay alive during times of stress. They store food, have social networks that allow them to move in with distant relatives during bad times, and employ such devices as food sharing, which comes in a variety of forms, including potlatches in the Pacific Northwest and social "giveaways" among the Hopi and Zuni, to avoid starving at the slightest shortfall of food. Humans establish a "standard of living" that is above mere subsistence. When they fall below this standard, they react.

The ability to react and to alter their environmental constraints—to change the carrying capacity—is one of the important ways humans are different from most animals. With other animals, when the numbers of a particular species go up, their predators' numbers increase also. As predators kill more of the overpopulated species, the animal population stops rising. Humans have not had significant predators for a million years or more. We do have another kind of predator: other humans. And this is where warfare enters the equation.

chapter three

ENTER CONFLICT

*T*he Mimbres Valley, located in the southwest corner of New Mexico, is a place of fertile fields watered by the small, clear Mimbres River, which flows out of the mountains to the north. The Mimbres people flourished around A.D. 1000, when there were more than a dozen major villages and many small homesteads situated up and down the length of the valley. The Mimbres people have been identified with their most distinctive pottery, the spectacular black-and-white painted bowls. Typically adorned with intricate geometric designs or pictorial images from daily life, these were used as food-serving vessels and often interred with the deceased. The Mimbres buried their dead close to their natal hearth, usually beneath the very floor they lived on.

In the early 1970s, during the first of a half dozen field seasons on the Mimbres, our dig camp was headquartered in a historic ranch house situated just above the river, right next to a very large, long-lived village dating to about one thousand years ago. My team was beginning to excavate on the big village site, but we were still exploring our surroundings. Several members noticed that directly across the river from us was a steep hill with a small, slightly flat area on top. Out of curiosity one day, part of the crew climbed the hill and reported back that it held the remains of approximately fifteen houses. The surface was littered with pieces of broken pottery that indicated that some of the earliest farmers to live in the valley must have settled there (around A.D. 200).

Such hilltop sites were known from other parts of the Southwest, but it did not make sense to us. Early farmers living on high, isolated knolls? Why live on the hill when they could have settled down the slope where we were camped? We were closer to water and farmland, and our location avoided the steep climb required to haul food, firewood, water, and everything else this community of perhaps thirty to forty people would have needed.

Archaeologists had puzzled over this "hilltop site" question for years, and my crew pondered it as we continued to dig. During the course of the next month, we made a fascinating discovery: Virtually every site of this same time period in the Mimbres Valley was situated on such an eminence. After we found another site located on a hill some seven hundred feet above the river floodplain, the rancher who owned the land we were digging on happened to mention that lightning frequently struck that hill. It struck so often, he said, that he actually lost a cow a year to lightning strikes on that particular knoll.

That bit of information stunned us. Those Mimbres hilltop locations were not only inconvenient but also dangerous in this land of daily summer thundershowers. Upon learning this, I began to suspect that the Mimbres people built these hilltop settlements because they had to. The possibility of prehistoric warfare was right in front of my eyes. The hills must have provided their communities with strategic defensive positions.[1] Suspecting that the hilltop villages were forts is one thing, it is quite another to have convincing evidence for warfare. As almost always with archaeology, I needed to put this find into a larger context.

I began to look at other archaeologists' work and realized that they also had found a good deal of evidence for warfare, even though they did not always recognize it. The Mimbres hilltop sites were not unique. These early farmer sites dating from 1000 B.C. to the first couple of centuries A.D. appear all over the Southwest. Many sites are clearly defensive, both in terms of their location and the presence of low, defensive walls. Archaeologists also find evidence of prehistoric warfare in the region in the form of massacres, scalping, and trophy head taking. This type of evidence spans a thousand years; even in a large area of the Southwest dating to the A.D. 800s, almost every site excavated was burned, another indicator of early intergroup conflict.

The prehistoric Southwest, long known as home to the "peaceful Pueblo Indians," was racked by war. Our Mimbres hilltop settlements were just one more example of it, even though they revealed only a few of the hallmarks of warfare. I began to think that if the Southwest was not peaceful, then there was little reason to believe any other place on Earth was peaceful for long. The whole idea of a peaceful past came into question.

Up to this point, I have used the word *warfare* loosely, but before continuing on this six-million-year journey through human history, I should clarify what I mean by warfare. Conflict among animals, especially chimpanzees, has the hallmarks of what I consider to be warfare. At the same time, not all human conflict is necessarily warfare. The word conjures up visions of conflict that involves armies with great pitched battles and professional soldiers, but feuding, ambushing, and raiding also are relevant. Many scholars define *warfare* in such a way that it refers to something that only complex societies employing metal tools can have. Anything else— say, a raid or two now and then—is not "real" warfare, they believe, but is something more akin to game playing and not a subject of much concern. Such an approach or attitude, however, confuses the methods of war with the results of war.

I think it's more useful to approach warfare with such questions as, Does conflict between independent political units lead to significant deaths and loss of territory, or result in some territory being rendered useless because it's too dangerous to live in? Are people spending a great deal of time and energy defending themselves? The answers to these questions reveal a very different concept of warfare. If fighting results in significant impacts on people, it is war regardless of how the fighting is conducted. To assume otherwise is either to sanitize or misunderstand the past. The world was hardly peaceful until someone in China or Mesopotamia hammered out the first bronze sword. Ambushing the neighboring village and killing a few of the men and women with stone spears and knives is serious warfare, especially if it occurs on a regular basis. Such ambush behavior is known throughout the world and must have been the most common form of conflict in the past, and so it must be a focus interest.

Not every form of conflict is warfare, and a few useful distinctions about conflict are valid. For example, homicide and feuding aren't warfare. People from the same society killing each other, a behavior not sanctioned by the society as a whole, is not warfare, although, admittedly, the distinction can be a gray one.[2] The frequency of fighting and the numbers killed in each single event must be considered together—they are, by themselves, not meaningful in deciding whether warfare existed or not. In some societies, like highland New Guinea and the Yanomama of Venezuela, warfare was extremely frequent, with raids, ambushes, or battles occurring annually or even monthly. Often these conflicts resulted in only one or two fatalities per incident. When the numbers are tallied over a person's life span, many of the adult males died fighting. The total of all the war-related events, including efforts at defense, reflects the intensity of warfare.

There is the popular idea that there are some "fierce people" who are more prone to making war and are somehow different from most of the rest of the people on Earth. The Comanche of the southern Plains and the

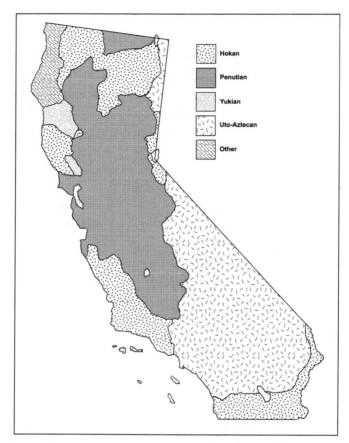

The distribution of California Indian languages shows repeated conquests by peoples who spoke unrelated languages, a pattern evidenced
throughout the world. Initially, much of the state was occupied by
Yukian speakers who were separated by the incursion of Hokan speakers, who were in turn eliminated in many areas by Penutian speakers,
and later by Uto-Aztecans.

Yanomama have been described as particularly aggressive and combative.
Others, including the Australian Aborigines or the Bushmen of South
Africa, have been considered more passive. These notions are part of pre-
conceived myths about human conflict and not based on reality.

It is one thing to define warfare, and another to find it. It is not easy to
see evidence of warfare in the past for a number of reasons. In El Morro,
the archaeological evidence for warfare was clear and stark, with massive
forts being the most obvious examples. Archaeology is not always so clear-
cut. In the quest to figure out our past, anthropologists and archaeologists
face the challenge of piecing together evidence from a variety of sources,

and like any puzzle, the process can be slow and painstaking. Until fairly recently, a considerable number of anthropologists and archaeologists were not inclined to look for evidence of warfare or ignored it when they did find it.

Much available evidence was recovered and interpreted by scholars who were often disinclined to see warfare or its consequences. As a result, finding past warfare is trickier than it might otherwise appear. For example, a castle is easy to recognize as an object of warfare, as are a sword and shield. But a bow can be used for hunting *and* fighting. When gathering information about past people, and when it comes to warfare, the real issue is knowing what to look for.

One of the most obvious indicators of warfare in the archaeological record is called "direct evidence of violence" found on skeletons. This includes arrowheads or spear points embedded in bones, or skulls with a major fracture from a "blunt instrument." Such evidence goes way back in time. The site of Shanidar Cave, in present-day Iraq, yielded a number of Neandertal skeletons dating from forty thousand to fifty thousand years ago. Among these, one had a stone blade stuck between two ribs, and another had evidence of blows to the head. These findings probably indicate violence, although other explanations are possible. Other clear-cut evidence for warfare in this time period is the fossilized human skeleton, called Skhul IX, recovered from a cave in Israel. In this case, the individual was speared in the leg and pelvis, as seen by the preserved damage to the bones, causing injuries that surely led to death. This unlucky person also may have suffered other wounds, which provides evidence of a classic form of warfare wounds as found among foragers—first immobilized by an arrow or spear, then dispatched by blows to the head.

Scalping, whether accomplished with a metal knife or a stone tool, usually results in long, straight cut marks on the skull bone itself. Scalping is really just a specialized form of trophy taking, and the taking of trophy heads was common in the past. During decapitation, the first two vertebrae usually go along with the head and do not stay with the body. When a skull has the first two vertebrae attached, or bodies are missing skulls along with the first two neck vertebrae, deliberate decapitation is the likely answer. Such was the case with a cache of forty-eight trophy heads found at the fifteen-hundred-year-old Cerro Carapo site on the coast of Peru. In a small cave in Kinboko Canyon, near Marsh Past in northern Arizona, a trophy head was buried about two thousand years ago as a grave good with an adult male at about the same time as the Mimbres Valley hill forts farther south. The head had been skinned, and the skin was carefully sewn up and painted—

fashioned so particularly and painted in such a standard way that this must have been a general practice. Trophy heads are depicted in almost identical fashion in nearby rock art.[3] Scalping was common enough in the Southwest at this same time that a special form of basket was woven to stretch and display the scalps. These scalp stretcher baskets were preserved only because of the very dry caves found in the area. In most of the world, such ancient evidence would have decayed and not be found archaeologically.[4]

Archaeologists sometimes recover bone showing very distinctive "parry fractures"—breaks that indicate the raising up of the arms to fend off a blow to the head. When an individual is about to be clubbed over the head, he instinctively raises an arm to deflect or "parry" the blow. The blow may well hit hard enough to break or fracture an arm but not cause a fatality. After the break heals, the bone still shows signs of the break. Such a fracture could result from an accident, but the overall frequency of fractured limbs can be computed, and when parry fractures are far more common than breaks from accidents would predict, we must conclude that they are from battle. The grave of the king who is known from inscriptions to have founded the ruling lineage of the Maya site of Copán was recently found, and he had just such a parry fracture. The archaeology suggested that the lineage was founded by conquest, and it is now clear he did not take power peacefully.

Not all evidence for warfare is as clear-cut as these examples. We assume that cannibalism was practiced when human bones have been treated in the same way people treated animal bones. In past times, in order to get all the nutrition possible from animals, the meat was cooked, leaving charred portions of the bone. As the carcass was processed, the bones were broken to extract the marrow, then sometimes boiled as part of a soup or gruel. All these types of processing have been found on human bones in many time periods around the world.

Some societies eat part of their dead relatives. Herodotus, the famous Greek historian, described the practice in the fifth century B.C. in Scythia.[5] The practice is better documented in the Fore people of highland New Guinea. Such consumption relates to preserving the spirit and linking the dead with the living. This behavior is extremely rare on a worldwide basis. Most of the time when humans eat other humans, they consume their enemies who have been killed or captured in battle, either for nutrition or as a ritual act. This practice is recorded almost all over the globe and as late as the seventeenth century in Europe. Historical examples of cannibalism include those from present-day Spain, Poland, and Bohemia, and prehistoric examples are known from Europe, Indonesia (Dayaks), Polynesia

These sling missiles demonstrate a widespread unwillingness to accept how common warfare was in the past. The cluster of sling missiles made of plaster (A) found in a 5000 B.C. site in Turkey are often believed to have been heated and used to boil water. Yet they (B) are identical in shape to the stone missiles from Hawaii used before European contact (C), and the lead missile made by the ancient Greeks (D) around 500 B.C.

(Maori), Melanesia (New Hebrides, Solomon Islands, New Caledonia, Fiji), Africa (Congo, Uganda, Ovimbundu), South America (Amazon Basin), Central America (Aztecs, Caribs), and North America (Iroquois). Some of this behavior is ritual and apparently only trace amounts of human flesh were actually consumed. For example, among the Huron, the entire village would participate in the torture and killing of a prisoner, culminating in the collective consumption of the heart, so this would not likely be archaeology visible in such cases.[6] When archaeologists find signs of cannibalism, it is almost certainly also evidence for warfare.

In spite of such considerable "direct" remains, much of the archaeological evidence for prehistoric warfare has nothing to do with bodies. Fortifications are the most common and obvious sign of warfare in the past. Settlements on hilltops surrounded by multiple walls, moats, and easily defended gates are quite convincing. The numbers of such forts can be impressive. There are more than one thousand hill forts, called *pa*, built by the Maori in New Zealand, and several times that many Iron Age (first millennium B.C.) hill forts in England. The Great Wall of China and Hadrian's Wall in England are obvious examples of fortification, even if there are no written records about them. In Peru, large, defensive walls many miles long also exist, which must have been built for the same defensive need. Bastions—portions of a fortification that project out—are also revealing.

When walls are studded with towers or other parts that jut out, defenders can shoot anyone trying to scale the wall. Such architecture leaves little doubt about the function of the wall itself. The earliest known examples of these walls are found in modern-day Turkey and date to 6000 B.C. These walls can be massive. Some walls around cities in ancient China were wide enough to accommodate a chariot and horses on top.

As I discovered in the Southwest, villages or towns can be better defended by being built on hilltops or upon narrow points of land. "Commanding the heights" is a basic military principle. In many cases, height alone was perceived to provide adequate defense. Many people around the world did not build defensive walls but instead built their houses connected so that the outer walls of the connected rooms provided a continuous defensive wall. This kind of defensive architecture is found in Southwest Asia and the American Southwest. The famous pueblos of the Taos, Acoma, and Hopi in Arizona and New Mexico were initially built in just this defensive manner—although now that peace prevails in the region, those communities have spread out and no longer present a defensive facade. Many prehistoric people took these defensive tactics one step further. They located their communities near their allies. By studying site maps and plotting settlement patterns over time periods, clear evidence for clusters of communities has been found. These "site clusters" are often carefully arranged so that one could signal from one site to the other, presumably for aid during attack. Often, when communities are clustered, the land between the clusters becomes hotly contested and thus uninhabitable. These relatively empty zones, or no-man's-lands, are found throughout the world among many different types of societies and are clear evidence for conflict. Empty zones have been recognized in the valley of Oaxaca in the last centuries B.C. when there was ample other evidence of warfare. They are found in the eastern United States in the late prehistoric period and in the Nile valley prior to the formation of the Egyptian state.[7] Sometimes, many of the defensive characteristics of prehistoric communities can be deduced without even digging.

When archaeologists excavate a site, they often find evidence of burning. Certainly, houses in the past were sometimes burned by accident, but when entire communities of hard-to-burn stone houses are charred, with all the people's possessions still in them, warfare must be suspected.[8] Burning is such a common act of warfare that in Mesoamerican writing the glyph signifying "conquest" depicted a temple being destroyed by fire. Archaeologists also recover caches of weapons—far more in number than would ever have been needed for hunting—or weapons that would not be useful for hunting. At one early farming village in the Middle East, a long wall along the edge of the village was excavated. Spaced along its interior, bucket-like pits had been hollowed out of the ground, and each was filled with hundreds of sling missiles. Another village had more than one thousand missiles piled in one room. This is evidence not only of warfare but also of stockpiling weapons in anticipation of attack.[9]

Shields and armor are found that were made exclusively for war. The range of materials used in their construction, in addition to metal, is ingenious: plate armor made from sections of bone sewn like venetian blinds made by prehistoric and historic Eskimo groups and worn under their parkas; long pieces of hide coiled around the body also from Eskimos; and armor woven from tough plant fibers in New Guinea. Shields were made not only of hide and metal; basketlike shields three feet in diameter were woven in the prehistoric Southwest. When scholars look carefully at these weapons and ask why people like the Australian Aborigines, who have so few possessions, would have so many weapons of war—special spears, special boomerangs, special spear-throwers, and shields and clubs used only for warfare—the importance of such weaponry becomes clear. The amount of effort and degree of care and skill used in making armor and other warfare-related items from around the world are often significant. In fact, this difference in "tool quality" can be very revealing. For example, if you make a digging tool and it breaks, you lose a bit of time out in the field. On the other hand, if your war club breaks in a battle, you are likely to die. In North America, among the Indians of the Plains, the best and strongest shield was fashioned out of buffalo hide, but not just any buffalo. The skin that covered the hump of a large male buffalo was carefully chosen. Then the hide was slowly smoked for days to make it stiffer and harder.[10] Making weapons and armor of the highest quality could save the life of the warrior on the battlefield. The archaeologist often sees meticulous care and fine workmanship reflected in the manufacture of weapons. This is clear evidence such items were intended for serious, deadly warfare, and not just ritual sparring.

An unexpected line of evidence for warfare is the presence of unburied or improperly buried bodies. One of the hallmarks of humans is our almost universal need to bury or otherwise formally deal with our dead. There are many different ways humans attend to the dead, but they all do something. We do not simply leave a body on the ground, or throw it in a ·ditch, or treat our dead disrespectfully. When humans treat the deceased in this manner, the body is that of an enemy or social deviant. Whenever archaeologists have recovered enough burials from a particular prehistoric culture, we can identify the normal burial practice. When we find bodies that deviate from this treatment in a manner we would consider disrespectful, we can suspect warfare as the cause. Hundreds of bodies tossed into ditches, as at the Crow Creek site on the upper Missouri, or stuffed into underground storage pits, or left out where their bones were gnawed by carnivores or rats, all bespeak of dead enemies, not relatives—or else a massacre that left no one alive to tend to the dead properly. On occasion, piles of bodies do show some attempts at burial. Dating to the same time range as the Mimbres hilltop sites and the trophy head from the Arizona cave, at a place called Cave 7 in southeastern Utah, almost one hundred people were killed in one massacre. It looks as if someone tried to bury some of the bodies, but most were not, and some still had knife points and the remains of other weapons embedded in them.

Sometimes this disrespectful treatment represents human sacrifices, almost surely of prisoners, because they were often buried with their hands bound, as found at the site of Teotihuacán near Mexico City.[11] The center of this great city was dominated by several monumental pyramids and temples. Near the Temple of the Feathered Serpent, mass human sacrifices of at least two hundred young men took place, probably in association with the dedication of the temple. The corpses were buried in and around the temple's perimeter in mass graves. Many individuals in these graves were found with their arms crossed and positioned behind them, presumably because their hands were tied.[12]

Visual art is another source of evidence for war. Rock art, painted and chipped into stone, and wall murals, beginning with the Upper Paleolithic cave paintings and continuing to the beautiful painted rooms of the Maya, often depict scenes of warfare, shields, and the like. Some pottery traditions, like the Moche pottery from the north coast of Peru, show battles, trophy heads, sacrificed prisoners of war, and men decked out with shields, weapons, body armor, and helmets. Imagery depicting dead, decapitated, and dismembered men is found carved in bas-relief on stone facings of public buildings in Peru and Mexico. Such public imagery certainly suggests that warfare was important. Demonstrating how successful a society had been at war was considered an important use of art.

There is little evidence in the archaeology of large battles that occurred away from residences. The remains of such events are so few and the remains so diffuse—some dropped weapons and the like—that they are almost never preserved well enough for archaeologists to recognize. Almost all that is known about such battles comes from historical and ethnographic accounts, so this aspect of prehistoric warfare is now lost, but it surely existed.

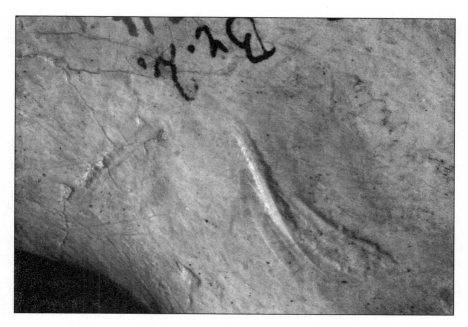

Many of the early human fossils show evidence of the bones being defleshed or butchered. Cannibalism was practiced world wide and goes deep into our past. The usual victim was a defeated enemy. This skull bone from the Neanderthal site of Krapina in the Balkans shows cuts made by a stone knife.

Moving along the human time line into the "historic" period, we find a wider variety of information about conflict than can be derived from archaeology alone. Early historical accounts, sometimes written by native people who learned the invading culture's language, are helpful, as is information recorded by early explorers. Accounts from anthropologists, missionaries, or government agents who learned the local language and kept diaries or made extensive reports contribute to the record. These latter sources can also include written accounts of oral traditions, legends, epic stories, and so on. The Bible, India's *Mahabharata*, Scandinavian epics, and Homer's *Iliad* were all told orally and only later captured in writing. All have warfare as important themes. One traditional story from the Hopi gives the flavor of such accounts and at the same time reveals details and aspects of some types of warfare, from the use of fire to the timing of raids.

Just as the sky turned the colors of the yellow dawn, Ta'palo rose to his feet on the kiva roof. He waved his blanket in the air, whereupon the attackers climbed to the top of the mesa and began the assault. There were many of them, so many in fact that they filled the village of Awat'ovi. . . . Running from kiva to kiva, they found that the men were inside. Immediately, they pulled out the ladders, thereby depriving those inside of any chance to escape. Now all of them had come to Awat'ovi with finely shredded juniper bark and greasewood kindling. Upon removing the ladders, they lit the bark . . . they ignited the juniper bark and the greasewood kindling, which they hurled into the kivas. Next, they set the wood stacks on top of the kivas aflame and threw them down through the hatches. Then they shot their arrows down on the men. . . . Now the raiders stormed into all the houses. Wherever they came across a man, no matter whether young or old, they killed him. Some they simply grabbed and cast into a kiva. Not a single man or boy did they spare.

Bundles of dry chili were hanging on the walls . . . the attackers pulverized them . . . and scattered the powder into the kivas, right on top of the flames. Then they closed up the kiva hatches everywhere. As a result, the smoke could not escape. The chili caught fire, and mixed with the smoke, stung most painfully. There was crying, screaming, and coughing. After a while the roof beams caught fire. As they flamed up, they began to collapse, one after the other. Finally, the screams died down and it became still. Eventually, the roofs caved in on the dead, burying them. Then there was just silence.[13]

In addition to oral traditions, there are ethnographic and other more recent accounts of the nature and intensity of traditional warfare from around the world. The tremendous impact Western society as well as other complex societies like China had on the people under observation prior to the arrival of anthropologists or other chroniclers makes these accounts problematic. Though many ethnographers attempt to describe the "traditional" society they set out to observe, their work actually reports how the elderly of the society lived when they were younger. Such research does not accurately describe the "pre-impact" situation, which was often several hundred years earlier. For example, the Germans had pacified the Samoan Islands almost one hundred years before Margaret Mead arrived as a young woman in the mid-1920s to do her famous study. Although there had once been considerable warfare, all was peaceful by the time Mead arrived, which is reflected in her rather idyllic portrayal of life on the isles. Earlier accounts present a very different picture. The Samoans had long fought among themselves and neighboring island groups. Missionary John Williams, in 1830–1832, recorded that one village had kept a record of 197 battles. One day he inquired about mountains in the distance being enveloped in flames and smoke and was informed "that a battle had been fought that very morning and that the flames which we saw were consuming the houses, the plantations and the bodies of women and children and infirm people" who had fallen into the hands of the conquerors. Samoa was at peace in the 1920s but at war in the 1820s.

The various kinds of tactics social groups have used through time to wage war is one more aspect of conflict. Raids are the most common form of warfare among noncomplex societies. The goal of a raid is to damage the enemy, with no intention of capturing territory or wiping out the enemy. Inflicting damage to the enemy while taking as little risk as possible is the modus operandi of raiding. The dawn raid, in which the attackers have the benefit of light but the victims are still asleep or unprepared, is a classic, worldwide behavior. Ernest Burch collected numerous accounts of warfare stories that elders among the Eskimos of northwest Alaska heard when they were young: "The most common procedure for achieving the tactical objective of [annihilation] was the surprise raid. This was executed by approaching a settlement on hands and knees under cover of darkness. . . . The ideal situation was for the approach to be made while everyone in the settlement was in the social center [an extra-large house] . . . if the attackers arrived too late, after everyone had gone home [from the social center] . . . the [attackers] would have to try and eliminate everyone in the village one by one, going from house to house and killing them while they slept."[14]

Even modern nation-states engage in raids. Winston Churchill was enamored with the concept of raids, and the World War II commando units were established to undertake them. Ambushes are really just a special kind of raid in which the goal is to surprise one or two individuals, kill them, and then run.

Pitched battles, in which large groups of combatants set up and square off, are less common, but all types of societies undertook them. Since such battles are riskier than raids for the attackers, they occurred less frequently. Ranging in size from fifty men on a side up to World War I's massive battles of the Somme, pitched battles are what most people today conceive of as warfare. Such encounters can sometimes end in a rout, when the defeated flee and lose cohesion. Under such circumstances large armies are annihilated or entire communities massacred. Alexander the Great's battle goal was always to attack so hard at one part of the enemy line that it would break and the soldiers scatter, then his army would massacre them as they fled. Some massacres in the past involved only fifty or a hundred individuals, but when the entire social group was wiped out, the event was more devastating than the rout of a large army.

Another aspect of warfare involves to what degree conflict is linked with other interaction among the opponents. Many societies trade or even exchange mates with another group during part of the year and launch raids on them in another. Planning a massacre treacherously disguised as a feast or celebration is an example of such shifting behaviors and is a recurrent theme around the world. An ethnographic account related to anthropologist Napoleon Chagnon in the 1960s by Kaobawa, a leader of a small Yanomama village, reveals how this could happen. Kaobawa's group, with few allies and under pressure from its enemies, tried to form an alliance with a neighboring group. This village was actually part of the enemy alliance and set about to take advantage of Kaobawa's desperation by inviting his group to a purported feast. When they arrived at the host village, "the men of Kaobawa's group danced both singly and en masse and were invited into the homes of their hosts. At this point their hosts fell upon them with axes and staves, killing about a dozen before the visitors could break through the palisade and escape."[15]

The Germans and Russians were actively trading materials useful in warfare until the day before the Nazis attacked in World War II. In the New Guinea highlands, raids often had to be planned in secret, excluding the men and women with close relatives among the group to be attacked, because they were expected to warn the intended victims. All types of societies from foragers to states have these friend-enemy dual relationships.

The evidence for and characteristics of past warfare come together, again, in Tikopia, that particularly appropriate example from the "paradise" of the South Pacific. In spite of the efforts to control population, including infanticide and periodic "explorations" for resettlement, the Tikopians could not control their numbers, nor were the sea and land of limitless bounty. In such a small society, with an entire island population of fewer than fifteen hundred people, severe resource stress would not be expected to result in warfare. If there were any place where people might starve when all other courses of action were exhausted, it would be a small island in the middle of nowhere. Yet there was warfare in paradise. At one time Tikopia had three political entities. In the mid-1700s, the group living in the least productive area of the island virtually annihilated the other two political entities or forced them to flee. We know from historical accounts that at least one other major act of warfare had taken place a couple of centuries previously. When Tikopia was not under a single political leadership, violent and annihilating warfare took place at least every few centuries.[16]

Having discovered that evidence for past warfare can be found just about anywhere in the world where reasonably good archaeological research has been undertaken—and historical and ethnographic accounts show the same thing—it was clear that the idea of a peaceful past was just a myth. With this in mind, I turned back to my two decades of research in the Southwest and wondered why all this warfare was occurring. The one common thread I found with all this warfare, including that from the Southwest, was that it correlated with people exceeding their area's carrying capacity. Ecological imbalance, I believe, is the fundamental cause of warfare. It is one thing to believe this but another to demonstrate this relationship. To do so, one must be able to show that there was such ecological imbalance. In addition, one needs to be able to provide an idea of how resource stress would lead to chronic and continuous warfare and not some other outcome.

Getting archaeological evidence of carrying-capacity stress requires being lucky and clever, so it is spotty. Evidence for climate change, which affects carrying capacity, is easier to find. In a place like the Southwest, where farming is, and probably always has been, marginal, climate deterioration should coincide with food shortages. The archaeology of the region as a whole shows that when the climate was good, the population grew and there was not much warfare. When the climate deteriorated, warfare intensified, as seen in El Morro where I encountered warfare and the rapid building of fortified towns. Warfare did seem to change with good times and bad times. Although my team had trouble assessing the level of carrying-capacity stress at the time the people lived on the hilltops in the Mimbres Valley, when we placed these sites in a regional context, it made sense. Warfare in the region was real and patterned. If the ancient people of the Southwest responded to changes in the climate with less or more warfare, then warfare was a result of some external event and not caused by anything intrinsic.

It is possible to describe a model of how human reproductive potential combined with limits to the carrying capacity results in ecological imbalance and warfare. If humans did not have mechanisms to keep from overexploiting their resources over the long run and could not keep their populations far enough below the carrying capacity to avoid being regularly subjected to food stress, starvation must have been a constant threat in the past. Once the notion of the inherent conservationist is recognized as a myth, it becomes obvious that humans would have encountered food stress on a regular basis. In fact, regardless of the type of human organization, this stress occurred in the past, as archaeology and history show.

Before starving, humans perceive themselves to be falling below what they consider their minimal standard of living. As I learned in Samoa, it

Armor was not restricted to people with metal. Eskimos live in the harshest environment on earth, and it might seem there would be no reason for war, yet surprise raids and ambush were so common they wore bone armor (left) under their parkas. And New Guinea highlanders made armor capable of stopping arrows out of fiber (right), belying the idea that their warfare was not serious and deadly.

may take several months for a food crisis to develop after a natural disaster, and such an impending crisis can be anticipated. People recognize what is happening long before it seriously affects them, and they react if they can. For most animals, natural disasters, disease, and starvation are the population limiters. Though human numbers are subject to disease and natural disasters (and there was little we would have been able to do about them in the past), starvation is a very different matter. Starvation is different because humans, with their brains and social structures, can do something about the fact that they are running out of food. Humans starve only when there are no other choices. One of those choices is to attempt to take either food, or food-producing land, from someone else. People *do* perceive resource stress *before* they are starving. If no state or central authority is there to stop them, they will fight before the situation gets hopeless. Resource stress in the form of hunger, and not starvation, is what precipitates warfare. If resource stress is the normal human condition, then warfare must have been an integral part of life most of the time in most places.

As human numbers go up, starvation and disease can possibly keep the population in check. This is one potential scenario, but it never seems to have happened in the past. It is hard to imagine an entire society that would let starvation control its numbers. Even the most passive of pacifists will admit that people will fight before they starve—especially if the threat of starvation is a chronic, recurring event. Even natural disasters that may result in food shortages can cause a reaction. Most catastrophes are more likely to have instigated warfare than to have caused groups to wait to see who would starve first. Rarely does starvation, or even its threat, run rampant without conflict developing.

This does not mean that warfare is inevitable. Humans could choose to starve, or the leaders could choose to let part of the population starve. The starving peasants in more complex societies, whether in China, Ireland, Japan, or the Yucatán, would probably have fought for food before starving, but they were usually not allowed to by the central government. On some occasions, there may have been no one in the vicinity from whom to take resources. An Eskimo band that ran out of food did not have the option of taking it from someone else if they had no nearby neighbors. Most people had other societies near enough that fighting and taking was always a possibility. When resources were critically short, fighting for them has been an option for humans for more than a million years.

If warfare was as common in the past as I suspect, then the biological consequences would be significant. From the point of view of each society, warfare is a means of obtaining more critically needed resources. From a larger perspective, warfare can be a factor in controlling population. The effects of warfare are as much indirect as direct. Raids, battles, and massacres do occur and result in significant deaths, especially of young males in nonstate societies. (Children are also often killed, but women are more often taken captive than killed.) The killing of young males does not directly control population much if the remaining men can take multiple wives. Archaeologists find that in many situations a small but significant percentage of the reproductive-aged women are killed. This would have a substantial impact on the society's growth rate. Moreover, men do produce food. If a group loses a significant number of men, then other members of the society may starve as a consequence. However, most of the effects of conflict on population growth are much more indirect.

In the American Southwest, for example, when warfare intensified in the A.D. 1200s, we know from skeletal analysis that overall health declined, particularly among children. At this time, people settled into large defensive towns, which increased the likelihood that if crops were bad, they were bad for all. There existed little means to share between communities. The population in the Southwest declined precipitously during this time period, but probably more from disease and starvation than from warfare itself. Similarly, in highland New Guinea, when a warring group is defeated, the survivors flee. Before they are settled and assimilated into another group, they are subject to exposure, malnutrition, and even starvation. Such defeats affected infant and female mortality rates, although the actual extent has rarely been measured. Conflict itself should not be considered a means of controlling population but as part of an overall process. Just because the population was reduced by disease and starvation does not mean that warfare was not a key component of the process and cannot easily be separated from it. Warfare, along with starvation and disease, becomes a component of population control—although trying to single out its direct effect is futile.

Although there is a tendency to think about societies as if they existed in isolation, people never live in isolation. There was never a time when great expanses of usable land lay empty around each society.[17] Almost no group in history had a carrying capacity that was fixed in space—they all had neighbors, and the resources of those neighbors were always a potential new source of resources. It was possible, and certainly did happen, that one group, or members of that group, could peacefully obtain resources in a time of need from neighboring groups. Those same neighbors see the situation in reverse. They see the first group's resources as potentially usable if *they* can get their hands on them. All social groups have neighbors around them, and those neighbors have the same potential provisioning problems as well as desirable resources. One can try to cooperate with one's neighbors to obtain food from them when needed, or one can compete with them and try to take food or land from them when needed. Most people did both at the same time; they cooperated and competed with their neighbors, depending on the circumstances.

What sets humans apart from almost all other animals is our ability to take resources from other groups, by group action. A large male bear can chase other bears from the best fishing spot along the river, and a male lion can defend its pride's territory from other lions, but humans develop this process much further. They can *cooperatively* take over the territory or resources of another group—either by killing them off or driving them from the resources. Such group aggression is not without risk, but it is achievable. The ability to engage in social cooperation sets up a dynamic among population growth, carrying capacity, and the potential for conflict.

Not only are human societies never alone, but regardless of how well they control their own population or act ecologically, they cannot control their neighbors' behavior. Each society must confront the real possibility that its neighbors will not live in ecological balance but will grow its numbers and attempt to take the resources from nearby groups. Not only have societies always lived in a changing environment, but they always have neighbors. The best way to survive in such a milieu is not to live in ecological balance with slow growth, but to grow rapidly and be able to fend off competitors as well as take resources from others.

To see how this most human dynamic works, imagine an extremely simple world with only two societies and no unoccupied land. Under normal conditions, neither group would have much motivation to take resources from the other. People may be somewhat hungry, but not hungry enough to risk getting killed in order to eat a little better. A few members of either group may die indirectly from food shortages—via disease or infant mortality, for example—but from an individual's perspective, he or she is much more likely to be killed trying to take food from the neighbors than from the usual provisioning shortfalls. Such a constant world would never last for long. Populations would grow and human activity would degrade the land or resources, reducing their abundance. Even if, by sheer luck, all things remained equal, it must be remembered that the climate would never be constant: Times of food stress occur because of changes in the weather, especially over the course of several generations. When a very bad year or series of years occurs, the willingness to risk a fight increases because the likelihood of starving goes up.

If one group is much bigger, better organized, or has better fighters among its members and the group faces starvation, the motivation to take over the territory of its neighbor is high, because it is very likely to succeed. Since human groups are never identical, there will always be some groups for whom warfare as a solution is a rational choice in any food crisis, because they are likely to succeed in getting more resources by warring on their neighbors.

Now comes the most important part of this overly simplified story: The group with the larger population *always* has an advantage in any competition over resources, whatever those resources may be. Over the course of human history, one side rarely has better weapons or tactics for any length of time, and most such warfare between smaller societies is attritional. With equal skills and weapons, each side would be expected to kill an equal number of its opponents. Over time, the larger group will finally overwhelm the smaller one. This advantage of size is well recognized by humans all over the world, and they go to great lengths to keep their numbers comparable to their potential enemies. This is observed anthropologically by the universal desire to have many allies, and the common tactic of smaller groups inviting other societies to join them, even in times of food stress.

Assume for a moment that by some miracle one of our two groups is full of farsighted, ecological geniuses. They are able to keep their population in check and, moreover, keep it far enough below the carrying capacity that minor changes in the weather, or even longer-term changes in the climate, do not result in food stress. If they need to consume only half of what is available each year, even if there is a terrible year, this group will probably come through the hardship just fine. More important, when a few good years come along, these masterfully ecological people will *not* grow rapidly, because to do so would mean that they would have trouble when the good times end. Think of them as the ecological equivalent of the industrious ants.

The second group, on the other hand, is just the opposite—it consists of ecological dimwits. They have no wonderful processes available to control their population. They are forever on the edge of the carrying capacity, they reproduce with abandon, and they frequently suffer food shortages and the inevitable consequences. Think of this bunch as the ecological equivalent of the carefree grasshoppers. When the good years come, they have more children and grow their population rapidly. Twenty years later, they have doubled their numbers and quickly run out of food at the first minor change in the weather. Of course, had this been a group of "noble savages" who eschewed warfare, they would have starved to death and only a much smaller and more sustainable group survived. This is not a bunch of noble savages; these are ecological dimwits and they attack their good neighbors in order to save their own skins. Since they now outnumber their good neighbors two to one, the dimwits prevail after heavy attrition on both sides. The "good" ants turn out to be dead ants, and the "bad" grasshoppers inherit the earth.

The moral of this table is that if any group can get itself into ecological balance and stabilize its population even in the face of environmental change, it will be tremendously disadvantaged against societies that do not behave that way. The long-term successful society, in a world with many different societies, will be the one that grows when it can and fights when it runs out of resources. It is useless to live an ecologically sustainable existence in the "Garden of Eden" unless the neighbors do so as well. Only one nonconservationist society in an entire region can begin a process of conflict and expansion by the "grasshoppers" at the expense of the Eden-dwelling "ants."

This smacks of a Darwinian competition—survival of the fittest—between societies. Note that the "fittest" of our two groups was not the more ecological, it was the one that grew faster. The idea of such Darwin-ian competition is unpalatable to many, especially when the "bad" folks appear to be the winners.

In the real world, the results of such a scenario might not be so dramatic. One population would not get that much bigger before the competition began, and most likely everyone would stop fighting before one side was completely killed off. With other animals, the more stable populations should win out over less stable ones.

In the extreme case, assume that humans were not capable of warfare and were more like rabbits or deer. If one social group, let's call them the "bal-anced" population, devised a set of mechanisms to avoid overexploiting the environment and to control its population, and the neighboring group did not, the neighboring, nonbalanced group would be expected to grow rapidly and overcrop its environment, and the population would periodically crash as a consequence. Let's call this group the "boom-and-bust" population. When it crashed, the population would decrease so much that surrounding areas of land would be left empty. The balanced group, on the other hand, would not go through such crashes. Each time the boom-and-bust people did, the balanced people would take over a bit of the depopulated territory, because they will grow when they safely can. Over time, the boom-and-bust people would be replaced and eliminated, but not by warfare.

This is how things might work in the animal world—but humans are not deer or rabbits. Since humans can fight, the opposite happens. When the boom-and-bust people boom, they can expand at the expense of their balanced neighbors. Perhaps just a little bit of expansion takes place. When their boom starts to turn into a bust, they will fight hard for new territory rather than starve, and they most likely will take some territory. After num-bers decline and conditions improve, they stop fighting. The balanced peo-ple do not get the opportunity to move into the empty territory of their more aggressive neighbors. Rather, the boom-and-bust people take over some of the balanced people's territory—who, as a consequence of the con-flict, will have fewer numbers. Over repeated cycles of this process, the boom-and-bust people would be expected to replace and eliminate the bal-anced people. And that is exactly what scholars have found in highland New Guinea, in tropical South America, and even in more complex societies.

So after considering the overall evidence uncovered in my own work and the work of other anthropologists, we see that life in the past was not as we thought it was—or wished it to be. Not only have two popular myths about human history prevailed, but they are intertwined. The myth of the "noble savage" living in peaceful harmony with nature is a naive version of the idea that traditional societies have been able to live below the carrying capacity and were able to control their populations so they wouldn't exceed the resource supply, but human societies have not been able to do this. And along with this misconception comes the myth of a peaceful past, which views warfare as occasional, minor, and almost gamelike. War in the past was frequent, serious, and deadly. If humans have been unable to live in ecological balance throughout history, then because they are intelligent and have no predators to control their population, they will compete for resources. There could not be a peaceful past if there was not ecological balance. The two myths are related, and neither is true because they are linked. The human inability to live in stable resource balance almost guarantees warfare. The nature of warfare and how humans cope with carrying-capacity stress differ depending on the type of society. These differences provide insight into the historical trend we are at the end of and what we can expect in the future. Before looking at how ecology and warfare relate among different types of human societies from ancient to modern times, our prehuman past must be considered.

chapter four

OUR EARLIEST PAST

*U*pstairs from my office at the Peabody Museum is the office of Richard Wrangham, a primatologist, which is a cross between an anthropologist and a zoologist who focuses on primates, especially the apes and monkeys. Whenever I have a question about chimpanzees, I go to Richard. We are both interested in warfare, but we approach it from opposite ends of the human developmental time line. Wrangham is engaged in studying the implications of chimpanzee warfare on our understanding of human evolution. He's thinking about the very beginning, before we humans were really humans. I, on the other hand, had not given much thought to the presence of warfare among human foragers or our early ancestors or protohumans. Until recently, my research and experience focused on egalitarian farmers or more complex societies. I was approaching the question of how warfare might have affected human evolution from what was, essentially, the "end" of the story—the last ten thousand years or less. Wrangham approaches the subject from the perspective of how intergroup conflict began, from a presumed early human ancestor much like a chimpanzee that lived six million years ago.

We each had limited knowledge of forager and protohuman warfare based on either ethnographic accounts or archaeological information, which forced both of us to improve our understanding of what happened in that gap in our collective knowledge. One day we discussed the importance of throwing rocks. There is quite a bit of archaeological evidence for early rock throwing. Wrangham told me that there was actually physiological evidence of selection among protohumans for the anatomical ability to throw hard and accurately. This was a small but critical piece of information.

Wrangham and primatologists like him—the pioneer, of course, being Jane Goodall—spend months at a time in the tropical habitat of chimpanzees. After a time, the chimps get accustomed to the presence of these humans and ignore them, so the chimps can be studied as they actually live. The primatologists learn to recognize each animal and follow them constantly. Each chimp is given a name, so that as new people are added to the research team they can be taught the names and continue to record individual behaviors. Primatologists have seen chimps make tools to get food, to form close friendships, to deliberately lie (pretend not to have food so they don't have to share), and to engage in many other humanlike behaviors. Several chimp troops have been studied continuously for many years, allowing behaviors that don't occur every week or even every month to be witnessed and for the frequency of such behaviors to be recorded. One behavior that has been observed repeatedly is deliberate and methodical attacks, resulting in the killing of chimps from other troops. Initially, this finding was quite a surprise. The behavior is now well established in multiple troops and is clearly not aberrant or unique.

Wrangham's accounts of chimpanzee killings—with stealthy surprise attacks; the use of overwhelming numbers; the determination to kill, often viciously, and not simply to scare and intimidate; and the significant number of chimps that die in these attacks—all sounded to me like human warfare. After many such exchanges with my colleague, I began to speculate about what warfare might have been like in our earliest protohuman ancestors. I have come to a somewhat different set of conclusions from Wrangham, but our overall concept is the same: Warfare has been an integral part of the human existence since long before we were humans. That this warfare has resulted in some biological impact on humans is certain, but just what that impact might be is far from certain. Wrangham feels strongly, and can make a very good case, that chimpanzees are genetically programmed not directly for warfare but for aggressive behavior, which leads to chimp warfare.[1] The question to consider is whether humans are too.

Theories are legion as to how humans, starting from an ancestor similar to modern chimpanzees, have come to be so different from the great apes—orangutans, gorillas, and chimps. Some scholars believe that a multitude of developments, each small, added up to cause this divergence, while others focus on a single key change as the catalyst. There are many theories of the key ingredient in what made us human: becoming bipedal (walking on two legs), the ability to make tools, leaving the rain forest to live in the open grasslands or savanna. The differences among these theories are actually not great, because almost all the proponents of these models would admit that our transformation from apes into humans must have been a process of coevolution, or feedback evolution.

The idea of coevolution revolves around the concept that as one trait evolves, it causes a different one to evolve as well, and as this second trait evolves, it causes the first to evolve more: A encourages B, and B encourages A in a sort of spiral or loop. For example, if using tools is beneficial to survival, and intelligence helps in tool use, then those individuals with more intelligence will be more successful at surviving and reproducing than those with less. Individuals who are more intelligent will, in the long run, have more offspring than those who are not. And the process continues around and around: As one becomes more intelligent, one can use more and more complex tools, which are even more helpful in surviving. Each change reinforces the other, so there is a coevolution of greater intelligence and more tool use. Each allows for more of the other, sort of like highway building: If a new highway is built, people will move to be near it, which then means more traffic, so the highway is enlarged, encouraging still more people to relocate near it, and on and on. Though such natural selection clearly existed in the human deep past, and virtually all realistic human-development models are of the coevolution type, the particulars are what is of interest, knowing which traits were important in this process and how they fed on each other.[2] Exactly how humans became human is a complex story and many of the answers are not yet worked out. Even so, one can paint a fairly clear picture of the broad pattern of coevolution that led to humans, and of particular importance is the role conflict might have played in the process.

Humans are members of the Primate order of mammals, along with lemurs, monkeys, and the various apes. Our closest ape relatives are the chimpanzees. About five or six million years ago, one group of chimps began to diverge from the others, eventually leading to modern humans. Though fossils from this span have been found for more than 150 years, the pace of discovery, especially in Africa, our communal homeland, has accelerated in recent years. The very early humanlike (or, more accurately, human-branch) ancestors are properly termed early hominids, like "Lucy" and the Australopithecines found in South and East Africa by Louis and Mary Leakey, Donald Johanson, and others. These creatures were bipedal, and some made tools, but they were small brained and small sized. Later members of the early human family were Peking and Java man, recovered as fossil skeletons from China, Southeast Asia, Africa, and Europe. These individuals are usually lumped into the category *Homo erectus*, who made the famous handaxes, were much bigger brained, and had body sizes about as large as ours today. Still later were the Neandertals of Europe, and contemporaries living in most of the Old World where it was not too cold. These protohumans all walked on two legs, made tools, at some point had fire, but they did not make art. Some Neandertals did bury their dead, but most apparently did not. In subtle ways, such as not making art or other decorations, these last of the protohumans did not behave as fully modern humans. Regardless of just how humanlike these ancestors were, they were all hunters and gatherers in one form or another, so this foraging for plants and animals was the way of life of most of human and protohuman history.

A good place to start looking at the coevolutionary process that led to humans today is with modern chimpanzees, because they are currently the best clue as to what the first protohumans were like. In fact, we humans are exceedingly fortunate that one of our closest, prehuman relatives still exists. From paleontology and genetic studies, scholars know that the human line separated from the chimpanzee line about five to six million years ago. There is reason to believe, based on ancient chimplike fossil skeletons, that chimps have not evolved as much from our common ancestor as humans have.[3] Thus, chimps are a potential model of a time when humankind had not yet diverged from the chimpanzee line. They are by no means a perfect model, because they too have had five million years to change.

It was Goodall who forever altered our perception of chimps with her pioneering observational fieldwork, begun in 1960 near Lake Tanganyika in Tanzania. Prior to this, primatologists had studied chimps only in zoos or from great distances in the wild. Goodall's breakthrough was to acculturate the chimps to her presence so she could get close enough to learn to recognize individuals and really observe their behavior. The study of these very same chimp groups is ongoing. Credit should also go to archaeologist Louis Leakey, who saw the wisdom of studying chimpanzees in the wild instead of in zoos and greatly encouraged Goodall as a young student to undertake her pioneering studies.[4]

Today, a number of additional long-term, ongoing studies have been undertaken by primatologists with very diverse groups of chimpanzees in West and Central Africa.[5] Thanks to this rich body of research, it is now clear that there are two distinct species of chimpanzees—the common chimps and the bonobos—each living on opposite sides of the Congo River in tropical Africa. This wealth of extremely well-collected information (some troops have been studied for about forty years) provides a level of understanding unavailable to earlier scholars. Scholars now know that chimpanzees forage in ways much like human foragers. They live in social groups, numbering approximately thirty individuals, roughly the same size as bands of human foragers. Primatologists have observed chimps teaching their offspring techniques for getting special foods, sharing some food, gathering a wide variety of food types from fruits to termites, and hunting. Observers confirm that chimpanzee society is not peaceful. In fact, chimps are one of the few mammals that fight as groups with other groups of the same species.

These long-term chimpanzee field studies have been a revelation to anthropologists. Chimps are not only much more socially complex than previously imagined, they also hunt and eat monkeys. Apes (including chimps) and humans descended from monkeylike ancestors but are not monkeys. Apes are larger than monkeys, more bipedal, and more intelligent, and they do not have tails. Chimps hunt such small monkeys as the red colobus. Some groups of chimps hunt a lot, which was an unexpected finding. Chimp hunting is coordinated. A monkey can easily get away from a single chimp, so the chimps work in teams. They surround monkeys, and some chimps chase one monkey into other chimps stationed in the surrounding circle. What is important is not that chimps hunt, but that they hunt as coordinated groups, requiring intelligence and communication ability.

An even more surprising observation is that chimpanzees fight with other groups of chimpanzees. A group of male chimps deliberately sets out to find an individual (usually a male) from an adjacent group. They surround the lone chimp and then kill it. Descriptions of these attacks are brutal. The lone male, pinned down and helpless, is bitten by his attackers' long canine teeth and pounded by their strong fists. Researchers sometimes don't get close enough to witness the actual attacks. When primatologists find bodies that have suffered such attacks, the corpses are mangled and even on occasion deliberately mutilated.

In this example from Goodall's study area, Sniff, the last surviving male in his troop, is attacked: "Six Kasekela males (the victorious group) screamed and barked in excitement as they hit, grabbed, and bit their victim viciously—wounding him in the mouth, forehead, nose, and back, and breaking one leg. [One male] struck the victim repeatedly in the nose... [another male] punched him. [A third male] grabbed Sniff by the neck and drank the blood streaming down his face. Then... two screaming males pulled Sniff down a hill. Sniff was seen one day later, crippled, almost unable to move."[6] He was never seen again.

Chimpanzees conduct deliberate raids, they use surprise, and they try to outnumber their enemies. When the odds are not enough in their favor, they withdraw. Chimps also use attrition: They kill the other males one at a time, but, over time, they can annihilate all the males of the other group. There have been enough long-term studies of several chimpanzee troops to estimate just how many chimps die from these conflicts. Current estimates are that about 30 percent of the males and a much lower, but still significant, number of females die from this intergroup chimpanzee conflict. This fatality rate from warfare is similar to what is found for many human societies, as I will discuss in the next chapters.[7]

Another similarity between humans and our ape cousins is the fact that chimpanzees are known to take over the territory of another group after they have killed all the males of that group. They also capture into their groups the females from these "conquered" groups. This behavior is parallel with human behavior. There is archaeological and ethnographic evidence that humans who lived in noncomplex societies in the past never took male prisoners but did capture females and incorporate them into their societies.

The observation of infanticide among chimps also parallels human behaviors. At least twenty cases have been observed; when considering the number of infants born in the half dozen troops under study, this means that about 10 to 15 percent of all infants die at the hand of other chimps in the studied groups. As I will discuss in the next chapters, infanticide was common in the past worldwide. Also, humans sometimes kill children when they defeat another group, even when they spare some of the adult females. Killing younger children is more likely, as they will not be economically productive for many years. Chimps kill the infants of other groups when they kill all the males and absorb the females. They kill infants from their own groups when dominant males want to be surrounded only by infants they have sired. Both males and females have been involved in some of these deliberate infant killings. Regardless of the reasons, infanticide is a partial check on chimpanzee population growth, just as it is among humans.

The way chimpanzees utilize their territories is similar to human behavior. Chimps spend almost all their time in less than half their territory. They have a typical range of about fourteen square miles yet spend almost all their time in only six square miles. They do so because it appears that the risk of ambush and death at the hands of a neighboring troop makes it too dangerous to forage in the outer fringes. In human terms, this outer edge of the chimp territory is a no-man's-land—an uninhabitable buffer zone between communities—a classic and common human response to chronic, endemic warfare. The observing primatologists confirm that chimpanzee "warfare" is dangerous and that the chimpanzees well perceive the risks. They will launch attacks on other individuals only when there is little risk to themselves, and they use buffer zones to reduce the risk of attacks by others.[8]

The major differences between human and chimp "warfare" are relative. Chimps are not very good at war, compared to humans. They usually attack only an isolated male, not a group of males, and they have a lot of trouble killing him. Rarely is a lone individual killed outright. Rather, the victim usually dies later from wounds inflicted by the much more numerous attacking party. In human terms, chimps ambush individuals with little risk to themselves, and they wipe out the opposing group by repeated efforts, not single massacres.

In another example from Goodall's study area, all six males of a group of chimpanzees were killed, one by one, over the span of many months, by the males of an adjacent group: "The raiders (a number of males from one group) rushed madly down the slope to their target. While Goliath (a lone male from another group) screamed and the patrol hooted and displayed, he was held and beaten and kicked and lifted and dropped and bitten and jumped on. At first he tried to protect his head, but soon he gave up and lay stretched out and still. His aggressors showed their excitement in a continuous barrage of hooting and drumming and charging and branch waving and screaming. They kept up the attack for 18 minutes, then turned for home. . . . Bleeding freely from his head, gashed on his back, Goliath tried to sit up but fell back shivering. He too was never seen again."[9]

Much of noncomplex society human warfare is similar to chimpanzee attacks. Massacres among humans at that social level are, in fact, rare occurrences, and victory by attrition is a viable strategy, as are buffer zones, surprise raids, taking captive females into the group, and mutilation of victims. The chimp and human behaviors are almost completely parallel. The use of weapons differentiates human conflict from that of chimps, giving humans the ability to kill much more quickly and surely. Superior communication skills allow humans to plan much more organized attacks, by using scouts, surrounds, alliances, and the like. These differences are really a matter of degree. The structure of chimp and of human warfare is the same; it is the differences between humans and chimps in general that separate styles of warfare.

Few mammals fight others in coordinated groups with warlike behavior. It takes a lot of intelligence to fight as a group. Direct field experiments have shown that chimps listen to the calls of other troops and count the callers to see if they are outnumbered. When they attack an individual, usually two or more chimps hold the victim down while the rest pound, stomp, bite, and tear with impunity. It takes a fairly high degree of intelligence to figure out who and how many should hold the victim down. Intergroup conflict among the chimps is not quite that simple. The other species of chimpanzees, the bonobos, seem to be every bit as smart as the common chimps, but they do not attack other troops. Although they have not been studied in the wild as intensely and for as long as chimps, bonobos do not appear to have warfare. Thus, intelligence in a species alone does not result in warfare, but it seems to be a necessary precondition for it.

The lack of warfare among the bonobos raises many questions. Another intriguing contrast is that bonobos do not hunt monkeys, even though monkeys are just as common in bonobo territories as they are in the forests the chimps occupy. Bonobos have been observed killing infant antelope when they encounter them hidden in the bush, and they seem to relish the meat every bit as much as chimps enjoy monkey meat. Bonobos appear not to hunt or engage in warfare because they do not know how to and/or are not genetically programmed to do so.[10] Nor do bonobos try to take over each other's territories. In fact, when different bonobo groups meet, it appears to result in more of a party than conflict. Intergroup competition does not seem to be a way ecological problems are resolved among the bonobos, and competition within groups (fighting for dominance) or between groups (warfare) is minimal or reduced compared with common chimps, or is nonexistent.

In spite of the many similarities between chimps and bonobos, important differences lie in their hunting and warfare. These two behaviors are similar between common chimps and humans, but not bonobos. There seems to be a correlation between group hunting and group fighting, which I believe is an important aspect of how we became human.

In addition to conflict, we must consider the ecology of chimp life. If humans are capable of rapid population growth and can quickly reach the carrying capacity of the land, what about chimps? Once again, the parallels between chimps and humans are strong. Humans today have no predators except other humans, and while this has not always been the case, it has been so for a long time. Chimpanzees also have few predators. In forested environments, there are leopards; in somewhat more open environments, there can be some additional predators like lions and hyenas. For the most part, chimps are a predator, not prey. Chimp numbers, like human numbers, are not significantly controlled by predators. The population growth aspect of chimpanzee ecology has been hard to study, because chimps are not doing well in the wild. Their preserves are small, and they often leave them to forage. Nearby farmers set snares to catch small game, and the foraging chimps sometimes accidentally get their hands caught in these traps, lose their hands, and then don't survive. Chimps are also hunted extensively for meat. Impacts like these, and the loss of territory due to development and logging, have prompted Goodall and others to issue appeals alerting people to the possible extinction of chimps in most of their once isolated territories. Also, chimps catch human diseases. In fact, polio, influenza, and other viruses are a major cause of death among chimpanzees. All these factors add up and keep the chimp populations low—so low, in fact, that not enough babies survive to reproduce the population, even in preserves. Thus, using ongoing field studies to determine what factors controlled chimp numbers before humans began to encroach so intensely on their territories is difficult, if not impossible, but some reasonable assumptions can be made.

Chimps are not inherent conservationists. They don't stop hunting monkeys and give the population a chance to recover once they begin to deplete their numbers. Nor do they limit the number of their own offspring, because they perceive their babies as having inadequate nutrition. Chimps are not human; they are controlled by the same processes as all other animals, or at least animals without major predators. Chimps are capable, when humans leave them alone, of reproducing to the point of vastly filling up their territories, but they never do or did. Starvation and, probably more commonly, inadequate nutrition resulting in disease kept their numbers in check. In fact, it has been observed that the more dominant females in the group, who have better access to food, have more surviving babies than the low-dominance females, suggesting strongly that access to food is a significant problem among chimpanzees, even when their numbers have been reduced due to human impact. In addition to disease and starvation, intergroup conflict and infanticide keep chimp numbers in check, a process that is very rare in the animal world.

In the past, chimp populations would have grown, starvation would have threatened, and chimp groups would have competed for territories as groups. Whether these factors are related depends on the unique circumstances of the chimpanzees' environment. The stresses and strains of encroaching humans into their once isolated territories make it difficult to quantify whether chimp conflict is driven by their outgrowing their area's carrying capacity, or is just an automatic behavior. I asked Richard Wrangham his opinion on the big question: How much of chimp warfare is genetic and how much is based on intelligent decision making? His answer was compelling.

Based on his observations, male chimps are genetically programmed to dominate others. They seem to enjoy dominating other males of their own group, but they usually do this in ways that are not lethal. They extend this behavior by attacking and killing the males of other groups. Wrangham likens this enjoyment to that of a sports team. The athletic victors seem to have the same type of pleasure that the chimps do when they successfully dominate or attack another. Wrangham points out that bonobos don't seem to have this dominance enjoyment. When both kinds of chimpanzees are observed in zoos, when there is no food shortage, no threat of attack by males of another group—in short, no reason to dominate—the common chimps still do so and seem to enjoy it. Bonobos, on the other hand, don't.

Wrangham explained that in the wild, each common chimp foray into enemy territory and potential attack is carefully calculated. Only when the odds are right do the marauding bands strike. There is no bloodlust behavior, no "irrational" risk taking as a result of being unable to control themselves. Chimps fight only when they figure they can easily win. Wrangham believes that this decision making about whether to fight or resist is not hardwired. It is intelligent decision making. Though male chimps appear to have a built-in enjoyment of dominating, this does not automatically lead to intergroup killing, what I consider to be a form of warfare.

If chimpanzees have a form of warfare, then it can be presumed that our forest-dwelling ancestors ("early hominids" or protohumans) probably did too, because humans and chimps are so similar. One could surmise that intergroup competition occurred over territory, because both chimpanzees and human foragers do compete over territories. These intelligent, group-living protohumans would have been a top predator, and their numbers would not have been held in check by large carnivores. Ultimately, their populations were limited by starvation, disease caused or compounded by poor nutrition (semi-starvation), or intergroup conflict. In other words, increased numbers of early hominids would have been met by competition among themselves. Such competition over territory would have encouraged some of our earliest ancestors to move out of the forest into the surrounding grasslands or savanna. This transition from one environment to the other is one of the keys to our becoming human. Just why the spread into more open land occurred is not clear, but there would have been an advantage to any group that could make the transition because of the reduced competition with other protohumans. Based on the animal fossils found nearby early hominid fossils in Africa, it is in the savanna that archaeologists have found the earliest protohumans.

The savanna is actually more resource-rich than the forest for protohumans, because it is composed of areas with trees as well as areas with grasslands and contains some riverine edges that provide still more different types of vegetation. In particular, the savanna has a greater variety of plant foods, roots, and seeds than found in the rain forest, and it has a much greater variety of animals that can be used for meat. These early hominids did not suddenly flood onto the savanna. Instead, they gradually began to occupy portions that enabled them to survive, primarily areas with trees or rocky outcrops. The savanna, unlike the forest, was home to large, group-living carnivores, in particular lions and hyenas, and the hominids sought protection from them.

Fending off a leopard is quite different from dealing with a pride of lions or a pack of hyenas. The savanna offered more opportunities, but also more risk. With proper behavior a chimp could learn to survive in regions with lions and hyenas. The group could forage in the heat of the day, when the large carnivores like to sleep, and hide when predators were spotted. In reality, the ability to survive must have improved by being able to flee to and sleep in trees or on rocks, as baboons do today. The archaeology reveals that the earliest bipedal hominids had long arms and toes that would have made climbing trees much easier than such activities are for modern humans.[11]

In the right locales, these protohumans would have been successful and their numbers would have grown. When population pressure increased, as it must have, some groups of these first savanna residents would have been forced to live in areas more and more marginal for survival—in particular, places with fewer or more dispersed trees, resulting in a reduced role for group competition or starvation in population control and a much greater role for predation. As with many other animals, population regulation would be controlled, in large part, by predation. This would have been a self-regulating world. When population was low, there would have been places to live with trees, so predation would be low. When the population grew, an increased proportion of the community was at risk, because they would be forced to live farther from trees. A self-adjusting balance would have been maintained.

Over time, the protohumans, broadly subsumed under the term Australopithecines, including the famous Lucy, continued to evolve, making them even more able to live in the grasslands. As they moved out and occupied the more open savanna, other skills and technologies were developed and mastered to make life increasingly sustainable outside the rain forest. These innovations coevolved and fed off of each other over millions of years. For example, protohumans developed defenses against the large predators. These defenses were not instantaneous and were never perfect, but gradually the strategies became increasingly effective. This improved defense system consisted sequentially of three main elements: throwing stones, using fire, and developing better weapons.

Archaeological evidence for throwing-stones—referred to as *manuports*—is found from some of the earliest hominid sites in Africa. Manuports are

Groups of male chimpanzees deliberately stalk and kill males from neighboring troops, eventually wiping out the other troop and taking over their territories. This photo, taken by Martin N. Muller, shows a victim of such an event lying splayed out after having been held spread-eagled by several male attackers while others pounded and bit him to death.

actually stones that are not found locally, so they must have been specially transported from other areas to the campsite. Most appear to be of a size and weight good for throwing, and they are common at a number of sites.[12] It has been suggested that the evolution of the human physique was dictated, in part, by the need to throw well. We do differ in musculature development from apes, and one of the ways we differ is in the arm, shoulder, and back muscles related to throwing an object. As strong as apes are, they can't pitch for the major leagues. Only humans have developed the ability to aim and throw a small projectile with accuracy.[13]

Though a group of protohumans probably could not have used stones to fend off a pride of hungry lions, they could have chased off smaller groups of less determined carnivores, and they certainly could have fended off another group of protohumans. In this case, the defenders have a great advantage in that they can stockpile far more rocks than attackers can carry. If this seems an unlikely form of defense, consider the earliest clear evidence for warfare in the Andean region of South America, the Ostra archaeological site. Located along the coast of Peru, Ostra seems to have had brush fences constructed along the two main approaches. The stones to support the fence were still in place. Behind the fences, archaeologists found hundreds of throwing-stones heaped in piles.[14]

Most paleoanthropologists would probably concur that the hominid ability to defend themselves against predators evolved substantially. I contend that this ability would have both reduced predation, resulting in more intrahuman competition, and provided the technology and social abilities for more complex warfare. Subsequently, the development of other weapons—especially spears—would have further increased the ability of hominids to fend off predators. Extraordinary preservation has enabled archaeologists to find several spears in Germany from around three hundred thousand years ago.[15] These weapons are surprisingly well made: tapered, with the weight forward of center so they can be thrown accurately. There is no reason to believe that spears were first used only at this time. We would expect thrusting-spears, spears that are pushed or thrust into the animal or enemy instead of being thrown, to have been used long before properly designed throwing-spears were widespread, because they would have required less skill to make and use.

Certainly fire would have provided an even better defense against predators, especially at night or while camped. Fire must have opened up large areas to human exploitation that were not usable before. Once fire had been in use, combined with other weapons, the "predator" problem would seem to have been solved sufficiently. This was a gradual process and would have varied in terms of the geographic terrain and the nature of the large predators inhabiting a given area. Nevertheless, humans did solve the predator problem and became a top predator themselves on the savanna, just as they had been in the forest.

Once these protohumans reached some level of abilities, they began to expand out of Africa and moved across much of Europe and Asia. Over millions of years, both in and beyond Africa, as a result of various traits that coevolved together, the human line slowly evolved greater intelligence, more use of tools, and the ability to communicate better. Each fed upon the other: Those individuals who were more intelligent found it easier to develop language; as using tools became more and more of a necessity for humans to survive, tool use helped to select for those with more intelligence; and so on. These same traits helped the human line survive in ever more varied environments. These traits aided humans in becoming better hunters. Intelligence and communication would have enhanced the ability to group hunt, and tool use would have made hunters more effective.

Once predation was no longer a major factor in limiting their growth, these early humans would have been like modern humans and chimpanzees. Human numbers are not controlled by predators, but by starvation, disease, and warfare. The protohuman populations would always grow to the point that their increased numbers stressed the carrying capacity; competition for resources would ensue, and conflict between groups would have been present. Intergroup competition would have been greatly intensified during this process.

Those groups that were most successful at warfare, either due to genetics or learned behavior, would be able to take over the territories of their neighbors, then their numbers would grow, and they would survive and spread at the expense of those groups that were less able and less successful at intergroup competition. Success in warfare would have been an important factor in determining which groups of early humans survived and which ones did not. The implications of this scenario are profound. Though evolutionary selection among humans for better tool use, more intelligence, better communication, and the like, could have existed in theory without conflict, conflict would have served to enhance these traits. In particular, conflict would have increased the value of big-game hunting as an adaptation.

As known from the primatologists' field observations, chimpanzees hunt monkeys, but they can also live without hunting. They hunt animals that are not dangerous, they do it without tools, and what meat they do get is not a critical resource to them. What separates modern human hunters from chimps is the human use of tools for hunting, and the importance of hunting for food—plus the fact that humans hunt animals that are dangerous, from elephants to wild cattle or even a polar bear. Each of the evolutionary steps in human hunting would have affected the nature of intergroup human conflict. Humans who began to use tools to hunt with would have also been able to use those tools to fight with. As people learned to hunt dangerous animals, those same skills would have been applicable to fighting other people as well. Stalking, fighting as a coordinated group, and being able to launch a projectile from a distance are all useful in hunting a bear or an elephant. And they are useful when executing an ambush on an unsuspecting camp of nearby humans.

The more a group became dependent on hunting large game—that is, game that takes more organization and better tools and hunting skills to bring down—the more it improved its ability to be successful at warfare. The people who concentrated on very small game, like rabbits, would not develop the skills or tools needed for large game, or for warfare. In the larger scheme of things, fighting humans is much the same as hunting large game. Groups that adopted a small-game-hunting strategy would be disadvantaged over those that chose a large-game strategy. Hunting rabbits does not prepare, train, or equip one to fight other humans. Even if a big-game strategy had been worked out, hunting small game would still be undertaken. A group of males that is well armed and travels away from the base camp to find and hunt large game is also, in the process, guarding its territory and going through the same steps it might take to launch a raid on or ambush a neighboring group. Ethnographically, all around the world, hunting small game is often executed with nets, and women are often involved. Similarly, fishing and shellfish collecting are also often performed by women as well as men. Only the hunting of large game is a specialized male activity the world over. With very few exceptions, it is these same men who engage in warfare.

The observational studies of bonobos in the wild reinforce these ideas. Bonobos neither hunt nor have warfare, so these behaviors do seem to be linked. It is possible that humans could have evolved like bonobos and become intelligent beings who used more tools, developed more communication, and did not hunt or have warfare. Obviously, we did not develop that way. Given that we humans started out as hunters, with intergroup conflict, and given that tools became ever more important to us, it seems that we evolved to better perform these behaviors—hunting and war—rather than evolving to lose the ability to do either.

For most of human history, the tools of the hunt were also the tools of warfare. As shown in the archaeological record, special tools were added just for warfare over time. First, humans developed shields and clubs, and perhaps different types of arrows for shooting people and animals. Later, swords, battleaxes, and maces become important tools in warfare. Even with more specialized tools, it is not easy to distinguish hunting tools from the tools of war. In fact, the tools of the hunt and warfare were so similar that archaeologists often cannot tell them apart.

Hunting had another consequence that was very important to human development. With big-game hunting comes the need to be able to share the food. Again, as shown from the observational fieldwork in tropical Africa, male chimps do not share meat well. When meat became a major component of the human diet, males had to learn how to share, which had profound implications for the nature of social relationships. Human males had to evolve the ability to control their behavior. They had to share with females, children, and other males. They may initially have been inclined to dominate others, but the desire to dominate and not to share had to be curtailed. Sharing, and the social behaviors of getting along that sharing implies, must have become ever more important as cooperative large-game hunting and the consequent increased reliance on the meat it provided became more important to early humans.

Other evidence reveals how this long evolutionary period—from a chimpanzee-like ancestor to modern humans—involved warfare as part of the process. Sexual dimorphism is important to consider. Differences in body size and shape between the sexes are known for many mammal species. The bigger, maned male lion; the antlered male deer; and the silver-backed, much bigger male gorilla are good examples. Today, men are typically physically larger than women and more heavily muscled. There appears to be, on average, less male-female difference in physical stature today than in the past. Differences in size among male and female chimpanzees, as well as our early ancestors recovered from fossils, are greater than those found the human sexes today. Sexual dimorphism has been a part of human history from the beginning.

In many species, the males are larger than the females, though in a few the reverse is true. The usual reason for this dimorphism is that the males fight with each other, usually over females, and size is advantageous. However, this difference in size is disadvantageous for other reasons. Bigger bodies require more food. Females are usually "sized correctly" for the adaptation, and males are "maladapted"—if it were not for the competition aspect. Among humans, archaeologists see sexual dimorphism throughout history whenever we have an adequate sample of skeletons.

Some of this physical difference between the human sexes may relate to sexual specialization. Hunting requires larger body size than plant gathering, for example. This difference in size could be due to competition, as is often the case with other animals. Nature films often imply that male lions lie around all day, make the females do the hunting, and then stroll in and take all the good meat from the kills. But this is not the entire story. The male lions are larger and have heavy manes because they defend the pride's hunting territories against other lions and keep other predators, like hyenas, out. The males patrol the boundaries of their territories and get into fights with other lions and often die in the process. In the lion world, there is a huge benefit to being big and strong and having a thick, bushy mane, which protects the vulnerable neck. Big male lions are not merely tolerated by the hardworking females; they are necessary for the survival of the pride.

Similarly, for much of human history having "oversized" males in the social group may have been a constant trade-off between their needing more food and their being better able to defend and expand the group's territories against smaller males in other groups. Thinking of two hypothetical groups, if one group had males who were the same size as the females, it would have made the best use of its resources. If a neighboring group had bigger, stronger males who dwarfed the females, that group would likely win when the two groups eventually began to compete—even if that group suffered more starvation in the long run because the males consumed more communal resources. This explanation seems far more likely than sexual dimorphism resulting simply from an ability to hunt larger animals, the only other reasonable explanation.

If warfare is included as an integral part of human evolution, then some of humankind's great advances—like fire—must be considered from a new perspective. Fire is a major way we differ from chimpanzees. It is not clear when fire was first controlled by humans. Some argue for the time of *Homo erectus*, a million or more years ago, and others see it occurring much more recently. Regardless of when humans actually mastered the art of using fire, it was surely a major leap forward. Fire was the first communal entertainment center. Prior to fire, you went to sleep when it got dark. Only with a full moon could you spend the night hours in a social situation. With fire, groups could sit around the campfire and talk, telling tales about the past, and in so doing begin to build an oral literature, and a group identity.

Fire provided much more than entertainment value. It protected humans from predators. Freed from having to live near trees, rocks, and other places of refuge, the entire world was then at our disposal—if we could figure out how to use this new means of self-defense. Initially, fire did one more thing: It protected those who had fire from other humans who did *not* have it and found it frightening. Groups of early humans with fire had a tremendous advantage, not only against wild animals but also against other humans. Those humans who had fire would have spread rapidly at the expense of those who did not. Remember, it is the *lack* of animal predators that creates the situation in which humans become the main predators of humans. Once protohumans had fire, they no longer had significant predators, and then the human world would have consisted of protohuman groups competing with other protohuman groups as the major means of expanding territories—and providing an important aspect of population control.

Dogs and their relationship to early humans is another aspect of our behavior that takes on new meaning in this light. Humans, unlike our chimplike ancestors, domesticated dogs, and it was not because humans like cuddly puppies, although that may have been why they were brought into camps or tolerated in the first place. Despite their reputation as "man's best friend," canines must have been the first domesticated animal for good reason. They surely provided much more than simple companionship in the past.[16]

A common explanation for dogs being domesticated is that they provided help with hunting. This theory isn't overly convincing, since many people throughout the world hunt without dogs, and for many types of hunting, dogs are not at all useful. Almost every society on Earth kept dogs, as shown from both archaeology and ethnology. It is possible, as some scholars believe, that dogs were first domesticated in areas where they *were* useful for hunting, and then, once well domesticated, were adopted by other people for other reasons. For instance, as a Peace Corps volunteer in Samoa, I had a dog. Dogs were kept nearly everywhere on the islands, but there was nothing to hunt there. The only useful role for them was as watchdogs. No one could get near my house, which had no walls, without my dog barking. Similarly, in places like the Peruvian Andes, large dogs are kept for protecting property and livestock, not hunting. Humans' desire for protection from strangers in the past would have been just as great as ours is today, if not more so. In the past, strangers would have almost always been enemies sneaking up to attack.

A much more likely explanation is that dogs were domesticated because of warfare—to serve as sentries and early-warning devices—and were thereby useful to all humans, regardless of whether the animals were used in hunting. Dogs would have played an important role as camp and village guards. All it takes is for a dog to recognize the local group of humans as its "pack" and all other humans as non–pack members; when non–pack members approach, it barks. In fact, this model explains the selection for dogs that bark, something that separates domesticated canines from their wolf ancestors. Dogs were selected by humans for their ability to bark, and though barking can be disruptive in hunting, it's critical for sentry duty.

Many of these ideas about the human coevolutionary process are conjecture, since there is so little hard evidence with which to work. As yet, we know virtually nothing about the ecological balance of these protohumans. There are serious debates about what early hominids ate, whether they actually hunted really large dangerous game early on or just scavenged the kills of other predators. There is hard evidence about early human warfare—not a great deal, but we do have some relevant finds that date from the last few million years. For example, there have been various suggestions that our two-million-year-old ancestors, Australopithecines, killed each other. Much of this evidence—bones that could have been used as clubs, and fossil skulls that are broken, perhaps from blows—is equivocal and not particularly convincing. The lack of archaeological evidence for protohuman warfare does not mean much. Warfare would never be recognized if chimpanzees were studied archaeologically. They don't use weapons to kill each other, and we cannot see their no-man's-lands from the things they leave around. Only when protohumans made and used enough tools in warfare would archaeological evidence of conflict be anticipated. Once humans were making more than just a few simple stone tools, about a million or so years ago, just the kind of evidence one would expect to be uncovered is indeed found. Virtually all the evidence comes from the fossilized bones of these early hominids themselves, and there aren't many of those. There are no tools archaeologists can definitely attribute to warfare at this time in the past. In fact, despite the paucity of evidence, it is remarkable how much skeletal evidence for conflict among protohumans there actually is.

In Europe the earliest fossilized human bones that have been found, dating back more than 750,000 years ago, were defleshed and probably cannibalized, most likely following an act of violence.[17] The oldest known human remains in Europe provide the oldest evidence for cannibalism in Europe. Dating from about the same time period, the Bodo cranium from Ethiopia shows much the same thing—probable cannibalism.[18] Several other fossils recovered and studied earlier in the history of anthropology— examples from Java, Choukoutien (China), Fontéchevade (France), and Ehringsdorf (Germany)—have depression fractures, which are evidence of violent blows to the head, and similar evidence from the skulls. These are less convincing because the analysis was done so long ago, many original specimens were lost during the Second World War, and the context of some of the other early finds was not adequately recorded.

Following the time of these *Homo erectus* protohumans, and getting much closer to the present, there is increasingly more archaeological evidence with which to work. About the time of the Neandertals, there begin to be many more skeletons to look at. These early humans lived in Europe and the Middle East from a bit more than one hundred thousand years ago up until about thirty-five thousand to thirty thousand years ago. Skeletons from this time period in Southwest Asia, East Asia, and Africa are not all classified as Neandertal, but they are equivalent for this survey. Of course, much of the rest of the world was also occupied by humans at this time, but because more archaeological research has taken place in Europe, archaeologists happen to have more to say about the ancient people who lived there. It's unlikely there was more or less warfare in other parts of the world.

Though not the same as modern humans, Neandertals had brains every bit as large as ours, were hunters of large game, and made a variety of stone tools. In particular, they made a stone tool that looks as if it was designed to be hafted to a spear. Based on all that is known about their behavior, Neandertals would be expected to have the same resource–population growth problems that later humans did. They were good hunters, able to kill large game—including the cave bear, a huge animal that weighed about sixteen hundred pounds. Neandertals also expanded their range into cold and difficult locales, suggesting the ability to grow their population in many different environments in part because they had fire. As a consequence, I would expect them to have experienced intergroup conflict—and that is what the archaeology reveals.

As was the case for earlier protohumans, about the only archaeological evidence we have to examine are Neandertal skeletal remains themselves. At this point, for the first time in human history, researchers can begin to question whether bodies were formally buried or not. Prior to this, there is no evidence that humans deliberately buried their dead, and the remains archaeologists find are basically just lucky preservation. In some cases, Neandertals deliberately buried their dead, but they may not have done so at all times and places. Shallow burials or the practice of simply covering the body with rocks may have been the norm. Later use of the Neandertal caves by others may have disturbed these burials, causing them to appear today as never having been "buried." Archaeologists have uncovered about three dozen Neandertal burials.[19] Many of the remains from this time period in Europe were not recovered from formal burials. This could be because the people died violently and were never properly buried. The fact that scholars find both burials and nonburials may be evidence of conflict, as it is for more recent times. The condition of the bone from these recovered remains is a more convincing, direct line of evidence of Neandertal warfare.

The site of Shanidar Cave, in present-day Iraq, yielded a number of Neandertal skeletons dating from forty thousand to fifty thousand years ago. One had a stone blade stuck between two ribs, and another had wounds on the head that probably represent evidence for violence, although other explanations are possible. More clear-cut evidence for warfare in this time period is the previously mentioned Skhul IX fossil from Israel, who died from spear wounds in the leg and pelvis. There are less convincing examples of violence from Monte Circeo (Italy), Broken Hill (Africa), and Ngandong (Java). A good case can be made that a mass burial occurred at the French site of La Ferrassie—such mass burials are likely the result of violence, because living in small social groups, as was typical of Neandertal foragers, it is unlikely that many people would die from disease or any other cause on the same day or two. Regardless of whether one accepts all or only the most convincing examples, more than 5 percent of Neandertal burials show violence of one form or another. This is about as high a rate of evidence for violent deaths as is found for much more recent skeletal samples from around the world. Since many violent deaths do not leave skeletal evidence, one can surmise that Neandertal deaths from warfare were about the same as the 5 to 25 percent for more recent foragers that I consider in the next chapter.

Beyond these examples, many of the Neandertal skeletons archaeologists have found are fragmentary. It has been proposed that this fragmentation may be the result of cannibalism.[20] In many cases, the bases or nasal passages of Neandertal skulls are broken out in places that would facilitate the easiest extraction of the brains, presumably for consumption. Other Neandertal bones are also broken in ways commensurate with butchering, as with animal bones that are broken to extract the marrow. The site of Krapina, in Yugoslavia, offers perhaps the best evidence for cannibalism in Neandertal times, although possible evidence exists for at least two other sites. Several specimens show evidence of cut marks, apparently for removing flesh.[21] If the preponderance of fragmented Neandertal bones does represent cannibalism, it most likely represents the killing and eating of enemies. Among modern humans, enemies can be treated as "not like us," and most recent examples of cannibalism victimized enemies, as discussed in Chapter 3.

Many aspects of ancient human behavior and evolution, from domesticating dogs to sexual dimorphism, very likely contain warfare components. Since there is plenty of direct evidence for warfare in the deep past, I believe that models of how we became human should include warfare as an important factor. Taking these ideas about the coevolution of intelligence and tool use, I can weave them into a vastly oversimplified story of how we might have become human from a chimplike ancestor. This story takes the generally accepted ideas of this process and adds warfare to it. In other words, if, as proposed, warfare played an important role in human evolution, how might human evolution have worked? Allow me to speculate about a few aspects of a very complex and far from well understood process.

Five or six million years ago, the earliest members of the human line, as opposed to the ape line, lived in a forestlike environment. Probably, like chimpanzees, the group suffered little threat from predators and regulated its numbers, in part, by conflict and competition with neighboring groups of humans. Eventually, these early humans began to use more open environments and began to move from the forest into the less-wooded savanna. At first, as they made this transition, early hominids may have been under predator threat, and their numbers were being regulated by those predators. Over the course of several million years, a coevolutionary process took place. Walking on two legs, which freed the hands for tools, increased intelligence, and increased communication ability seem to have evolved in tandem. Along with this walking, talking, and tool use process came an ever-increasing reliance on hunting animals for food, as opposed to almost exclusively foraging for plants, as with the chimpanzees. At some point, there was a reduction in the number of predators that were partially controlling the early humans' numbers. Minus major predators, other humans became their main predators, and intergroup conflict would have been a significant component of the coevolutionary process from then on.

The better hunters were the better competitors, the more intelligent early humans were better competitors, the better communicators were better competitors, and so forth. The ability to compete successfully evolved along with these other traits, each reinforcing the other. Conflict cannot be separated from our evolutionary trajectory any more than the selection for intelligence or communication ability can be separated from the process. They all became intertwined.

The ability of humans to live in large groups carries advantages and disadvantages. One of the advantages is better defense. The larger the group, the safer all are from attack. On the other hand, the more people who live together, the sooner they use up the food in the vicinity. Large groups can hunt communally, and life is less boring when more people are around. Yet too many people cause too many disputes. There are always trade-offs involved as social groups enlarge. Intergroup conflict factors surely played a role in determining group size. All these factors coevolved for millions of years, until the last thirty thousand to forty thousand years. By that time, humans had achieved the intelligence, communication ability, population growth rate, ability to make and use tools, skill to hunt almost any animal on the planet, and capacity to engage in organized intergroup conflict that are found in people today.

Before concluding this chapter, I must add a few more things about protohumans, especially the last of these early hominids, the Neandertals. They were successful—in fact, they were *very* successful. Neandertals spread over much of Earth prior to being fully modern humans. Some places, like the very northern latitudes, the Americas, the Oceanic islands, and Australia, were not colonized until humans were fully human. Scholars know from the archaeology that protohumans lived throughout the rest of the world. These early hominids were certainly capable of reproducing fast enough to spread all over and to spread into new ecological zones. Having started in the tropics, they could survive in deserts, on mountains, and in the cold. At the same time, in spite of this ability to grow and spread, the actual population growth rate for these protohumans and early humans was very slow. On average, it may have taken one hundred thousand years for the world's population to double throughout the last million years. In contrast, the world's population has more than doubled in my lifetime.

I am reasonably confident that for most of this almost-million-year span these protohumans had such rudimentary cultures and language that they could not have been acting as true conservationists. They would have had no means to devise or enforce cultural rules that would keep their populations well below the carrying capacity. For most of this time, their numbers were controlled in the same way other animals' are, by starvation, disease, accidents, and, of course, in the case of protohumans and true humans, by warfare. Only in the last forty thousand years or so has the world been inhabited by fully modern humans—creatures so much like us that they had the intelligence, culture, and language capabilities to change their relationship to their environment in ways that their ancestors could not.

In many critical ways humans are like chimpanzees. Chimps reproduce and run out of resources in their territories; human reproduction can potentially outstrip our resources as well. Food is never unlimited for chimpanzees, nor is it automatically plentiful for humans. Humans and chimpanzees are both intelligent, social animals that live in groups and so are capable of, and undertake, group-based conflict against other groups: warfare. And yet humans are not chimpanzees, no matter how many genes we have in common, or how similar we are in some ways. Humans are not only more intelligent, we have much more complex social systems. Or, more likely, we have much more complex social systems because we are much more intelligent. Perhaps the most important difference is that humans live in a world in which every society is surrounded by very intelligent, social animals with lots of tools, including weapons. We humans are surrounded by other humans.

If one thinks of "human history" as the time when humans were fully modern in intelligence, had fully developed language ability, developed art, and acquired the ability to make complex tools, then human history began around one hundred thousand years ago. Many scholars believe that these changes took place in Africa, with these modern humans then spreading over Earth. Other scholars suggest that humans all over the world evolved in tandem to a fully modern state. In any case, by about forty thousand years ago, most of the world was occupied by fully modern people. These earliest humans were nomadic foragers. And it is to foragers, both past and present, that I now turn—to see how humans coped for thousands of years with ecological problems and to examine the role warfare played in their lives and adaptations.

chapter five

WARFARE AMONG FORAGERS

As a college student about thirty-five years ago, I was in southern Utah on a camping trip with some friends, hoping to paddle a canoe to Rainbow Bridge as the newly created Lake Powell was filling up behind Glen Canyon Dam. The landscape in this part of the country is stark: dramatic undulating expanses of bare sandstone, with huge mesas looming in the distance. A few short junipers and pines grow here and there, but the vegetation is mainly sagebrush, and one can see for miles—when the weather cooperates. On this trip our vision was impaired by a sudden spring snowstorm.

As we drove along a deserted sandy track, it began to get dark and very cold, and the wind was whipping up the snow. We had to find a place to camp. A few hundred yards away was a sandstone mesa that paralleled the road. We could just make out its vertical face in the darkening sky. Someone spotted a shallow opening in the cliff. We pulled off the dirt road, grabbed our food and sleeping bags, and headed for the cave. Soon we were inside, had a fire going, and began cooking dinner. The snow swirled outside as the wind howled, but we were warm, safe, and dry. I have never felt better around a fire than I did that night. It did help to know that we had down sleeping bags to keep us warm and plenty of food. Nevertheless, we could relate to our ancient ancestors who would have found the cave equally attractive and comfortable.

It was soon clear we were not the first humans to find this shelter. We saw stone chips and broken fragments of spear points in the sandy floor. Our cave had been used by people many thousands of years ago—only they had to hunt and gather all their food and make warm clothing out of animal skins and plant fibers. We couldn't help wondering how anyone could have survived during this time of year. No plants were yet blooming, and it was bitter cold and muddy where the ground wasn't frozen or covered in snow. Animals, if any were around, would have been lean after a long winter. We did not see how anyone could even hunt in this weather.

The people who had used this cave in the deep past did not store any substantial amounts of food; they had to move around regularly to find something to eat, regardless of the weather. Thanks to recent ethnographic research, anthropologists know that groups of hunter-gatherers had worked out many successful means of staying alive and had knowledge of their environment that my friends and I certainly did not possess. Life could not have been easy for those ancient people, since resources were few and sparsely located. There could not have been many of them. They would have had little reason to fight each other. Sitting by the fire in that cave so many years ago, I could not have been presented with a more vivid glimpse of the traditional hunter-gatherer way of life—clever people with great environmental knowledge, who must have lived in ecological harmony with their surroundings.

As scholars are better able to examine and figure out the past, it's becoming increasingly clear that this vision of the ancient forager lifeway is incorrect. Caves all over the world, just like the one I slept in that cold spring night, preserve not only the chipped-stone tools and sometimes the rock art of past hunter-gatherers, but their skeletal remains as well. Enough examples of these bones showing evidence for violent deaths and massacres suggest that this ancient lifestyle was not necessarily a peaceful one.

The basic human social grouping for more than a million years was a small band of people, usually forty or fewer residing in one group, who survived by foraging—or regularly moving around—hunting, and gathering their food. They did not farm domesticated crops or herd domesticated animals, nor did they intensively use or depend on any one particular wild resource that they processed and stored. Traditional foragers were able to utilize wild plants and animals by not living in one place for very long. They continually moved camp, typically never staying much longer than perhaps a few weeks or so in one location.[1]

Usually, based on ethnographic examples of forager societies that have been studied in recent times, the men in the group were related, and the women came from other nearby groups. Forager technology was clever but simple, typically bows, many different types of baskets and cord bags, boomerangs, spear-throwers, nets and snares, sandals made from hide or cordage, a few ornaments of shell or bone, a water container made out of an ostrich-egg shell or similar material, and perhaps a musical instrument fashioned from a piece of wood and some cord. Specially selected stones chipped to make knives, scrapers, and spear points, and maybe a bone awl, were all that was needed in the way of tools to make other tools. Forager houses were ephemeral, and there was a strong division of labor. For the most part, men did the hunting and the women collected plants. Among surviving foragers known from ethnography, much of the group's daily calorie count was derived from plants, so the contribution made by the females to the group's diet is significant. Children and adolescents in forager societies made a small contribution to the diet, in contrast to the children of farmers, who do help produce significant calories.[2]

A typical forager group, say, twenty-five to thirty people, builds a camp in an area that has some useful resources. They then go out from the camp in small groups, usually women with women, and men with men. The women tend to focus on plants and the men hunting. This description is, of course, oversimplified—for example, men gather honey when possible, and women do not pass up the opportunity to capture a small animal. Food is brought back to the camp, processed, shared to some degree, and consumed. Little, if any, is stored for long in most situations. After a number of days, the particular locale is stripped of food, or the trips away from camp become longer and longer in order to gather enough food. At some point, the decision is made to move camp to a less exploited area. The entire group moves, and everything needs to be carried, including babies. There is a continuum between having many camps, each used for only a short time, and camps that are used for long periods. Which approach is taken is influenced by the nature of the resources. Only in certain circumstances is it possible to stay long in one place. The extreme, almost never attained by foragers, is to stay in one place all year—a sedentary lifestyle.[3]

With all this moving around, the number of children a forager female can have is severely limited. Not only must she go out each day to forage, but she must periodically carry the children to the new camp. If a baby is nursing, it must be carried by the mother on her daily foraging efforts, while older children can sometimes be left with others, a grandmother or some portion of the group not going out that day. Depending on how far the walk is to the new camp, even older children may need to be carried, at least partway. It is not practical for foragers to have children spaced very close together if camp movement is at all frequent or daily foraging trips far. Spacing children about four years apart is a common practice among modern foragers, as is assumed to be the case with earlier foragers.

This earliest human social organization was egalitarian. Within forager society, who one's parents are does not matter; there are no differences in status and no special access to resources based on birth—at least in comparison to other, later types of human societies. Foragers have no perma-

The !Kung (Bushmen) of southern Africa are among the few surviving foragers on earth. They have amazing knowledge of the plants and animals available to them. Here, a woman with her child is collecting tubers using a digging stick. In spite of the marginal environment and environmental knowledge, the !Kung, like all other foragers, focus on short-term needs and not long-term ecological balance.

nent leaders, no meaningful differences in wealth, and no social institutions beyond that of the group itself. The only major difference in "wealth" or "position" among traditional forager societies is that sometimes some men in the group had many wives, while others had none. Only a few items are individually owned—a stone axe or objects used for religious purposes, for example—but there are few items to be owned in the first place. Everyone must carry all he or she owns, so no one owns much. Land and resources are usually considered communal property, not owned by an individual or even a nuclear family.

Anthropologists have classified this type of social organization and way of life the *band* level of society. "Band" refers to the group's social organization, but such societies are also often termed hunter-gatherers—referring to their lifestyle or lifeway—because they do not farm. Farming of domesticated plants and animals—a process that involves sowing, tilling, harvesting, and storing—is a recent human invention. I prefer the term *forager*, because in the recent past some social groups were hunter-gatherers but lived in permanent villages and were more complexly organized. So foragers are hunter-gatherers who do not have permanent settlements and are organized as bands. I use this distinction because many hunter-gatherers "farm wilds." The plants or animals in their region were so dense and abundant and were used so intensively that the people were able to live in one place and harvest the wild plants and animals as if they were domesticated. They wound up with lifestyles very similar to those of farmers, and can also be termed sedentary collectors. The most famous of these "farmers of wilds" or sedentary collector societies are the peoples of the northwest coast of North America, where humans heavily relied on fishing and hunting marine mammals. Other examples of "farmers of wilds" abound. The Jomon people of Japan, dating from around 10,000 B.C. to A.D. 1, also specialized in seafood, the California Indian intensively collected acorns, the Natufians of the ancient Middle East harvested wild grains. Although these peoples were not true farmers, ecologically they behaved like them and are best understood in those terms, rather than as foragers.[4]

Only occasionally do foraging bands join to form larger units, usually when food is plentiful for the purpose of finding mates and conducting some trading. No organized efforts or decisions are made at more than the basic coresident unit. Foragers do not join forces to accomplish things. Examples of forager societies that exist today, or very recently, are the !Kung Bushmen, traditional Eskimo groups, Australian Aborigines, the Paiute and related groups in the Great Basin of Nevada and Utah, and the Hadza of east Africa. The band of foragers is most relevant to the human distant past, because until relatively recently on the scale of human history, all humans were foragers. No humans farmed before twelve thousand years ago, so for at least the last million years or so (exactly when the human lineage became *human* is debatable), we were all foragers.

Among anthropologists there are a surprising number of theories about how foragers actually live. This range of ideas includes viewing foragers as idyllic "noble savages" (a concept formulated in the nineteenth century) all the way to the belief that their lives were hard, brutish, and short. None of these theories was based on any actual evidence, or else they were founded on information that was sparse and strongly biased. Anthropologists began systematic studies of foragers only early in the twentieth century, and much of this information was problematic on two counts. First, early ethnographers were usually more interested in investigating kinship terminology (what name did you give your mother's brother as opposed to your father's brother?), religion, and ceremonies than in discovering the economics and demography of the foragers. Second, most of the groups studied were no longer living a traditional forager lifestyle when they were interviewed but were already heavily impacted by Europeans. Much of the past "uncovered" by these early anthropologists was actually reconstructed by interviews. Such interviews can reveal a great deal about ceremonies, social organizations, and the like, but they provide much less information about the true nuts and bolts of forager society—specifically who gathered what foods, how much was obtained each day, how often there were shortages.

Not until the 1950s did anthropologists begin to implement more behavioral ethnographic field studies, the goal being to study foragers as they actually *behaved*, rather than as was recounted or remembered.[5] One of the more famous, if not the first really serious behavioral ethnographic field study, was conducted among the !Kung Bushmen of South Africa.[6] Many of these field studies involved biological anthropologists, using established methodologies biologists use to study such animals as lions, wolves and, especially, the great apes in the wild. This kind of research resulted in a much more meticulous methodology. These researchers considered such questions as, Exactly how much time did it take to get how much food? In order to find the answers, they had to follow foragers on their daily routines and note just how much time was spent obtaining food and exactly what its nutritional value was. The researchers had to determine who was gathering which particular food—an adolescent, a pregnant female, or a forty-year-old man—what they did with the food, if the food was shared, and with whom. These types of ethnographic field studies have a major influence on the way anthropologists think about the forager way of life. The problem is that most "modern" foragers have long since come into contact with more complex societies, and how applicable these studies are as models for foragers who lived in the deep past is questionable. This is still a hotly debated topic.

When considering modern foragers, three groups come most readily to mind: the Bushmen (!Kung) of the South African Kalahari Desert, the Aborigines of Australia, and the Eskimo (Inuit) of the Arctic. These groups have been studied extensively, especially by researchers using behavioral methods. Each society reveals something unique about how foragers survived within their particular ecological environments as well as about the nature of forager warfare.

One thing that our three examples of modern foragers have in common is that these groups (as well as others, who are less well documented) live in difficult environments.[7] Most, like the Bushmen and the Australian Aborigines, live in deserts. The Eskimos occupy an incredibly harsh, unique environment. All the remaining forager societies in the world today live in what can only be termed "marginal environments." Some marginal environments may not appear so to us. This is especially true of tropical forest environments. Even though they are filled with plants, animals are scarce and most of the vegetation is not edible, so it is very hard to obtain a balanced diet in these forests. It is so difficult that it is not clear whether tropical forests can be occupied without obtaining some food from people living outside the forests. Tropical foraging today is intertwined with adjacent farmers, and such classic foragers as the Pygmies of the Ituri forest in Central Africa have a close symbiotic relationship with the adjacent farmers—so much so that there is disagreement over whether they should be used as an example of a "traditional" foraging way of life.[8]

Foragers did not always live in marginal regions. If everybody was a forager at some point in the deep past, then foragers must have lived in many better places—most other places—on Earth. The archaeology shows there were foragers living throughout Europe, Southwest Asia, and China—not deserts, not the Arctic, but where most humans today live. These "better places" were taken over by farmers over time. What was once forager territory was long ago plowed under or now has cities built upon it. Farmers and the colonizers—more socially complex societies—have taken over the regions that were once home to foragers. Even though scholars know that the foragers were there, there are no ethnographic accounts. Finding archaeological evidence of foragers can be difficult because they did not make permanent houses, pottery, or other things that last long enough for archaeologists to study them. The older an archaeological site is, the more it has decayed, the more ephemeral it is, and the more likely it has been plowed under or built over. Archaeological traces of foragers are hard to find, because there were, in fact, very few foragers in prehistoric times. These are people who truly left no "footprint" at times.

An empty Coke bottle falls from the sky and is found by a band of slight, easygoing, laughing people—the !Kung of the Kalahari Desert.[9] Of all the foragers alive today, perhaps the !Kung of South Africa best capture the imagination of modern Western society. The general public has an idea of how foraging people survive with few possessions and little conflict in a harsh, arid environment from movies like *The Gods Must Be Crazy* (with its metaphorical Coke bottle), as well as in the famous anthropological documentary *The Hunters*.

The !Kung speak a derivation of the language family called San and are not closely related to the Bantu speakers who inhabit most of Africa. San speakers occupied much of Southern Africa before the Bantu speakers, including the Zulu, arrived. Although each small group among these few remaining San speakers has a different name, they are often lumped under the generic category "Bushmen." While some consider the term to be pejorative, Bushmen is in fact what they call themselves today when speaking English. Their languages are classified as San and they are usually lumped with the linguistically related Khoikhoi speakers, who were called Hottentots in the past. These latter represent the people living along the coast and inland prior to the movement of Bantu speakers into the area in the last thousand years or less. Combined they are termed Khoisan speakers, but when I discuss all the Khoisan speakers, I simply use the term Bushmen.[10]

The !Kung and other Bushmen living today in the hot, dry Kalahari Desert have become the epitome of the traditional forager, exemplars of our ancestry for tens of thousands of years. They are probably the best studied foragers living today, thanks to many exhaustive ethnographic studies, some carried out by my colleagues at Harvard. In fact, right outside my office in the Peabody Museum is an exhibit about a group of !Kung foragers. Museum visitors learn of the !Kung's ingenuity, their minimal set of tools and equipment, and their integration with the natural environment. The viewer is also informed that in spite of their severe desert surroundings, "food is plentiful and life is easy" for the !Kung. The exhibit reports that they work fewer hours per day than any farmers or members of industrialized nations anywhere on Earth. The !Kung of today are peaceful, and modern !Kung may enjoy ample food most of the time, but the !Kung of today do not necessarily represent the !Kung of the past—nor do they provide a particularly good model for how humans lived in the past. Every day I walk past an exhibit that presents a fascinating yet incomplete story about the !Kung and other foragers.

In addition to capturing the public's imagination, the !Kung are especially important to the scholarly community. The study of these desert survivors forever changed our methods for working with foragers—as well as anthropologists' perceptions of the forager way of life. The !Kung studies initiated by John and Lorna Marshall, Irven DeVore, and Richard Lee, followed by John Yellen and Henry Harpending, among others, broke new ground in the field of ethnographic study. The old, traditional model of anthropology—which was to sit comfortably in the shade and interview old members of the social group—was shattered by their methods. Though such "old school" information can be invaluable, it can provide only certain kinds of information. If you are interested in what people do, you need to observe them doing it.

This new breed of researchers was particularly interested in how foragers

These Australian Aborigines have cut down a tree to extract the honey from a beehive. Foragers all over the world are known to harvest plants, animals and collect honey in ways that do not optimize the regeneration of these resources. This is done in spite of ideals about living in harmony with nature and not using more resources than needed. When such goals require significantly more work than other means of food procurement, they were often not implemented.

made a living for its value as a model of how humans would have made a living over the last million years. These cultural and biological anthropologists followed the !Kung throughout the day. They watched and timed the women when they foraged for plant foods and accompanied the men when they hunted. The researchers then counted and weighed what the !Kung had foraged and were able to determine just how many calories were procured for every hour of effort. Such a methodology resembles what biologists do with animal populations. Primatologist Jane Goodall pioneered this method in her field studies of chimpanzees. This intense scrutiny was not performed because the researchers did not trust the !Kung to tell them the truth. The !Kung, who did not have watches, were not in a position to provide such answers—nor could you and I if we didn't read the labels on our food packaging or constantly consult our watches.

What these pioneering anthropologists discovered shocked many scholars in the field. Instead of working from dawn to dusk, barely eking out enough sustenance to survive, the !Kung spent less time procuring food than did almost all the farmers known around the world. The researchers found that the !Kung devoted fewer than four hours a day to foraging and could simply sit around the camp talking and enjoying each other's company the rest of the time. If the !Kung were any model, foragers did not have it hard—they were not stressed by the limited resources of their environment. And these particular foragers were living in one of the least hospitable places on Earth, the Kalahari Desert. Imagine how easy life would have been in more temperate or well-watered environments.

This observation raised the obvious question: Why would foragers, who have it so easy, ever begin to farm if tilling, sowing, and harvesting were so much more work? Farming developed the world over, appearing, remarkably, at just about the same time everywhere—between nine thousand and twelve thousand years ago. This new perception of our forager past swept through the anthropology world and the scholarly community in general. Today, Paul and Anne Ehrlich, with Gretchen Daily, write about modern society's ecological problems drawing a comparison with the "easy" lifestyle of the !Kung foragers. Even a 2001 issue of *National Geographic* described the Bushmen of the Nyae Nyae district of northeastern Namibia as "conservation icons living in perfect harmony with nature."[11]

Knowing about the need for population control in order to live in ecological balance, we would assume that if the !Kung population grew, their ability to live in harmony with nature would be threatened. The question is how they keep their population in such perfect balance. This question has been the subject of careful census data on birth rates and infant survival, and computer model building of how such population control might work. The conclusion that most scholars have reached is that the !Kung space their children far apart, resulting in an overall low net growth. This birth spacing occurs somewhat naturally, because the !Kung must walk long distances to find food and a mother can carry only one infant while doing this. In spite of this long interval birth spacing, if there is some growth in the population, then some other not currently understood mechanisms must have kicked in to reduce birth rates even further. A combination of lifestyle and social mechanisms enables the !Kung to live as close to ecological nirvana as is known, in spite of their difficult environment. Here we have our mythical inherent conservationists in the flesh.

Unfortunately, this scenario is not true. Why this fairy tale is so readily accepted is not clear, but it must relate to a desire in our modern, collective consciousness to find some ecologically benevolent humans somewhere on Earth. The !Kung found living in the center of the Kalahari *do* spend only a few hours of the day foraging for food, at least most of the time. That does not mean they did so in the past, nor that they were then, or are now, living in ecological balance.

The initial estimates of actual !Kung foraging times were based on observations made only during a few months in one year. The researchers were not there observing the !Kung throughout the year, over many years. A good crop, whether it is a corn crop in Mesoamerica or a wild mongongo nut crop in the Kalahari, results in less work than usual, anywhere in the world. In order to put these studies in proper perspective, we have to know how typical were the year and season of the year studied. In reality, the initial study itself was not completely valid. Before continuing with the argument, I need to explain that this !Kung fieldwork was a pioneering study. Now, almost fifty years later, it is possible to recognize its flaws with much more experience and comparative information generated because this initial work was so revealing. This is how science proceeds. The researchers themselves are the first to admit that our understanding is an ongoing undertaking and that early mistakes are not evidence of failure, just first steps in the process.

Some of the problems in this groundbreaking research changed scholars' estimate of how easy life was for the !Kung. For example, the anthropologists who followed the women as they foraged sometimes assisted them. On some occasions, they loaded the women into their pickup trucks and drove them where they wanted to forage. Even more important, as Irven DeVore, the director of one of these pioneering studies and now at Harvard, explained to me, he and his colleagues did not take into account the amount of time the !Kung spent processing the food they collected. As it turns out, subsequent research has shown that collecting and processing combined take much more time than originally estimated. In fact, the !Kung spend more time in camp than most other foragers studied, which is not surprising since much of their diet includes nuts, which require lots of processing.[12]

Another important point not fully factored into the initial 1950s studies is that these modern-day !Kung were not living in isolation—they had cotton cloth and iron tools. They had technology that was more efficient than their traditional technology and that required less effort to make and maintain. In the past, the !Kung certainly must have spent considerable amounts of time creating tools and clothing, rather than sitting around the fire socializing. Another factor is even more revealing: The !Kung are now surrounded by herders and, more distantly, by farmers. The herders and their animals can survive in the arid area only because water holes, called boreholes, were drilled throughout the region in the 1950s. This desert was not at all hospitable to the herders prior to European technology, and it was surely more difficult for the !Kung to live there as well.

The !Kung living in the Kalahari in recent times were not a biologically closed system. Early ethnographic observers noted that they did not exchange mates only with other foraging groups. Instead, !Kung women would marry out of the foraging group into the herder societies around them. This is a very important observation, because other foragers around the world have been observed to have significant growth rates, sometimes as high as 2 percent, while the !Kung seem to have very little growth. If, for example, one woman in ten married out of the foraging community into a herding community, it would reduce the reproductive rate of the foragers by 2 percent. That is very close to the estimated number of women marrying into herding communities in Richard Lee's initial !Kung study in the early 1960s. Some of the most fertile and reproductively valuable members of !Kung society were being removed from the reproductive pool. It would not take much of this regular siphoning off of women at their childbearing peak to reduce dramatically any group's overall growth rate. Looking at the actual demographic statistics shows the same thing. !Kung women average about 4+ children each. Modern foragers rarely have infant mortality rates as great as 50 percent, with most having rates below 40 percent, and most of these deaths are due to diseases that may not have existed in the prehistoric past. In the past, a forager woman who had 4+ children would, on average, have had more than two survive. Overall, we would expect the !Kung population to have grown.[13]

Modern !Kung people are demographically below where they probably used to be in the past, they have better technology than they used to have, and they were studied for only a limited time with methods that may have overestimated their ability to forage. They do not live in ecological balance. That vision of the "ideal" !Kung way of life is more a matter of wishful thinking—or myth—than reality.

The early !Kung would have had a positive growth rate and would have been periodically confronted with food stress as a consequence. Neighboring societies in more well-watered areas may have grown even more rapidly and lived in even larger groups. When confronted with food shortages, those neighbors may well have tried to encroach on the lower-density desert-dwelling foragers—who would have had to defend their territory with force and stay put, or just push farther into the desert until there was no place left to go.

In generalizing from the !Kung and other forager examples, I am interested in three ecological issues: Can they keep their populations stable over the long run? Can they keep from degrading their environments? And do they have true conservationist behaviors? Generally, do these "modern" foragers maintain an ecological balance, and if so, how? The consensus among scholars has been that they do manage to stay in balance with their resources, but I disagree.

Though the !Kung are the classic examples of ethnographic foragers and field studies focusing on them have presented us with evidence about the way foragers live (or might have lived), other forms of evidence of forager interaction with their environments exist. For example, there is archaeological evidence for foragers burning the natural vegetation because the plants that came back were more of the kind the animals they hunted could eat. This would not necessarily degrade the environment, but it certainly changed it and much of the grasslands of the world came about this way.[14] Such evidence is found in North America, Japan, and Australia, and on various islands throughout the world.

There is also archaeological and ethnographic evidence for net hunting, in which all the animals in an area are systematically driven into nets and killed. This procedure does not automatically degrade the environment, but it could easily overexploit particular localities. Archaeologists have evidence for direct overexploitation of resources like turtles and shellfish among foragers, from places as diverse as Southwest Asia, South Africa, and California. Archaeologists find that the shells in excavated shell middens, essentially "trash heaps," get smaller over time. Researchers have found that turtle shells get smaller and more rare, all pointing to overexploitation of such easily acquired resources and the resultant need to harvest younger and smaller forms.[15]

Another fascinating line of evidence is the way food is distributed within a social group. As societies around the world became more complexly organized with hierarchies and class structure, research has shown that some social classes ate much better than others. If food was plentiful, one would expect all members of a group to eat well. Scholars find unequal access to food among some forager societies in which food was known to be in short supply. For example, among the Pygmies of Central Africa, a recent study showed that women consumed less protein than men and had overall poorer health. Even among the Pygmy men, leaders consumed more protein than the nonleader adult males.[16] In this case, good food was not abundant, even in spite of recently introduced new technologies.

In order to have a stable population, foragers would have to maintain very low reproductive rates.[17] The low birth rates among modern foragers have been assumed to exist because of the need to birth-space so the women could forage far from camp and still carry a child. For early foragers who lived in better environments, this may have been less of a constraint. In richer environments, the distances between food sources would have been less. The more meat in the diet, the less the women would have had to walk each day. They would not need to have spaced children so far apart, and the groups' growth rates would have been higher.

Infanticide is another factor in forager demography that must be considered. Infanticide was common among all foragers for whom there is relevant information, including most forager groups in Australia, where scholars estimate that the number of children was reduced by about 30 percent.[18] Infanticide was common among all Eskimo groups and was significant among South American foragers like the Ache, 14 percent of the boys, 23 percent of the girls.[19] There is evidence for prehistoric infanticide from coastal foragers in South America.[20] This information makes it clear that the need for foraging women to walk long distances did not result in birth spacing at appropriate intervals to result in a stable population. There is no ethnographically known population of foragers with zero population growth, nor are there any known mechanisms that would work to keep the populations in perfect balance.

Foragers do not live in isolation, nor have they ever in the past, just as with the !Kung today. No one—except for people on very small islands—ever lives in isolation. Not only does almost everyone on Earth have neighbors, but these neighboring groups often find themselves living under very different circumstances. Rather than asking, Can any group of foragers stay in ecological balance for an extended time? the real question should be, Can *every* group of foragers in a region stay in ecological balance? I believe the answer to that question is unlikely, if not downright impossible. Once one group gets out of balance, competition would ensue.

Such foragers as the !Kung embody the myth of the peaceful past because modern foragers are peaceful now. They also embody the myth of the ecologically balanced noble savage, since they are living well below the carrying capacity today. Since these circumstances result from the impact of complex societies on the foragers, foragers today are not representative of foragers in the past. What we can know about foragers in the past must come from archaeology or very early historical accounts. Past war and ecology have to be gleaned from the earth or ferreted from old manuscripts, but the evidence is there. Evidence for warfare is more easily found, and it is clear and strong.

The San or Bushmen of southern Africa are often portrayed as completely peaceful. This rock art battle scene is one of many pieces of evidence that contradict this notion. Competition over resources was prevalent here, as elsewhere among foragers.

... we were unexpectedly intruded upon by a very numerous tribe, about three hundred. Their appearance coming across the plain, occasioned great alarm. ... On the hostile tribe coming near, I saw they were all men. ... In a very short time the fight began. ... Men and women were fighting furiously, and indiscriminately, covered with blood, two of the latter were killed in this affair. [The battle ended with at least three killed, and a counterattack was planned for that night.]

... and finding most of them asleep, laying about in groups, our party rushed upon them, killing three on the spot, and wounding several others. The enemy fled ... leaving their war implements in the hands of their assailants and their wounded to be beaten to death by boomerangs.[21]

This nineteenth-century account of a violent encounter between Aboriginal foragers was written by William Buckley, who escaped from a penal colony on the southern coast of Australia in 1803 and lived for thirty-two years among the Aborigines. He provides a rare glimpse of what forager warfare might have been like in the past. Information about forager warfare is scanty—just as all information about foragers is limited. There are fewer forager cemeteries to discover how they died, few houses to have burned, few foragers are known to have made fortifications, and most modern foragers were studied long after they had been impacted by colonial people. Yet this picture of Australia two hundred years ago hardly speaks of a peaceful past.

Archaeology reveals burials with evidence of violent deaths and even massacres, and specialized weapons useful only for warfare have been found. From the prehistoric art painted and chipped onto cave walls, archaeologists find imagery depicting battles. There are ethnographic accounts of indigenous people fighting other indigenous people, not just the colonizers, as in the Buckley account from Australia and others from Southern Africa. As resource richness declines, ethnographic evidence for warfare also declines, until there is little evidence for warfare in extremely marginal areas. In such places, like central Australia, battles between foragers have been observed, but the participants are really only going through the motions. As soon as someone is injured, the fighting stops. Or shields are used only ceremonially, not for serious combat.

Among the !Kung today not even that amount of vestigial warfare is found. But the !Kung of today are not the !Kung of the past. Historical accounts and archaeology provide a picture of the !Kung that contrasts sharply with the "friendly" desert people of today. Until about two thousand years ago, the !Kung, or their San-speaking relatives, lived over much of Southern Africa, not just in the Kalahari Desert. Around that time, they obtained goats, which were first domesticated in Southwest Asia, then spread to the tip of South Africa. At some point thereafter, the Bantu speakers arrived in the region with their cattle and crops. Finally, in the 1600s, the Europeans entered the scene with their farms and guns. Over this span of more than five hundred years, the original Bushman population declined precipitously in the impacted areas, and the descendants of some of these people became part of the modern states of South Africa, Namibia, and Botswana, while a few, such as the !Kung, retained their foraging lifestyle—but only in the extreme desert.

Today, these vast areas of Southern Africa are predominantly occupied by European-derived British and Dutch, as well as Bantu-speaking Zulu and Herero people. The most productive geographical areas of the !Kung's former territories are no longer occupied solely by Bushmen. When the Europeans arrived, some of the Bushmen were goatherders who lived in relatively large groups. Warfare was prevalent, as is known from early historical accounts and rock art.

These historical accounts of the 1600s–1800s reveal that groups of small Bushman bands joined together and defended their joint territory and even had no-man's-lands around them. The Bushmen defended their territories against other Bushmen into the nineteenth century, with a Dutch recorder noting, "Every armed man is considered an enemy" and "If two Bushmen [from different groups] are approaching each other, their arms will be put down within range of site."[22] When the Herero (Bantu speakers) began to invade Bushman territory in the 1800s, they were met with raids and warfare effective enough that the Herero retreated.[23] There is also rock art from South Africa depicting battle scenes. This art predates the arrival of Europeans, but beyond that, determining the date of the images is difficult. In addition to the historical accounts of actual warfare, scholars know that some leaders of the Bantu farming groups used Bushmen for their personal guards. It is doubtful that any group notorious for being peaceful and friendly would be selected as palace guards. The early Bushmen fought each other and were extremely capable of fighting the Europeans and the Bantu farmers. The very earliest accounts by the Dutch and British attest to the military skill of the San-speaking Bushmen. They obviously did not learn the art of warfare from the Europeans. They, like the people they fought, had developed these arts over millennia.

These historical accounts attest to resource stress in Southern Africa. The !Kung people, who now occupy the center of the region's desert, were living there because other San—more overcrowded, perhaps more aggressive groups—were occupying the wetter areas. There are Dutch accounts of stock-herding peoples, known as Khoihkoi today, raiding rival groups, who were in turn raided by nonherders, whom we would classify as Bushmen. The herders "when they caught any of them killed them without mercy and threw them to the dogs."[24]

As expected, the wetter areas of the region were contested and fully populated. The modern !Kung reside in the desert because they have to. Their ancestors had slowly been forced to occupy more and more marginal areas as the better land was taken over. Like all other places on Earth, the better areas were occupied first, and the marginal areas inhabited only when there were no alternatives. Certain Bushmen behaviors are evidence for resource stress. They defended territories and even owned particularly productive trees, a sure sign that resources were not unlimited.[25] There is no evidence that the !Kung or their related groups at the time these early historical accounts were written were living in ecological balance, nor were they peaceful.

In addition to southern Africa's Bushmen, the people who live in the Arctic regions of North America are foragers. Arctic foragers live in a broad sweep along the north coast of Alaska, Canada, Greenland, and part of Siberia, and are generically referred to as the Eskimos. The word *Eskimo* derives from an Algonquin word for these people of the far north. There are many individual groups, including the Netsilik and Copper Eskimo of Canada. Sometimes all Canadian Eskimos are referred to as Inuit, and the Kalimiut and Nuvuk and all other northern Alaskan Eskimos as Inupait.

In this harsh environment one might expect that Eskimos would not need social mechanisms of population control. Natural factors probably did have much more of an impact on the Arctic foragers' demography than on that of many other foragers living under different climatic conditions. In the frigid north, even a slight mistake could result in death. A boat capsized by a whale, a leak in a kayak, or just getting lost in a snowstorm would almost certainly be fatal. Starvation in such a difficult and unpredictable environment was a constant threat. Remember, the most famous Eskimo of all time, Nanook, ran out of food and starved to death on the ice. (Even having a rifle didn't help.)

In spite of these hazards, Eskimo populations did grow, and there were some mechanisms to control it. As known from the early ethnographers, infanticide was regularly practiced, especially with girls, and served as a significant check on population growth. This was a conscious decision by the birth family based on the ability to support the baby. Using estimates of completed family sizes and the efforts for territorial expansion, it is clear that infanticide and starvation alone did not keep populations in balance.

Almost all the early Arctic anthropologists and explorers recorded incidences of warfare and stories about warfare among the Inuit (Eskimos). Based on ethnographic collections, historical drawings, and archaeological finds, researchers know that the Eskimos had tools used exclusively for warfare, most dramatically body armor. The armor was made from pieces of bone and ivory cut into plates and worn like a coat of mail armor. In addition, Eskimos had very powerful recurved bows made from bone. The high quality of these bows and their rather limited use for hunting suggest that warfare was a significant factor in the development of this piece of equipment and its widespread ownership.[26]

In the 1960s, anthropologist Ernest Burch compiled a very complete description of warfare among the Eskimos of northwest Alaska, probably the best summary for any foraging people.[27] Since that warfare had ended about ninety years earlier, Burch drew his information from historical accounts and secondary accounts from older Eskimo men. These Eskimos fought with closely related Eskimo societies, with Siberian and Southwest Alaska Eskimos, and with Athapaskan Indians of the interior. Burch estimates that there was warfare at least once a year somewhere in the region. His study group had the special term "great warrior," and an attacking party could number as many as fifty men, although fifteen to twenty were the norm. A raid could take ten days or more to complete because of the distances involved, the raiding party always had a war leader, and it was generally recognized that the better-disciplined unit always won.

Burch learned that coastal and inland villages were often located with defense in mind—on a spit of land, or adjacent to thick willows, which provided a barrier to attackers. Tunnels were sometimes dug between houses so people could escape surprise raids. Dogs played an important role as sentinels. The goal in all warfare among these Eskimos was annihilation, Burch reported, and women and children were normally not spared, nor were prisoners taken, except to be killed later. Burning logs and bark were thrown into houses to set them on fire and to force the inhabitants out, where they could be killed. Burch's study reveals that the surprise dawn raid was the typical and preferred war tactic, but open battles did occur. These took the form of lines of men facing each other; sometimes sawtoothed clubs were used, and armor worn; the bow and arrow was the preferred weapon. Alliances were made between groups within Burch's study area, especially when the enemy was numerous

Archaeologists working on the Saunaktuk Inuit site on the Beaufort Sea, in the Northwest Territories of Canada, have recovered the remains of skeletons of many women and children that show evidence of violent death and dismemberment.[28] Historical accounts recorded about this location recount that the people were attacked by Athapaskan Indians from the south when the men were away. A massacre occurred, including torture, which fits well with the archaeologically recovered remains. In another historical account, the Ahtna Athapaskans claimed to have slaughtered the Chugach Eskimos on Mummy Island in Prince William Sound in the nineteenth century.[29] Everything about this information implies serious and deadly warfare among Arctic foragers.

Though quantified numbers are not available, various accounts that are somewhat supported by archaeology indicate that a significant number of polar people appear to have been killed in warfare. In spite of all the natural hazards, the practice of infanticide, and the constant possibility of starving, the population of Arctic foragers still grew to the point that deaths resulting from warfare were part of the process of regulating their numbers. This does not mean that starvation would not have controlled the Eskimo population had there been no warfare, or even that infanticide might have kept the numbers in perfect balance. It just means that this did not happen. The Eskimos were not living in ecological balance, in spite of the difficult environment, and warfare was one of the mechanisms that ultimately were controlling the number of people.

From one of the coldest places on Earth to one of the hottest, the forager groups studied in Australia for the most part share with the Eskimos the characteristics of living in a harsh climate as well as the generally held perception of their being peaceful people—more into dreaming than fighting. Foragers occupied the entire continent of Australia up until the last couple of centuries. In fact, Australia is the only continent in which farming was never indigenously developed.[30] Carbon-14 dating of archaeological sites shows that Australia was occupied for more than forty thousand years. In that time, the early Australians developed many different languages and cultures. Lumping these various groups together under the rubric "Aborigines" oversimplifies a very complex situation. This variability among the ancient Australians is of interest, because patterns can be observed in the differences found in the nature of their societies. Looking at the entire continent, instead of a single social group, has its merits.

No foraging group in Australia has had an extensive, careful documentation of its food quest. The few estimates researchers do have for the amount of time actually spent foraging range from three to seven hours per day. Some lower estimates include only the food quest, while the higher numbers include food-processing time. To show just how varied the lifestyles are among the Australian Aboriginal groups, the proportion of the diet gleaned from hunting ranges from 30 percent to 70 percent. Thanks to many early ethnographies, scholars do know a great deal about the Aboriginal social structure and religion. The role of dreaming, the importance of sacred places like Ayres Rock (Uluru), and the very complex relationships among kin, including naming rules and special rules of behavior toward particular types of relatives, are hallmarks of the Aboriginal way of life.

The ancient Australians had very limited tool kits, consisting mainly of items made of wood and chipped stone, including knives, spears, wooden bowls, ceremonial objects, and axes. They had no pottery or cloth. Most groups foraged by moving around very large territories. The Aborigines

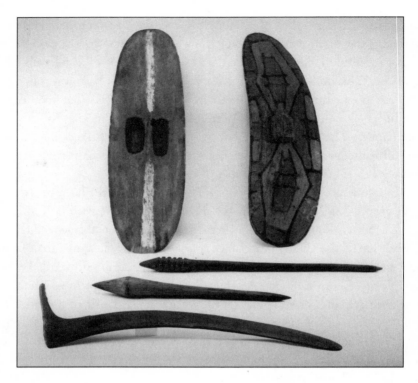

The need to walk great distances for food and carry children resulted in the Australian Aborigines having one of the most minimal tool kits known. Yet, they had heavy wooden shields (shown here front and back), heavy war clubs, and a hooked boomerang used exclusively for war. The threat of conflict was so great that the bulk of their tools were weapons.

made use of a great variety of plants and animals, including things that most of us would not consider food—like the famous witchety grub, an insect larva that was consumed in large quantities by some groups. A wide variety of skills and amazing resourcefulness are needed to survive as foragers in the hot, dry Australian Outback.

The prevalent "Aboriginal model," popular among many anthropologists today, portrays the early Australians as peaceful and terms what warfare they did have as stylized and not lethal. Based on recent ethnographic observations, when a conflict between groups arose, a formal battle was arranged: Both sides lined up and fought, and as soon as one individual was injured, fighting was terminated and the disagreement considered settled. Aboriginal populations are believed to have been in a zero-growth mode for millennia, and it is thought that territories were fluid and vast, with complex kinship arrangements allowing people to move from one area to another when resources were either abundant or failed. The traditional perception among most of the anthropologists who studied Australia's Aborigines was that there were low densities of people, few possessions, and little, if any, reason to fight.

This model does describe the Aboriginal people, for example the Arunta, living in the most marginal areas of the continent—again, desert regions—as observed by anthropologists in this century. But that does not mean the model describes what life was like overall in Australia in the past. There is a big difference between the recent situation—with population loss, new technologies, and social groups being studied in the most marginal environments—and the precontact situation, especially in the environmentally richer zones.

There are a number of different lines of evidence to support the belief that warfare among the early Australian Aborigines was, in fact, common. Some of this evidence is only tantalizing, other examples are more substantive, but in total there is a lot of it. Ethnographic material in many museums collected soon after the British arrived in the late 1700s reveals that Aborigines had a number of tools used exclusively for warfare. They used spear-throwers, generically known as woomera in Australia, and boomerangs, of course. Some Aboriginal people had a special boomerang, called a hooked boomerang, that had the gentle U of all boomerangs but with a sharp, pointed extension coming off one end. They used the particular boomerang only for warfare, and it may have been used more as a club than as a throwing weapon. Many tribes also had clubs used only in warfare.

Some Aboriginal groups used two different types of spear-throwers. One was heavier and used for slinging long, heavy war spears, while the other, lighter thrower was used for slinging smaller spears at game. According to their own ethnographic descriptions, one spear-thrower was used for hunting and the other for warfare.[31] Many Aboriginal people had shields. These were relatively small, but as a defense against spears launched by spear-throwers they would have been quite adequate. In recent years, such shields were used in ceremonies. The idea that people would invent and maintain heavy, strong, well-made, functionally good shields to be used only for dancing is absurd. The fact that there is ethnographic documentation of these specialized weapons makes this evidence for Aboriginal warfare unimpeachable.

There is precious little for archaeologists to discover for people with such sparse tool kits. Nevertheless, we find additional evidence, such as rock art depicting Aboriginal peoples fighting. Rock art is hard to date, but some styles are estimated to be many thousands of years old, and images of conflict apparently come from all periods. Enough examples show evidence that the nature of the warfare changes over time, becoming more complex in the last four thousand years.[32] The fact that there is enough rock art showing warfare even to be able to try to make such inferences speaks volumes. Direct evidence for conflict has been found in human skeletons that display signs of violent deaths. Since the Aborigines did not use the bow but engaged in hand-to-hand combat, the evidence consists of fractured skulls, as it does elsewhere in the world.[33] Since only a small fraction of all warfare deaths should show up on skeletons, this skeletal evidence reveals just how common prehistoric warfare was on the Australian continent.

Finally, early historical accounts exist of warfare among the people living along the coasts of Australia. These locales, especially in the southeastern part of the continent near present-day Victoria, are the best-watered and most productive areas, and not surprisingly they are where most Australians live today. The overall Australian environment has a shocking polarity in its extremes, differences that existed for the last few thousand years. In the 1800s, the central desert region's population density was as low as one person per one hundred square miles. In Victoria it was closer to one person per square mile, so in some places the land was able to support one hundred times as many people as in other regions.

Archaeology and early historical accounts show that the Aborigines in these well-watered areas lived in larger groups, often numbering one hundred people, and two thousand five hundred are known to have come together for special events. They built fish weirs more than three hundred feet long and dug complex ditches to entrap great quantities of spawning eels going upriver.[34] A fish weir cannot be built just anywhere. The ditches covered several acres and required considerable work. Not surprisingly, when the early Europeans arrived in the late 1700s, they encountered Aborigines who defended their territories from other Aboriginal groups. The colonizers also observed the existence of no-man's-lands between the territories of native groups and noted that warfare appeared to be common— with alliances formed between groups and special neutral locations where trade could be carried out safely. Some people in these neutral locations would still post guards at night in fear of attack.

One of the earliest descriptions of Aboriginal warfare is by escaped convict William Buckley, cited earlier. In his account of living with the Wathaurong, beginning in 1804, Buckley describes warfare that often blended into feuding—a man being killed for running off with a woman, for example. He also describes night attacks and massacres, fear of attack, the need for allies, and cases of treachery and the like. Many Aboriginal women were also killed, and sometimes joined in the fighting. "The next day we moved on to another fresh water lake of considerable extent, where we camped, not very much at our ease, as we saw another tribe on the opposite shore. In the middle of the night we heard a dreadful uproar in that direction, and in the morning learned that those we had seen before dark had been fallen upon by some others whilst they were sleeping; so on hearing this we went to their assistance. On our arrival a horrid scene presented itself, many women and children laying about in all directions, wounded and sadly mutilated. Several of the poor creatures had rushed into the lake and were drowned." On another occasion, Buckley, along with a few families, was set upon by a party of sixty men: "My old friend . . . had a spear sent right through his body, and then they hunted out his wife and killed her dead upon the spot. The savages then came back to where I was supporting my wounded friend; who seeing them approaching, sprung up, even in the last agonies of death, and speared the nearest assailant in the arm. My friend was, of course, dispatched immediately, with spears and boomerangs; as was a son of his."[35] Buckley had undoubtedly led a tough life, but even he seems to have been overwhelmed by the level of violence he encountered. Even assuming that the numbers are not exaggerated, there may have been five hundred people involved in a battle he described. From Buckley's account I estimate at least nine killed, or almost 2 percent of the total involved. Since he describes such events as common, the total deaths over time for each group must have been substantial.

More detail of competition and conflict exists among Aboriginal foragers from the Arnhem Land region near the northern coast. Resources were much more abundant than in the center of the continent, and human densities were higher. The Murngin were studied in the early twentieth century. Using interviews, ethnographer Lloyd Warner was able to reconstruct the number of people who died in warfare in the late 1800s. During a twenty-year span, about the time an adult would have been a fighter, in an overall population of about three thousand people with about eight hundred fighting-age males, Warner estimated that about two hundred had died in warfare. Though some of this fighting might be considered feuding, and a single event might involve only two or just a few people, the overall result was that about 25 percent of the men died in warfare, which is not unlike what is found for the intense warfare of New Guinea farmers. The Murngin had terminology for six different types of fighting, including names for surrounding a camp in a night attack, a general open fight, and a pitched battle. In two well-recorded pitched battles, roughly fifteen men were killed in each, and at least one battle involved luring the enemy into a trap where they were surrounded.[36]

This convincing evidence of warfare among the Bushmen, Eskimos, and Australian Aborigines far from exhausts known cases of forager warfare. There is archaeological evidence for forager warfare from around the world, but only a few instances are further enlightening. One of those is from early Europe. Sometime between 40,000 and 30,000 B.C., Neandertals were replaced in Europe by what is often described as "the fully modern humans," known colloquially as Cro-Magnon. Arguments rage whether this was an in situ evolution—that is, the Neandertals evolved into modern humans—or a biological replacement—biologically different people from Southwest Asia and Africa replaced them—and whether, if it was replacement, it was peaceful and gradual, or rapid and competitive. The Upper Paleolithic period lasted from 40,000 B.C. until around 12,000 years ago, when the world began to warm up and the great glaciers that covered much of Europe began to retreat. Even the subsequent time period, the Mesolithic (10,000–6000 B.C.), was still the domain of foragers.

Starting with the Upper Paleolithic period, the time of the famous cave paintings of France and Spain, scholars begin to uncover lines of evidence in addition to blows to the head or cut marks on bones, although these continue, including fifteen possible cases of cannibalism.[37] The site of Dolní Věstonice in Czechoslovakia, dating from twenty thousand to twenty-five thousand years ago, where art objects were produced in great numbers, also provides a window on warfare at that time. The well-known "village" consisted of a very large structure obviously occupied by many families, similar to the Iroquois longhouses, surrounded by some smaller structures. The entire area was surrounded by a wall or fence of mammoth bones. Typically this sort of barrier is used ethnographically around the world for defense. A number of multiple burials—several people placed in the same grave at the same time—have been found at Dolní Věstonice, especially mass burials of fighting-age males, a number of whom also have wounds to the head. It is unlikely that several males in their prime would die from disease at the same time. They could have been killed in a failed mammoth hunt, but death from warfare is certainly more plausible. This "village" was located on a high point of land—hills provide a good deal of defense, especially against spear-throwers, the best weapon of the times. Almost every line of evidence for warfare I would expect to find for this type of forager has been identified at Dolní Věstonice.

Among the bison, horses, deer, and other animals depicted at Lascaux, Cougnac, Pech-Merle, and other cave sites are a few primitive representations of people.[38] Among these are a number of portrayals, some more convincing than others, of humans being speared or otherwise dead or dying. Such images are common enough that art historians refer to them as the "killed man" motif. Known from the French caves of Cosquer, Cougnac, Gabillou, Lascaux, Le Placard, Pech-Merle, and Sous-Grand-Lac, these incredible images date from at least twenty thousand years ago. This is not an inconsequential number of examples. Interpreting rock art is hardly a cut-and-dried process, and others would argue that this interpretation of warring humans in Paleolithic paintings is all wrong. However, it should be pointed out that in many traditional societies the depiction of humans is much less "realistic" than for animals. In addition, humans are virtually never shown in Paleolithic art in groups engaged in an activity. Thus, we would not expect to see scenes of battles in Paleolithic art even if they were a common occurrence at that time. Nor would we particularly expect accurate renderings of humans being killed, if humans are not depicted accurately in other contexts.

A final piece of evidence for warfare from the Upper Paleolithic comes from Sudan. When the Aswan Dam was built, a great deal of archaeology was undertaken along the Nile River in Upper Egypt and Sudan. From this research scholars know that toward the end of the Paleolithic, about ten thousand to two thousand years ago, a graveyard was used by foragers along the Nile. Evidence was found there for warfare as intense as any known from anywhere in the past. The graveyard held the remains of fifty-nine people, at least twenty-four of whom showed direct evidence of violent death, including stone points from arrows or spears within the body cavity, and many contained several points. There were six multiple burials, and almost all those individuals had points in them, indicating that the people in each mass grave were killed in a single event and then buried together. This evidence shows a level of warfare that exceeds almost all the other known examples from any time, anywhere, in the past.[39]

After the great ice sheets melted, the Upper Paleolithic people of Europe readapted to more moderate climatic conditions during the time referred to as the Mesolithic. Archaeologists have uncovered evidence for warfare in this period. The Mesolithic site of Ofnet in Bavaria has the remains of a massacre of about thirty-eight men, women, and children who were killed in one event.[40] Most of the individuals in the group were bludgeoned to death: Their heads were cut off and possibly a few were scalped. Then the heads, with parts of the neck still attached, were buried in two pits. It appears that an entire social group was massacred, since social groups at that time would rarely be expected to number more than forty people. It has been estimated from burial evidence from Brittany dating to about 6000 B.C. that about 8 percent of all deaths were due to warfare, and from a Mesolithic site in the Ukraine the number rises to 15.9 percent. Of course, only a portion of war deaths will be evident in skeletal remains. Other Mesolithic sites also have piles of heads, but nothing as dramatic as Ofnet. Warfare deaths have also been noted in the Ukraine, Denmark, France, England, Switzerland, Spain, and North Africa. Also, Mesolithic cave art from the Castellón region of Spain shows pitched battles.[41]

From very early times in Europe, there is evidence of individuals who were victims of lethal wounds, mass burials, cannibalism, massacres, and warfare depicted in rock art. I would not expect to find much more evidence than this, given how few remains foragers leave archaeologically. The evidence found for foragers in very early Europe is about the same as for the Australian Aborigines. Warfare among foragers has not increased over time; it has always been there.

Starting around one hundred thousand years ago, modern humans spread out of Africa, but it was only in the last fifteen thousand years or so that they spread into the New World, after the glaciers began retreating. These later foragers of the Americas are of interest because a great deal of research has been done there. In North America, some of the oldest skeletons known show evidence for violence. Of fewer than a dozen of the oldest human remains recovered in the New World—dating to more than eight thousand years ago—three died violent deaths or were recovering from violent blows, including the famous Kennewick Man, who had a spear point in his pelvis. The Spirit Cave male was recovering from a depression fracture to the side of the skull at the time of his death. Also from Nevada, a young male about sixteen to eighteen years old from the Grimes Burial Shelter, dated to about nine thousand five hundred years ago, was killed by a knife wound to the chest.[42] Later in time, around the Santa Barbara area in California, skeletons dating to more than two thousand years ago show considerable evidence for warfare, including blows to the head and spear and arrow points embedded in bones. As much as 5 percent of all skeletons of men have spear points in them.[43]

Past foragers lived in much more hospitable places than modern foragers are found today. Foragers were capable of rapid population growth in the past. This is clearly evident in their expansion out of Africa and subsequent populating of almost the entire world—foragers' rapid populating of the Americas and Australia being the most dramatic examples. There is no evidence that any region with foragers ever attained zero population growth over the long run, nor any sign that they were able to maintain ecological balance. Since foragers could not—and did not—achieve this balance, I would expect conflict to ensue, which is supported by the evidence for forager warfare.

From the earliest foragers found archaeologically to historical accounts of foragers from all corners of the globe, the evidence shows that they fight and kill in deadly earnest. Pitched battles in which the sides lined up and fought were few. Attacking-party sizes were small, specialized weapons were not overly common, and few defensive fortifications were used. Yet there are numerous skeletons from forager archaeological sites showing evidence of violent deaths; there were some massacres, some specialized weapons, and, on occasion, defenses and defensively located communities. Forager warfare was socially charged, with evidence of trophy taking, especially heads, and warfare imagery existing in the form of rock art. Although surprise raids and ambush were the common methods of forager warfare, overall death rates from intergroup conflict were high, as seen in the 25 percent warfare death rate from the Murngin of Australia and the more than 40 percent for a prehistoric Sudan community.

Despite humans' much greater intelligence, with which they might have been able to assess their population growth and regulate their numbers, despite their ability to hunt, collect, and eat many more types of food, which could raise the area's carrying capacity over that of chimps, and regardless of humans' greater communication skills, which could be used to adjudicate disputes, early foragers were not able to live peacefully. Rather, each local group optimized its own living situations and grew and competed for resources. Greater intelligence led to a greater ability to make weapons. The ability to eat more foods resulted in population growth. Communication skills could also be used to form alliances and plan attacks. Deaths from warfare among foragers are about as common as conflict fatalities primatologists find among chimps. All this indicates that becoming fully human and expanding over the globe did not result in foragers' ability to live in ecological balance or in peace.

Foraging was *the* way of life for most of human history. Farming—the great transformation that began about ten thousand years ago—resulted in most of the world becoming occupied by farmers to this day. Since farmers obtain far more calories per acre of land than do foragers, there should have been ample food available when farming took off as an adaptation. Were farmers able to take this great bonanza of food and live peacefully with their neighbors? Was the agricultural revolution also a peaceful revolution? To see how all this unfolded, it is to the early horticulturists I turn next.

chapter six

CONFLICT AND GROWTH
AMONG TRIBAL FARMERS

During the autumn of 1970, I was working on a field project in the northern part of Turkey's Fertile Crescent, where archaeologists believe agriculture first began. This was a semiarid region of spectacular vistas—rolling hills with higher rocky mountains in the distance—dotted with picturesque villages here and there. Fences did not exist, and vast expanses of the Turks' meager wheat and barley fields spread out all around us. The occasional camel caravan would pass the site—we had the only motorized vehicles for as far as the eye could see—and the area had a distinctly barren, empty look to it.

Our dig was an ancient village occupied between 6000 and 5000 B.C., and we were particularly interested in recovering fossil pollen and carbonized plant remains, hoping to understand the diet of the early people who had lived there and the climate at the time. In the course of our work, we found evidence of oak and pistachio trees in these carbonized plant and pollen remains. From such information it was possible to reconstruct the "natural" state of the region, meaning the way the land had looked before significant human impact, as an oak-pistachio woodland: a land of grasses with an abundance of large trees spaced about.

In my description of the modern-day environment around the dig, I omitted one key observation. I walked to the top of the site with my binoculars one day and spotted a *tree!* Over thousands of years, this once tree-covered Turkish woodland had become almost devoid of any and all trees. These trees, for which we found abundant archaeological evidence, were desirable trees, since acorns and pistachio nuts would have provided food. Even acorns, though bitter and requiring extensive processing, would be a valuable food source. Yet all the oak and pistachio trees were gone, long since plowed under the vast expanse of open fields. If there is any question

just how much environmental degradation farming societies can do to the
environment, even in the absence of modern technology, try finding a tree
in many parts of the Middle East, even where archaeologists *know* trees were
plentiful six thousand years ago.

Though the realization that farming and herding had degraded the environment was hardly an original concept, the devastating effects of that process became clear to me at that moment on the hill. What was *not* clear
thirty years ago, however, was what the implications of such a drastic environmental change must be and why the transformation from one ecological
environment to another happened in the first place. The question of the
ability of the land to support these people, or how they may have had to
cope with an increased scarcity of water, farmland, or food, did not enter
my thinking in 1970.[1]

In prehistory, the foraging lifeway lasted for well over a million years, but
then the pace of change accelerated. What has been termed the "Neolithic
revolution"—the transition from foraging to farming, perhaps the most
dramatic change ever in human behavior—occurred in the Middle East
beginning around 10,000 B.C. Independently, a little bit later in time, the
same revolution took place in China. In the New World a bit more than six
thousand years ago, a surprisingly similar shift to farming—with such
crops as corn, beans, and potatoes—occurred, again independently, in
Mesoamerica (present-day Mexico) and South America.[2]

Though foraging as a means of subsistence seems foreign to those of us
living in the modern world, farming as a lifestyle is quite familiar . . . or is
it? Actually, farming is much more than just sowing and harvesting, and the
process took thousands of years to perfect. Initially, wild plants had to be
selectively planted and harvested so that genetic traits made them more useful, a process anthropologists term "domestication." For example, judging
by the corn found in sites in Mexico that date as far back as 4000 B.C., the
progenitor of corn had only a few small kernels on each puny cob, and
these kernels fell off as soon as they were ripe. If farmers waited a bit too
long to harvest that early corn, they got nothing. Modern corn, on the
other hand, after centuries of selective breeding, has hundreds of kernels
on each cob, and they never fall off. The domestication of animals followed
a similar process. Wild pigs and cattle were large, dangerous animals, and
the first sheep had no wool. Once selectively bred, these "new" animals were
much more docile and useful than the wild ones from which they derived.

The key to much farming is growing something that can be stored and
having the technology to do it, for example, storing grain so it will not rot.
On our dig in Turkey, we found the remains of elaborate storage buildings

The people of the Mimbres Valley in south-western New Mexico (ca. A.D. 1000) had periods of less and more warfare which correlated with climate change and environmental degradation. This drawing of the designs on one of their bowls shows a decapitation scene. The costume of the executioner suggests this was a ritual act. Worldwide most such ritual killings were of captured enemies.

with raised stone floors and rows of air shafts to keep the wheat cool and dry. In fact, those ancient Turks expended much more effort in building storage rooms than their own living rooms. Food that stores well is often very dry. In order to be consumed, such food must be processed, usually ground, and then cooked. Foragers had very minimal tool kits. In contrast, the farmer tool kit included a vast array of elaborate technologies, including grinding tools, presses to extract the poisons from tubers, pots for boiling. Farmers also needed to "grow" their clothing, either by raising sheep or llamas for wool or planting flax or cotton, and of course these fibers had to be processed into wearable goods. Being a farmer is not simply a matter of having a handful of seeds; it means having all this technology worked out. In order to develop and facilitate this complex horticultural process and the new sets of skills that proceeded right along with it, the first farmers had social organizations that are often described as tribes. This anthropological terminology represents a problem because we colloquially think of the word *tribe* as meaning a related group of people rather than a type of social organization. One can refer to the Paiute tribe, which was organized socially as a band, or refer to the Kwakiutl tribe, which was organized socially as a chiefdom (see Chapter 7), or to the Hopi tribe, which was in fact organized socially as a tribe. A perhaps better term, but one that is not always accurate, is sedentary-egalitarian societies. The problem is that not all tribally organized people were sedentary, for example the Plains buffalo hunters, nor were tribes perfectly egalitarian, so I stick with the word *tribe* here for this type of social organization.

Tribes are much larger groups than forager bands, and most tribes are farmers, or farmerlike, in their subsistence strategy. Tribes, like foragers, do not have hereditary leaders, but unlike foragers, they have social organizations that cross-cut kinship lines and provide a kind of social "glue" that helps keep the larger units within the community cooperating instead of competing. Such cooperation was necessary, for example, in order to build and maintain irrigation canals and raised fields—and fortifications. What can be considered "organized religion" occurs with tribes, while most band-level religion is based on individual or ad hoc behavior. Farmers have religious groups or institutions that transcend the life spans of any individual.

Anthropologists know a good deal about the early farmers, because sedentary people leave much richer archaeological records than foragers. Farmers began to stay in one place and work the same ground for generations; they created permanent settlements, cemeteries, and fortifications; and they built the first shrines and temples. As a result, the tribal farmers' past can be characterized in far greater detail than that of the roving bands of foragers.

Farming boils down to one major accomplishment: Humans are able to get more calories from an acre of land. Farmers may have to work extremely hard to get those extra calories, by sowing, harvesting, and processing the food, but they do get them—and the consequences are profound. By keeping the population low, societies that adapted to horticulture could find their resources abundant. On the other hand, the population could grow immensely because each acre can support far more people who farm than forage. In fact, farmers can be ten to fifty times more dense than foragers. If the population does rise and the land begins to be used intensely, farmers can begin to affect the environment in ways far beyond what foragers ever did.

The archaeology makes it clear that all over the world and in all time periods the initial farmers experienced population explosions. Their numbers never remained low for long. There are many obvious reasons for fast growth among farmers. Women do not need to forage very much away from the village, and there are more people to serve as baby-sitters, so the need to space children far apart is eliminated. Farmers spend a lot of time processing food: They grind wheat into flour and bake bread, grind corn into tortillas, or boil rice until it is soft. Since these are great "first foods" for babies, farmers' infants can be weaned earlier than the offspring of foragers. By not having to move camp often and with stored food available, ailing individuals don't have to keep up with the group and are more likely to recover from illness. All in all, these factors would be expected to lead to more rapid population growth for farmers than foragers.

But there's more. The value children bring to farming societies exceeds that of foragers. All people may want children, but farmers can put them to work better and are even more motivated to have them. As observed from ethnography, young foragers are not very productive. Hunting takes skill and practice, and few men under the age of eighteen are very successful hunters. Indeed, few men of *any* age are really good hunters. In most groups, the few best hunters get most of the game. Similarly, collecting wild plants is not a simple matter of just picking up nuts or digging roots. Knowledge of exactly where and when to do it is essential, and an experienced woman can be much more productive than a younger one. Among foragers, children under the age of twelve are not very food productive, and even teenagers are not great contributors. With farmers, things change dramatically. There are numerous small farming tasks that can be undertaken by children that then free up adults for other tasks. Though it is difficult to estimate, the consensus is that by the time farmers' children are ten years old they are producing as many calories as they are consuming, if not more.

There are even more subtle reasons why farmers want to have lots of children. For one thing, the farmers' social milieu is competitive. Decisions constantly arise about who has rights to farm which land, or who has access to water. Large families with lots of in-laws result in a more vocal, influential presence. In most societies, big families and successful families are synonymous. Finally, in a world without Social Security, children are an old-age pension. Parents want to make sure that enough of their offspring survive to take care of them as they age. Though this is a concern of foragers as well, it is a greater concern for farmers, because the tribal social group is no longer the kin group, and an individual is less likely to be taken care of by the group as a whole. For farmers, the benefits of large families are significant.

As tribal farmers spread over much of Earth they displaced resident foragers and began to compete with one another. This re-creation of the early farming village of Ch'iang-chia (Pan-p'o Neolithic) in China shows typical moat and palisade construction that protected such villages worldwide.

Although the potential growth rate for foragers can be substantial—and over time can be exceedingly large—farmers are in another league. What gives them the edge seems to be the combination of the advantages of farming, a more sedentary lifestyle, more prepared foods, larger social groups, and stored foods. All these factors under the right circumstances can lead to substantial growth. When all this is combined with the economic advantage of children in many farming situations, the results can be explosive. As discussed in Chapter 2, one of the fastest growth rates on record was found among the Hutterites of South Dakota, who had completed family sizes of nearly ten children on average for a couple of generations. When new territory is available—the American Great Plains in the 1800s, where the Hutterites lived, or Caribbean and Pacific islands when first colonized—farmer-society growth rates can be particularly substantial. Rates as high as 3 percent annual increase are known. Although many of these instances were accompanied by somewhat improved medical knowledge, they preceded the advent of modern twentieth-century medicine. Such rates mean that a group's population could double every generation. Doubling every 25 years means that in 100 years there would be 16 times as many people, and after 200 years there would be more than 250 times as many. Now, there is no known rate of increase for 200 years under such circumstances, but the potential for explosive growth among farmers is clearly there.[3]

With such growth rates, it would not take long to fill up an area, regardless of the group's technological gains. Growth rates may fall, as in parts of Japan, because of the shortage of land and the desirability of fewer children. With rates this high, a group's population limits would be reached so rapidly that there would be little time for even partial cultural adjustments of any significance to kick in. As demonstrated, there is no evidence that most social groups ever completely got population growth under control to begin with. I would expect such rapid growth among farmers to be accompanied or followed by considerable conflict—and often by subsequent population collapse. In fact, this is precisely what the archaeology and historical accounts show for early farmers.

Farming populations can grow, affect their environment, and then suffer the consequences in ways that make clear that they were neither conservationists nor able to control their population growth in spite of being highly sensitive to their surroundings. This is particularly evident in the American Southwest, perhaps the best archaeologically understood area of the world. The Southwest is dry and sparsely vegetated, offering the perfect parameters in which to find sites, and well-preserved ones at that. Archaeologists have worked in the region for many years and have produced an astonishingly rich record of the area. There are historical accounts of the Southwest's early people, beginning in 1540, and some of their descendants are still living in the same places with great knowledge of their past. These early inhabitants were farmers until very recently and for the most part were organized as tribes. The Southwest is a terrific place to attempt to understand how farmers came to be there and how they operated. It is also a good place to examine the relationship among carrying capacity, climate, and warfare.

As director of a project for the Mimbres Foundation, I returned to New Mexico in 1974, to survey the Mimbres Valley for archaeological information. Although now semiarid, this region at one time was much greener and better watered than it is today. Away from the river's floodplain and the flats above it, the sides of the valley are punctuated by steep hills, knobs, and ridges, and there is a sense of enclosure and isolation all around. Like the other prehistoric people of the Southwest, the Mimbres lived in small villages and farmed corn, beans, and squash.[4]

As part of our survey, the crew selected sections of the valley according to land quality, concentrating on areas near nice bottomland, then sections along small tributaries, and finally in really hardscrabble areas. We walked and recorded all the prehistoric sites found on the three different types of land. Using styles and designs of broken pottery discovered on the surface, we were able to date most of these sites and could translate their size into the number of inhabitants living in each. Taking our estimates and extrapolating to the entire valley, we were able to work out changes in valleywide population sizes from A.D. 200 to 1400. At the same time, my crew excavated on sites of each period. We screened the soil for animal bones, sieved the dirt and ash from hearths and other burned places to get pieces of charcoal, and extracted pollen grains from the dirt floors. All this information revealed a great deal about the environment during each time period. What we found showed a classic pattern of farmer behavior.

From A.D. 200 to about 1100, the population in the Mimbres Valley increased by about ten times. An increase of that size seemed dramatic for the time, but in reality it took a growth rate of less than 0.5 percent to accomplish it—and many societies have grown much faster. From the archaeology, we could observe that along with this growth came an increased need to find places to farm. Initially, around 200, all the village sites were located near quality farmland. Then, slowly but surely, more and more sites were situated in areas where farming would have been more difficult. Finally, in the later time periods, we found small sites situated where the only way to farm was to build small terraces to catch a bit more rainfall runoff.

At the same time, we discovered that the Mimbres hunted increasingly fewer deer and other large animals. Rabbits, which reproduce rapidly, began to dominate the animal bones we recovered. We could almost literally see the valley being denuded. Charcoal and pollen from plants that grew along the floodplain began to disappear from the deposits. Firewood, initially from these same plants, became wood from the hill slopes. Cottontail rabbits, which would have used this denser foliage cover as habitat, were replaced by jackrabbits, which are adapted to more open terrain. The river regime was so changed that water-loving muskrats and sycamore trees were both extincted from the valley. In short, the human population in the Mimbres Valley grew and increasingly ran out of farmland, then denuded the surrounding area for more places to farm, for firewood, and for construction wood—all of which we could see in the recovered pollen, charcoal, and animal bone. Then, around 1130, our survey revealed that the population crashed—not completely, but valleywide by half. From that point on it continued to decline, until the Mimbres Valley was completely uninhabited by around 1400.

By comparing climatological records and the archaeology, we could see that peak population growth in the valley occurred when the climate was very benign for farming around 900–1150. Even so, this group of tribal farmers was outstripping the environment in every way. Once the climate began to revert to the less favorable long-term average, the Mimbres people were unable to support themselves and the population numbers declined.

The Maori of New Zealand built hundreds of hilltop forts. This one, visited and drawn by Captain Cook's expedition, was built on a natural arch. Although such forts were very inefficient places to live, in the past they were a way of life for much of the world as the only means to survive constant warfare.

With the arrival of the Little Ice Age around 1300, the climate turned much colder, and then the numbers really plummeted.

Judging from the archaeology, there is not the slightest hint that the Mimbres, like all other farmers, wanted to or were able to control their population growth. They could not predict the coming bad climate, nor would they have been able to observe that the animals and vegetation changed over time. This scenario took about nine hundred years to play out—that's more than thirty generations. Things would not have changed much in any twenty-five-year period. The Mimbres people probably had little idea what was happening to their world, any more than my friend Sila did in Samoa. Any individual family was motivated to have lots of children instead of trying to reduce the total number of people in the valley.

California provides another archaeological example of the same process. Beginning at 10,000 B.C. California was occupied by foragers. Human densities were low and the people did not seem to be having much effect on the environment. For example, fur seals were breeding on the beaches a bit south of San Francisco and the pups would have been very susceptible to being taken by foragers. No boats were needed, just clubs. Yet for thousands of years the seals and the early Californians coexisted. It would appear that the foragers were so few that they did not kill enough pups to reduce the herds to the point that the seals needed to abandon the mainland and breed only on offshore islands, as they do today. Since the pups were seasonal, this may have been an annual bottleneck in the food supply that kept the human population down. However, at some point the bottleneck was overcome by finding a food that was available or storable at the time of year of the former bottleneck—probably acorns—and the people became sedentary collectors. Group sizes increased and more people began to take the fur seal pups. Around 2000 B.C., the seals stopped rearing their pups on the mainland. Then the now much more numerous people began to exploit shellfish more intensely, allowing less time for them to mature between harvests. The average size of shells in the shell mounds declined over time. The human population along the California coast become more sedentary and began to act more like farmers, seriously impacting their environment. As I discuss later, it was about this time that there was an increase in warfare after this transformation.

What we uncovered in the Mimbres Valley and what happened in California has been repeated many, many times in other places around the world. Consequently, some general statements about the effects of non–socially complex farmers on the environment can be made. First and foremost, such farmland eventually becomes an ecological disaster area. Farmers are not innately different from foragers, but the conditions for their behavior are different. Just as foragers can recognize that overhunting will cause problems in the future yet still overhunt, farmers can realize that poor farming practices will cause problems in the future and continue the behavior. In the case of foragers, it would have been hard for any individual to see the impact of his behavior. Even if one hunter tries to avoid killing pregnant female animals and uses the carcass well, game will be depleted if there are more than a certain number of hunters. If a hunter's family is starving, he will kill the pregnant female deer. The same issues and behaviors face farmers. Their world is small. Overgrazing their sheep or plowing that results in flooding downstream is hard to perceive as harmful to the environment. Even if certain practices are recognized as harmful, it's hard to resist if their families are hungry.

To put this in a modern context, if it takes fifty years for a pine tree to mature, only 2 percent of the trees can be cut down each year or, at some point in the not-too-distant future, you'll run out of trees. Any logger in the Northwest can do this simple math and reach the same conclusion. There is tremendous desire and effort made to cut trees at a higher rate. We can wonder why people would be so ecologically shortsighted, but they are. It's a question of scale and time. From the point of view of the logger, the rate he cuts is immaterial since he cannot cut down the entire forest, and he is not going to live forever. He needs the trees to make a living in order to feed his family now. The fifty-year or one-hundred-year consequences of cutting down too many trees is irrelevant to the logger's immediate problem, which is why we have such conflict between the loggers and the environmentalists today.

Similar situations certainly faced foragers and farmers in the past. Based on their individual time scales and personal needs, and from their particular perception of the impact their actions had on the environment, they may have seen no problem—or were able to live with it in order to survive. The real difference between the foragers and farmers is a matter of numbers and technology. If farmers are ten to fifty times more dense, they will degrade the environment many times faster than foragers, even if they are just as ecologically "well behaved" on an individual basis.

The situation is even worse than that: Farmers use technology that stresses the environment much more than that of foragers. More wood is needed to cook crops that have been dried out and stored, and wood is consumed to fire pottery, burn clay to make bricks, and heat lime to plaster walls. Farming tends to denude the landscape during part of the annual cycle in ways that foraging never does, and domestic animals can be a terrible scourge on the landscape. All this behavior can very quickly wreak havoc on the environment, even without the impact of irrigation, terracing, or the more intensive farming techniques that come with more complex farmers.[5]

It is, in part, the differences in technology among the various early farmers or "almost farmers" that result in the differing levels of "conservationist behavior" perceived today. People who are not actually real farmers but behave much like them, in that they have permanent villages and store large quantities of staples—such as acorn gatherers in California or salmon fishers in the Pacific Northwest—are the least destructive of the farmer or farmerlike types. They do not have domestic animals, they do not plow, and although their numbers can be large, they rarely approach the numbers of many true farmers. Interestingly, it is such sedentary collectors who are most likely to be considered inherent conservationists.

Next come the farmers of the Americas. Without significant domestic animals, except in the Andes where llamas were raised, their impact was less than is often the case of early farmers in the Old World. Moreover, you do not plow without draft animals, and the absence of plowing probably reduced their impact on the environment. Equally important, the people of the New World did not begin farming as early as those in many places in the Old World. A comparison of farming in Mesoamerica with the advent of horticulture in the Middle East or the eastern Mediterranean is relevant. Sheep and goats were domesticated, and wheat and barley were grown in the Middle East from around 7500 B.C. on, if not a bit earlier. The environment in the region has endured close to ten thousand years of impact, and the islands of the Aegean were only slightly behind.

In Mesoamerica, by contrast, effective farming seems to have occurred no earlier than about 2500 B.C., and without domestic animals. Humans have been farming in Mexico for half as long. The rocky landscapes and the treeless vistas of the Aegean and Middle East are, to a significant extent, a consequence of those many thousands of years of horticulture. The contrast is even more striking in North America. Effective corn farming really reached the Eastern United States only after A.D. 500 or even a bit later. The first Europeans encountered a North American environment that had been intensively farmed for fewer than one thousand years. There was obviously no past "oneness with nature" in the Middle East, because of the clear impact humans have had on the environment. In contrast, the low population densities and marginal farming found in aboriginal New England left much less obvious and dramatic impact on the land.[6]

Rapid growth, large populations, and a technology that impacts the environment more than that of foragers almost ensures that a time of scarcity will ensue after farmers have been in a region for just a few hundred years. The Middle East did not suddenly experience ecological stress after the complex societies of Mesopotamia had been around for a while. The region must have become stressed soon after farming was well established.

In North America, most of the indigenous people were either farmers or people who treated wild species as if they were domesticates. In 1492, the regions along the rivers of the Great Plains, the Eastern woodlands, and the entire Southeast and the Southwest were all the domain of farmers, not foragers. There must have been well over one hundred farmers for every forager living in North America when Christopher Columbus arrived in the New World. By that time, North America's farmers had also been forced to cope with population growth, environmental degradation, and climate change. Warfare would have been the consequence of such factors, as it was everywhere else around the world. No "oneness with nature" was capable of overcoming these events.

The one potential way farmers could have avoided the resource stress–conflict cycle is by developing social rules that limit growth. Without a central "government," such rules can be enforced only at the tribal level by

A camel train passing the prehistoric site of Girikihaciyan in southeastern Turkey. The earliest domestication of plants and animals took place in the Middle East. Almost 10,000 years of farming and herding have denuded an original oak-pistachio woodland, and today only a few trees can be seen in the distance.

social sanctions, not authority. More complex societies are far more likely to develop some mechanism to deal with the population growth problem than are independent egalitarian farmers, where children are an asset and large numbers a defense against aggressive neighbors. It is no accident that scholars have never been able to demonstrate the existence of such social rules for zero population growth that worked in simple farming societies.

A final problem farmers face is both a result of warfare and its cause. Farmers, or similarly organized tribal people, develop buffer zones between their territories. Scholars see these no-man's-lands in the Amazon, the New Guinea highlands, the Southwest, and the Great Plains—basically everywhere competing groups have been observed. Since crops are vulnerable to destruction by an enemy, and since egalitarian farmers have limited ability to organize boundary defenses, tribes tend to leave areas of unfarmed land between competing groups. These buffer zones are essentially fallow fields. After a number of years, they begin to look very attractive to farmers, whose own fields have ever-decreasing yields without a rest. The motivation to take over the buffer zone and farm it becomes greater and greater over time. The way to take a buffer zone is to eliminate the people on the other side. Even if a relative peace develops temporarily between competing groups, the no-man's-land will become more and more tempting. One side will eventually attempt to take it, starting the process of intergroup conflict all over again.

Further compounding the problems farmers face are changes in climate. In the case of the Mimbres people, our archaeological evidence showed that a good climate interval led to a large increase in population, and a subsequent poor climate interval led to a precipitous decline. Such fluctuations certainly must have affected tribal farmers all over the world and in all time periods. Less well understood, but probably even more dramatic, was a crisis faced by the earliest farmers in the Levant, along the eastern edge of the Mediterranean. Around 8000 B.C., as farming became established in the region, the archaeology shows that there was a great increase in the number of villages and their size, as well as the increased presence of public/ceremonial architecture and even the production of what scholars would consider "luxury goods." After a thousand years or so, there was a dramatic change. The number of sites and their sizes and "grandness" were radically curtailed. Though archaeologists do not see full-scale abandonment, there seems to have been a major population decline. The best explanation to date for this situation is that a climatic shift must have severely hurt the ability of the inhabitants to farm, which devastated the Levant.[7]

My own work uncovering the villages of early farmers in Turkey is revealing. I was digging sites that held a level of romance one rarely encounters on archaeological field projects. Working alongside us in the early seventies were workmen hired from a nearby village, which consisted of clusters of houses made of mud brick with flat roofs. Our Turkish helpers herded sheep and goats and were still plowing their fields with wooden plows pulled by oxen. As twentieth-century scholars, there we were uncovering the origins of agriculture, which had changed the world. At the same time, we were surrounded by people living a lifestyle that was little different from that of the ancient farmers we were studying. Working in that superficially idyllic setting, we often felt as if we had been transported back into the time span our trenches were revealing.

Turkey's earliest farmers built templelike structures or shrines with beautifully painted murals on the walls. They also carved realistic figurines and stone carvings of animals and humans. They bred sheep, goats, cattle, and pigs, and grew wheat, barley, lentils, olives, grapes, and lots of other foods we still eat today. Our research did not uncover any plows; it is not clear when plowing started. We did find round doughnutlike stones, which we assumed ancient farmers used to weight their "digging sticks" for planting crops without plows. Small holes are poked in the ground with the sharp end of the stick and seeds are dropped in, or the stick can be used to dig up the roots and tubers of wild plants. With the plethora of new foods, plants, and animals, these early farmers had the time to construct and adorn those impressive ceremonial buildings—and found no need for warfare.

Today, farmland all over Anatolia, modern Turkey, and the rest of the Middle East is severely degraded. The environment of the early farmers was much different from what I encountered in the 1970s. For many years I felt that the way of life we witnessed there was little changed from what it had been in the past. We had uncovered some sling missiles, which were molded out of plaster and found in piles. I even commissioned Veci, one of the workmen, to make me a woolen sling, and he showed me how shepherds used them to hurl stones at predators threatening their sheep. We found no direct evidence of warfare in our excavation project. And, again, why should we have, given the prevailing anthropological theories of the day?

At the time, our crew never tried to find a defensive wall around the village we were digging. Archaeologists now know that a number of villages of the same time period in the Middle East do have such walls. And then there's the problem of the sling missiles, those surprisingly accurate projectiles. One of those other defensive sites had thousands of similar missiles stored in strategically located pits dug behind the base of a long wall. Those missiles were not used to herd sheep. It now seems obvious to me that many sites around Anatolia of that time period were built defensively, with rooms massed together so that the dwellings themselves formed a solid outside wall and had to be entered from the roof. Other sites had mud-brick defensive walls, some with elaborately defended gates. Sling missiles are found on lots of these sites, often in great quantities, and are clearly not for protecting flocks of sheep.

Some of these Anatolian sites had been catastrophically burned and are known for mass graves, unburied bodies, and traumatic wounds. In the seventies we assumed the "doughnut" stones we uncovered were digging-stick weights, even though, ethnographically, no one uses anything like a stone-weighted stick to plant or collect plants. They do look exactly like the round stone heads attached to wooden clubs—maces—used in many places in the world exclusively for fighting and still used ceremonially today to signify power. The queen of England holds a ceremonial mace as a badge of office. Those "digging-stick weights" were actually mace heads! Thirty years ago, I was holding mace heads and sling missiles in my hands, totally unaware of their implications.

The reason the local Turkish villagers we worked with live in undefended settlements today is that the state provides for their defense, although the number of guns the Turks kept illegally was quite impressive. A fresh look at the archaeology conducted throughout the Middle East reveals that not every site at every time was fortified, nor are all burned. Anatolia and the rest of the Middle East must have seen the vagaries of intensity of warfare we find in many other places and times. Clearly, the early Turkish farmers were not living in the Garden of Eden. When our crew was working there, we had been intrigued by the rustic charm and simply did not think to question the harsh reality of the social-political climate in which those ancient people must have lived. The transition to agriculture—one of humankind's great milestones, which forever changed us and the world—did not begin the way most scholars think it did. Just what happened, and the role warfare played in the process, is an unexpected story.

The development of farming has captivated archaeologists for well over a hundred years, and it's an intriguing question. Why, after tens of thousands of years of being biologically human with the same skills and intellect modern humans possess fully in all respects, did humans become farmers very rapidly? An oversimplified vision of the way foragers might have become farmers is that a few clever people developed domesticated plants and in some places animals as well. When foragers saw these innovations, they imitated their neighbors and became farmers themselves. This is not what happened. Groups that had agriculture were able to increase their populations more rapidly than foragers, especially when the farmers had a well-adapted complex of crops and technologies. When this confluence of having the crops and animals well suited to their environment occurred, the farmers' populations exploded. They spread rapidly, replacing the foragers who had previously occupied vast areas of the globe. This was not a peaceful process.

The world had not been filled with foragers who became farmers. Descendants of farming groups expanded and took over most of the world. The so-called Agricultural Revolution was much more than that: It was a major repopulating of large portions of the world. This transformation is one of a series of changes in the human condition that very much define who we, as humans, are—and one that, in reality, involved considerable warfare.[8]

The process of farmers taking over from foragers was complex. It is best understood in Europe, then in Southeast Asia, but there is evidence that the same process took place in Mesoamerica and Africa. The reason farmers could spread was that they had potential for rapid population growth. The consequences of these phenomena have not always been so obvious. To illustrate, visualize the foragers and the farmers. If the group of farmers is capable of growing its population very quickly while the foragers are rela-

The Yanomama of the jungles of Venezuela and Brazil live in fortified village compounds. Here preparing for a dance ceremony, they are carrying the same spears they use in inter-village warfare. These tribal farmers have very high death rates from warfare, even though only a few people are killed in any particular combat. Most fighting is in the form of surprise raids, and women and children are often killed in such raids.

tively stable, and the farmers tend to be in a larger group to begin with than the band of foragers, the farmers will try to expand into the range of the foragers when they run out of available farmland. By being organized into larger groups and being able more quickly to replace losses due to warfare, the farmers will easily prevail. The more the farmers encroach, the more resources they gobble up, and the more mouths there are to feed, which leads to still more encroachment. The numbers of the roving band of foragers will continue to dwindle as their territory shrinks and they lose members of the group from warfare.

The replacement of foragers by farmers was rapid where anthropologists can measure it: Good estimates are about one mile of new territory every year along the boundary between the two ways of life.[9] This is a remarkably fast process. In five hundred years, farmers could have expanded five hundred miles in every direction from their original territory. Entire continents could have been colonized in a millennium or so. In only a few places can it be observed whether or not this process was accompanied by conflict. Of course, the details of this process are more subtle than I have described. The farmers incorporated foragers, especially forager women, into their societies as they went, and some nonfarmers did convert to farming. Genetically a mix of spreading farmers and converted locals occupy the world today.

In many parts of the world it is difficult to determine how much of the historically known warfare was a result of the impact of European expansion and conquest of much of the world and how much was a continuation of indigenous farmer warfare, the distribution of languages is very enlightening. Linguists have developed maps showing the way languages appeared and disappeared over time on all the continents, but only rather recently were the implications of these language distributions realized. They are like a fossil remnant of past humans interacting with each other. Scholars can often see that one language or language family has spread at the expense of others, and such language spreads are known from many places in the world. Some replacements are very ancient, while others are recent and were actually occurring when Europeans first entered the scene. The languages of the present-day people living in an area can tell us a lot about how and when those people got there.

Language maps do not always show evidence of the spread of one social group over the territories of other groups. For example, in highland New Guinea there are hundreds of languages all mixed up with each other, strongly suggesting that no one particular group has been overwhelmingly successful at expanding into neighboring territories. A similar pattern holds for part, but not all, of early California. There were hundreds of different languages spoken in California at European contact, almost as many as the rest of North America combined. Conversely, the distribution and dominance of Bantu-related languages in Africa, and the Austronesian languages of Southeast Asia and Oceania, clearly show the expansion of groups of related people over vast distances.[10]

Several of these linguistic radiations are reasonably well documented. In Southeast Asia, for example, archaeology shows that foragers were present from the time of *Homo erectus* over a half million years ago and that they used boats to get to New Guinea and Australia by at least forty thousand years ago. So scholars are sure that Southeast Asia was fully occupied by foragers for a long time. Linguists also know that there were a great number of different languages spoken throughout this entire area. Today, almost all the peoples in the area speak languages that are part of the Austronesian language family, and they are related in such a way that it is clear the original speakers lived in the South China area and radiated outward. This process seems to have begun around 4000 B.C., when the Austronesian speakers moved to the Philippines, then Borneo, and then into Melanesia.

A branch of these Austronesian-speaking people began long-distance voyaging and populated the far-flung islands of Polynesia, finally reaching Hawaii around A.D. 300 and New Zealand around 800.[11] Never in human history has such a large area that was not devoid of inhabitants been populated by related peoples in such a short time. Australia and the Americas were rapidly populated, but there were no people living there when it happened. The spread of the Austronesian language family was one primarily of replacement. One way or another, the foragers were replaced or assimilated by farmers.

Whenever researchers have good information about how this language spread and replacement process actually worked, it is associated with warfare. This stands to reason: Why would one group give up its land, often the best land around, and peacefully move away? Much more realistically, one group expands and replaces the former inhabitants. Most likely, the indigenous groups that remained in the marginal areas did not move into those less desirable locales. Rather, the only speakers of the original language who survived in the area were living in the marginal places to begin with. In other words, people were killed in the process. These replacements took hold presumably because the encroaching population had some advantage that translated into either military superiority or faster growth. For instance, if one group had a social organization, leadership, or new tactics that allowed it the advantage, it would take over territory. Or if the group simply outgrew the competition and fought, it would also prevail. Understanding the implications of the language distributions presents a fascinating map of past conflict.

In addition to the spread of Austronesian-speaking farmers over Southeast Asia, other "great diasporas," as they have been termed, included a radiation out of the Middle East into Europe, across North Africa, and east into Pakistan. The Bantu speakers, who were farmer-herders, spread over Africa, and a final major language spread was Uto-Aztecan-speaking farmers moving north from central Mexico as far as southern Utah. Where we have good information in Europe, Africa, and Mesoamerica—North America, these farmer spreads were accompanied by significant warfare. Many of the first farming villages in Europe, from southeastern Europe to Germany and Belgium, were fortified with palisades or walls. Arrowheads are scattered around some of these fortifications, showing that they were attacked, with the attackers concentrating on the gate areas. In Germany, massacres are also known, with thirty-four bodies at Talheim, fifty dead in a ditch at Vaihingen, and trophy skulls and war dead in the hundreds at Herxheim. The foragers did not give up their lands easily, and there is little evidence that there was peaceful interchange. The important point is that these farming populations grew quite rapidly and ran out of resources, which is why they expanded. The initial farmers in all parts of the world were decidedly not in ecological balance.

The question is whether, once in control, the farmers were able to stay peaceful. Was their typically tribal social organization conducive to warfare, or toward mediation and consensus? Looking at farmer-tribal warfare from around the world should help answer these questions.

Tribal warfare tends to be a lot like forager warfare, with an emphasis on raiding, ambush, and surprise attacks. Classic forms of tribal-level conflict include the dawn raid, picking a person off when he leaves the village alone, or even inviting the enemy to a feast and slaughtering them all. Since people organized as tribes are more numerous and live in larger, sedentary communities, we find for the first time many fortifications in the archaeological record. We also find evidence for more elaboration of warfare: more pitched battles, war leaders, and war ceremonialism, and evidence of massacres, more alliances for making war, and more contested no-man's-lands.

Ethnographers have discovered that people, especially tribal farmers, fight when we would not expect them to. A tribe can increase its area's carrying capacity by building an irrigation canal, clearing a forest, building terraces, and the like. These projects are a lot of work to build and maintain, but in many times and places they can be accomplished to make more food available. Studies in places as diverse as New Zealand, Peru, and Sarawak in Southeast Asia have shown that groups choose to fight for existing resources rather than create additional ones.[12]

This does not mean that members of tribal-level societies would rather fight than work, just that many people were more fatalistic than we are today. When people have a good chance of living into their seventies, as we do, they try to make it happen. When a person could very likely die soon from disease, accidents, starvation, or perhaps witchcraft, the risk of death from warfare could be less troubling and seem less costly. If a group thinks it might have a reasonably good shot at taking some resources from its neighbors, and the alternative is constructing a massive irrigation canal that may never be completed because of the cooperation required or could be washed out by a flood soon after completion, a quick attack on the neighbors can appear to be a better plan of action. This linkage between carrying capacity and warfare has been strong among farmers, and there are numerous examples of how the process worked.

Turning again to the prehistoric Southwest, my fieldwork in New Mexico showed that the Mimbres people experienced warfare when they first became farmers and then later suffered food stress. Looking at the Southwest overall provides a clearer picture of how population growth and warfare relate to resource availability. From the archaeology, scholars know that around A.D. 900, the warfare that had gone on in the region for centuries ceased. For the next two hundred and fifty years, we find little evidence for warfare anywhere in the Southwest. This happens to be a time of great population expansion, with most estimates having the population growing fivefold in this interval. The largest and most impressive buildings ever constructed in the Southwest were made at this time by the people in New Mexico's Chaco Canyon. This must have been a time of peace and prosperity, but the good times did not last.

Beginning around A.D. 1150, but really taking off in the mid- to late 1200s, we find archaeological evidence that there was a complete transformation and warfare became ubiquitous and intense. During this interval, virtually everyone in the Southwest moved into very defensive villages. The famous Mesa Verde cliff dwellings are examples from this time period. We find that sites were sacked and burned, and bodies were not formally buried. The rock art and mural wall art show a concern for warfare—scenes of fighting and men carrying large shields and weapons. Even more telling is the evidence from settlement patterns revealing that the communities formed alliances and clustered together, leaving large in-between areas unoccupied. Around 1250, the region's population began to decline markedly. Entire areas were completely abandoned and considerable migration took place by 1300. The population of the Southwest withered to about one-fifth of its peak. This is a very short version of a well-worked-out story. These occurrences took place from southern Colorado and Utah, down through southern Arizona and New Mexico, and into northern Mexico. At Casas Grandes in Chihuahua, Mexico, the largest site in the greater Southwest, a major massacre took place in the late 1300s or a bit later—the town was sacked and destroyed and hundreds of people were killed. By 1540, when Coronado reached the area, he found nothing like the great towns of Chaco, nor nearly as many people.

Considering the archaeological evidence, changes in carrying capacity in the prehistoric Southwest derived from changes in climate appear to have led directly to increases and decreases in warfare. Though the local climate was not constant from 500 B.C. to A.D. 900—and in particular on a worldwide basis there was deterioration around A.D. 500—no changes seem to have been dramatic enough in the Southwest to have precipitated either a crisis or especially good times, as the population neither rose nor fell dramatically. Beginning around A.D. 900 was a time known as the Medieval

Warm Period in Europe, a period when the world was wet and warm—perfect conditions for farmers. Again, this was when the Vikings expanded into Iceland and Greenland and Europe's great cathedrals were constructed. This period of prosperity in Europe corresponds with the time of peace, prosperity, and massive building efforts in the Southwest. The benign climatic conditions led to the population increase in the Southwest, since it was possible to farm in more localities than before and there were fewer bad years.

When the climate turned poor again, it did do so with a vengeance. The Medieval Warm Period came to an end around 1200, and not long thereafter the first signs of the Little Ice Age were seen in Europe. Famine was recorded in England in 1317 as crops did not mature due to the cold. I believe the same thing happened in North America. The Southwest has never been a great place to farm. When it became colder and the growing season shortened, things really fell apart—as reflected in the increased archaeological evidence for warfare during this time period. Competition for the best farmland, and perhaps each other's stored foods, began. As the conflict increased, the response was to build large defensive sites—which, under the circumstances, was the worst possible thing to do. Jamming people into one place made everybody more vulnerable. When the crops failed, they failed for all. The surrounding region's wild plants and animals, which would have balanced a diet focused on corn, would have been quickly depleted, and everyone's diet would have suffered greatly. At this time, there is archaeological evidence for anemia in children and bad health in general throughout the region. My belief is that some combination of poor nutrition, deaths due to warfare, and probably actual starvation decimated the Southwest's population.

In biological terms, this situation would be described as a temporary increase in population above the long-term sustainability of the environment, followed by a population crash. Such cycles are seen with deer, rabbits, and other mammals. When such a crash happens with humans, it is accompanied by very intense warfare. Humans will fight before they will starve, although the fighting may intensify the starving. In the prehistory of the Southwest there is a link among climate, population growth, and warfare. A shift toward a good climate for farming led to rapid growth, a change toward a poor climate led to the population being far too large for the region, and warfare was an important component of reaching a new level of population more commensurate with the carrying capacity. This scenario, or ones very much like it, has probably been played out hundreds of times the world over. This is a long-term process that can be seen only when there are good historical records or very good archaeological information—or both.

Ethnographic accounts provide additional insights into farmer warfare. Some of the most interesting studies were conducted in the highlands of New Guinea. The coast of New Guinea had long been known to Asian and European traders and explorers. Inland rose steep, almost impenetrable, jungle-covered mountains that were essentially unusable and very sparsely inhabited. What no one realized was that well into the interior of the island, beyond the mountains, lay broad, rather flat valleys that were highly productive, filled with people, and almost totally cut off from the rest of the world.

In the 1930s, a party of European gold seekers trekked to the top of a New Guinea mountain range and settled down for the night. After the sun set they realized that the valley below was dotted with countless flickering campfires. That highland plateau was the home of thousands of people who had been farming these mountain valleys for thousands of years with only minimal interaction with the groups living along the coast. The gold hunters and the highland farmers could scarcely believe the other existed, and the initial encounters were peaceful, apparently because the New Guineans thought the Europeans were gods, ghosts, or something otherworldly. The farmers realized their error pretty quickly, and the prospectors soon realized that they had entered a dangerous, brutal world of constant warfare.[13]

The New Guinea highlands are an extraordinary place: The population density is extremely high, and life revolves around farming yams and raising pigs. The political units are groups of a few hundred individuals belonging to clans; the males tend to be related and women come from nearby groups. Warfare is endemic, with formal battles, ambushes, and even occasional massacres, going on almost continually. According to ethnographic studies from the 1960s, an individual group might be involved in a dozen battles in a single year and come to the aid of allies several more times. Battles seem indecisive. For instance, a battle may be broken off if it starts to rain heavily. If a combatant is killed or seriously injured, that may also be occasion to stop fighting for the day. This lack of decisiveness lulled some early ethnographers into seeing this pattern of chronic conflict as not really "warfare." The researchers viewed it as something more akin to "play fighting" or as simply a means of allowing the men and boys to "get it out of their systems." Nothing could be further from the truth.

In fact, anthropologist Carl Heider, who performed one of the early, important studies of the region beginning in 1961, came away from his first stay in highland New Guinea thinking that the warfare was not particularly deadly; he titled his book *Grand Valley Dani: Peaceful Warriors*. After Heider had revisited his study subjects over almost a decade, he reached a very different conclusion. Initially, Heider's field studies had taken place between battles that had changed the political, demographic, and ecological landscape; only later did he gather evidence of just how real highland warfare was. More careful investigation of the issues—gained by constructing genealogies and then asking how each person died, or carefully working out histories of early wars and battles—revealed a very different world.[14]

Such research shows that New Guinean men see their warfare as very dangerous and frequently experience nightmares about being isolated from their compatriots and bludgeoned to death. This fighting is nasty. For instance, arrows are smeared with excrement in the hope a successful hit will cause infection. And it is deadly: 25 percent of the men and about 5 percent of the women die from warfare. About 30 percent of all independent highland social groups become extinct each century because they are defeated.[15] These groups are either massacred and killed, or the survivors of a particularly deadly encounter flee and take refuge with trading partners or distant relatives. This last place on Earth to have remained unaffected by modern society was not the most peaceful but one of the most warlike ever encountered.

The next least-exposed group of tribally organized farmers are the Yanomama of Venezuela. Ethnographic descriptions of the frequency, intensity, and deadliness of their warfare are virtually identical to accounts from New Guinea. The Nuer and Dinka of East Africa and the Kalinga of Southeast Asia also document historical tribal warfare, so there are good examples on almost all continents. The problem with many other examples—such as the Iroquois, parts of Melanesia, the Great Plains of North America—is that the observed warfare took place in the light of European impact. Because these cases are controversial as to cause, and because there are many cases in which European impact cannot be a prime factor in the warfare, I focus on those examples.

In the 1960s, anthropologist Napoleon Chagnon studied the Yanomama, a horticultural, hunting society living in the rain forest in the upper reaches of the Orinoco River in Venezuela and Brazil that, although in contact with Europeans, had not yet been brought under governmental control. He found intense, pervasive, and continual warfare. There have been suggestions that this warfare was a consequence of recent impact by traders, missionaries, and even the anthropologists themselves. Yanomama warfare has become controversial because people such as Patrick Tierney have accused Chagnon of exaggerating or even instigating this warfare. Accusations that imply the Yanomama were peaceful in the past are without foundation and demonstrably untrue as the account below and the work of other researchers all show. Yet these accusations are taken seriously by many, not because a convincing case was made about anything Chagnon did but because they appeal to our desire to have a peaceful world and our belief that indigenous peoples were peaceful. Firsthand accounts of Yanomama warfare—including the vivid account below from a twelve-year-old girl who was taken captive in the 1930s—as well as other historical documentation assembled by scholars that are removed from the controversy show that, if anything, more violent and intense warfare than that recorded by Chagnon took place among the Yanomama long before he got there.[16]

> Suddenly I heard shouts: the enemy, the enemy. . . . The men had gone running to meet the enemy . . . [the men of the group put up a poor fight and flee, leaving the women and children to the enemy] . . . we could not flee any more; the Karawetari [the enemy] were by now quite close [the women and children were surrounded and captured] . . . from all sides the women continued to arrive with their children, whom the other Karawetari had captured. They all joined us. Then the men began to kill the children; little ones, bigger ones, they killed many of them. They tried to run away, but they caught them, and threw them on the ground, and stuck them with bows which went through their bodies and rooted them to the ground. Taking the smallest by the feet, they beat them against the trees and rocks. The children's eyes trembled. . . . They killed so many. . . .[17]

Ethnographic accounts show that the Yanomama live in fairly small groups, usually fewer than one hundred people, and farm primarily plantains, bananas, and manioc. Hunting is very important, and animal protein is valuable to them. They live in fortified villages made by building their houses in a circle, which opens onto a central courtyard. Warfare among the Yanomama is endemic. Raids and ambushes are the norm, inviting another group to a feast and then attacking them is known, and massacres do occur. Women are often captured by the victors, but the children of these women are often killed. Alliances between groups are in a constant state of flux, with the allies of one day becoming the enemies of the next. Death rates due to warfare are high—about 24 percent of the men and 7 percent of the women. It is very hard to determine the number of children killed, so overall estimates are speculative.[18] As with other band- and tribal-level societies, some of the warfare appears almost playlike, with skirmishes and attacks that result in only a minor injury or two. Organization is weak. Attacking parties will break up before reaching their destinations and fights are often poorly coordinated. No armor is used. Even so, among the Yanomama, social groups are divided up and eliminated, many people are killed, good fighters are recognized as such and feared even by people in their own community, large buffer zones (some thirty miles wide) between settlements are maintained, villages are fortified—and the people hate the warfare.[19]

Another example, this time from North America, provides further evidence for the intensity and lethality of tribal warfare. In southern California beginning around 2000 B.C., people living along the coast began to behave much as farmers do and so are relevant here. The Chumash and other tribes treated oak trees as a crop, harvested shellfish, ocean fish, and sea mammals, and lived in permanent, large villages with special sweat lodges.

Though it is easy to see how land resources could have been overtaxed, the ocean is much more subtle. Popular misconceptions abound about the seas being an unlimited resource. Shellfish can be harvested only at a controlled rate or they decline in numbers and size, because people harvest the largest first. This phenomenon is observable in the archaeological sites along the southern California coast where there are shell mounds filled with thousands upon thousands of broken pieces of shell. These early California Indian sites are also the dirtiest I have ever encountered—the dirt is greasy and sticks to everything, because these shellfish had to be cooked and the cooking water was thrown out onto the shell mound. After hundreds of years and thousands of cooking events, the soil has absorbed this residue. Over time, the average size of the shells found in these mounds, regardless of species, declined, as the human population overexploited the sea.

The southern California Indians ate so many small shellfish, making it increasingly hard to collect the same amount of pounds of shellfish meat, even though great quantities of large fish and sea mammals were available. They had Pismo clams and abalone, but they also ate plenty of small mussels. Ocean fishing required boats, which were hard to make where there was so little wood. The Indians did make ingenious boats with sewn-together planks sealed with naturally occurring bitumen, or tar. Fishing would have been dangerous and unpredictable. But that was not the only problem. There was the weather.

As known from long-term climatology studies, El Niño events, in which ocean warming in the southern Pacific influences the world's climate, have been occurring for centuries. Such an event would have upset everything, causing torrential rains and floods on land and a warming of the ocean, resulting in changing the fish species. As observed in modern times, El Niño could be followed by a period that was the reverse and drought would result.[20] Longer-term events, like the Medieval Warm Period and Little Ice Age, would more than likely have upset the balance of people and resources. The southern California coast could support a lot of people, and there were a lot of people for the last several thousand years. Anything that went wrong would have precipitated a crisis.

Archaeologists find some of the highest incidences of violent deaths of any prehistoric people ever studied along the Southern California coast at this time period. The proportion of such deaths changed over time—due either to changes in social structure and the intensity of warfare, the impact of climate change, or the presence of new competitive groups to the south. In any case, direct skeletal evidence of violent deaths in the area surges from around 5 or 6 percent up to about 18 percent of all adults when there is also skeletal evidence of poor health.[21] Skeletal evidence for violent fatalities would actually be much lower than total warfare deaths, because skeletal remains only sometimes provide such clues. So much for a Southern California Garden of Eden.

This sampling of early farming societies illustrates that simple farmers live in a world of warfare. Drawing from these examples, and from what scholars know about similar societies, several general statements can be made. Farmer warfare from the historical record was almost always described by the participants as conflict over women or revenge, and on a short-term basis appeared to be more like "play" war than "real" war. When queried more carefully, the majority of participants in these conflicts admitted to economic reasons for the warfare, and some even suggested that economics were the dominant reason.

When the long-term consequences of tribal warfare are examined, major shifts in the ownership of resources become clear, and that is demographically very important. Time and time again, both archaeologically and historically, death rates due to warfare of 25 percent of the men over their adult lives, and perhaps 5 percent of the women in addition to many children, are recorded. Anthropologist Lawrence Keeley was able to tabulate the amount of land lost or gained in one generation for five egalitarian societies. The figure ranged from 5 to 60 percent, and averaged 30 percent. This is a significant amount of change among territories over the long haul. There is also evidence that societies are completely destroyed by defeats. Farmer-egalitarian warfare very often results in the development of large, unusable no-man's-lands, which result in unstable intergroup relations.

Buffer zone widths range from about a half mile for the Dani of New Guinea to twenty miles for Yanomama of the Amazon and the prehistoric farmers of the Southwest.[22]

Warfare among farmers organized as tribes is some of the most violent, not just in terms of the number of fatalities but also in that it resulted in a constant—almost daily—threat of attack. Tribal-farmer warfare is more institutionalized and organized, just as tribal societies, in general, are more institutionalized and organized than foraging bands. In tribes, as in bands, there is no specialization. Every adult male, with few exceptions, is expected to fight. Undoubtedly, some individuals are recognized as great warriors in tribes, but few are exempted from the fray.

Farmer warfare was simple, direct, and deadly. Rarely were prisoners taken in tribal-level warfare, except for women who were integrated into the victors' society. The goal is annihilation of all men, women, and children, although men were the primary target. The limited organizational structure of tribes means that there were not campaigns, sieges, and the like. On offense, each man brought his own food and carried his own weapons. On defense, the women could take an active part in the fighting.

Tribal-level warfare was not constant in the past. Conflict rarely disappeared for long in the archaeological record, but there were times when it became especially virulent. These time spans seem to coincide with climate change, or the aftermath of rapid growth in population, which may have been the result of technological change or climatic optimums. The fact that these correlations can be observed strongly implies that farmer warfare has real causes and is not sparked by revenge, the innate need of males to release pent-up aggression, or other such explanations that would be immune to changes in climate, ecology, or population size.

The development of farming and the spread of farmers over much of Earth set in motion the potential for even more rapid population growth than any seen for forager-level societies. At the same time, farmers were capable of degrading their environments in ways that foragers could not. Even if the climate did not change for the worse, farmers tended to deteriorate their environments by their actions alone, increasing the stress on resources. Compared with foragers, farmers set the stage for even more endemic and intense competition between groups. The early horticulturists inflamed a situation of war and ecological imbalance into one of even *more* war and *more* imbalance.

In a way, tribally organized farmers without central authorities were in the worst possible situation. Being sedentary, these societies were capable of very rapid growth. Even though they often did practice infanticide, each farming family recognized the benefits of having lots of children, so they would grow whenever possible. Lacking strong leadership, the group was unable to enforce effective social behaviors. For instance, if any single family, or even an entire village, actually attempted to get into ecological balance by not overusing resources, there was nothing to keep its neighbors from doing so. It did not pay to be a conservationist, and the early farmers were not—at least not to the extent necessary to avoid constantly pressing their locale's carrying capacity. Stressed for resources, as shown from the archaeology, farmers would have been almost continually beset by malnutrition-induced diseases and outright starvation, and the need to engage in infanticide and warfare.

The invention of farming did not result in peacefulness, even though it greatly increased the resources available to humans and, in theory, provided great motivation to practice conservation. For example, if you have a big investment in houses and other facilities, you don't want to have to move, so you'd better take care of what is around you. The great agricultural revolution did not produce a revolution in intergroup relations. Warfare continued with the advent of farming and, if anything, became more common and deadly than forager warfare.

Over time, as tribal societies grew larger, they began to evolve new types of social organizations, and out of this process strong leaders emerged. With such central authority came the opportunity to exert control over the entire population as no form of government had ever before in human history. The development of these much larger, much more complexly organized social groups presented a new chapter in human relationships—and still more dramatic changes in the lifeway of most humans. Complex societies with their strong central governments could potentially control population growth, might be able to foresee and prevent ecological imbalance, and might even enforce peace on the populace.

chapter seven

COMPLEX SOCIETIES

*W*e started climbing at about 11,750 feet above sea level—actually, staggering is a better description. Our Peruvian workmen carried everything, all our digging equipment, our shovels and screens, even our lunch. It was all I could do to take one slow step after another up this hill high in the central Andes. Gasping for breath as I came to the summit another 750 feet higher, our party came upon a massive stone wall. After climbing through a broken-down section of this enclosure, we encountered another hulking wall, and then a third. Inside these formidable barricades were the remains of thousands of small, round stone houses within the perimeter of Peru's Hatunmarca archaeological site. Six hundred years ago, scores and scores of people had lived on this hilltop, jammed into this forty-acre space, and would have had to walk long distances up and down the steep incline to farm, fetch water, and gather firewood or llama dung and everything else they needed to survive. Even by the standards of the prehistoric Andes, this was one terrible place to live. These early Peruvians must have been terrified of something to barricade themselves in like that on this lofty promontory.

The research team I was visiting was able to understand a great deal about the people who dwelt in these mountains.[1] Known as the Wanka, they were ultimately conquered by the Inca and eventually abandoned these extraordinary high fortress towns. It's not clear whether the Wanka initially built these settlements out of fear of the Inca or each other.

Up to that point in my career—this was the late 1970s—all my other field experiences with warfare had been much more subtle. I'd certainly learned that prehistoric societies could have warfare without living in enormous, fortified towns surrounded by massive, concentric defensive walls. With the development of complex societies, warfare takes on a new dimension. Fortresses, defensive walls hundreds of miles long, and weapons and armor expertly crafted by specialists all give the warfare of complex societies a different visibility. Almost all archaeologists recognize the huge Peruvian forts like Hatunmarca as evidence for significant warfare, but the question of how common and deadly conflict was among complex societies—and the impact it had on these societies—is not as easy to see as those giant stone walls.

Peru's Wanka were organized as a chiefdom and were conquered by the Inca, who were a state-level society. Both these much larger social groups present a vivid contrast to the smaller, egalitarian bands and tribes. Across the span of human history, there has been a steady succession of the different ways groups have organized themselves, and these societies have become increasingly more intricately organized as the number of people living in them has grown. A dramatic change from the point of view of ecology and conflict in human social development came, not just with the agricultural revolution but with the development of these much more complexly organized groups.

By calling these social groupings "complex societies" anthropologists are considering the number of social institutions and the rules and mechanisms for hooking people together found within them. Complex societies have a maze of such institutions and many means of linking them together. Chiefdoms and states can be complex in terms of their groupwide social structures. They may contain castes, kings, courts, Kiwanis clubs, politburos, political parties, paramount chiefs, and peasants. Individuals within the chiefdom or state may lead much less complex lives than their counterparts in a tribe.

The Hopi, as members of a tribe embedded within a state, lead some of the most complex lives imaginable. They have particular and different relationships with their mother's family (their clan) and their father's family, they have differing relationships with people of their pueblo and also within the mesa on which their pueblo is located, and, finally, with the tribe as a whole, a population of only a few thousand people. At the same time, they are likely to belong to one or more religious societies, which sets up another series of relationships and involves long and complex ritual events that are time-consuming to study, to prepare for, and to undertake. All of this religious observance is built into a complex annual calendar with many differing groups having to work together and coordinate their activities to stage the annual set of religious and secular events. My life, in the highly complex nation-state of the United States, is trivially simple by comparison.

Complex societies also have different social classes—elites and nonelites—and they are hereditary; you don't earn your status by your deeds.

This wall remnant is one of three that surrounded this 300+ acre hilltop site, situated at more than 12,500 feet above sea level in the central Andes. The inhabitants of this 700-year-old site were eventually conquered by the Inca.

The Industrial Revolution changed this somewhat, with accomplishments becoming important in defining status, while "breeding" and "family" still continue to matter, especially in Europe. Ancient states also had elites, but even more important, they had bureaucrats—people who were not true elites but had more wealth and status than the peasant farmers. This new "middle class" enforced the laws, kept records, managed building projects, and ran the armies of the state.

Leaders in both states and chiefdoms have the power to enforce their orders, which in some states are codified into laws. The members of chiefdoms and states pay taxes or tribute. In one way or another, some portion of what an individual makes or grows is taken from him and used to support other people in the group. Often, a portion of this tribute is given back to individuals when they participate in public efforts, like building an irrigation canal or temple. These centrally controlled resources are also used to support the specialists, individuals who do not farm or fish but who are scribes, priests, generals, weavers, and bureaucrats. This combination of tribute and specialists provides the means and technology to build pyramids, palaces, roads, and castles—the massive public works projects that are one of the characteristics of the complex societies.

"Chiefdoms" are the relatively less complex of the two complex-society groupings. The earliest chiefdoms were found in the Middle East by 5000 B.C., and by 2000 B.C. in the Americas. Samoa is considered a classic chiefdom and still functions that way today, although almost all modern chiefdoms have been subsumed into nation-states. Unlike the band-level foragers or the egalitarian tribal farmers, chiefdoms, as the name implies, have strong leaders or chiefs. And since the leadership is hereditary, both maternal and paternal kinship lines are usually very important in these societies.

Much larger than tribes, chiefdoms often contain fifty thousand or more people, and all known examples, both archaeologically and ethnographically, contain at least several thousand individuals. The large public works—temples, burial monuments, elaborate irrigation systems, hillside terracing for farms—that archaeologists see for the first time with chiefdom-level societies exist because the chiefs have the means and the ability to force people to work, as well as the need to enhance their own prestige and support growing numbers. In addition to serving social functions and demonstrating the power of the chiefs, these public works allowed for an increase in carrying capacity beyond what tribes could have accomplished in the same locale. The leaders of chiefdoms are closely tied to religion and play a central religious role. Equally important, in all the cases of chiefdom societies anthropologists know about, chiefs compete intensely with other chiefs. Though tribes do compete, they do so as a loose group. Chiefs compete personally. By killing or capturing a chief, the victor takes the losing leader's subjects and land. As in the game of chess, the goal is to capture the king, not take all the pawns. Chiefdoms are also precarious and allies are critical. No chief is safe if his enemies gang up on him, so it behooves every chief to have as many allies as possible. To gain allies a chief must appear strong, and one way of demonstrating strength is to look wealthy. The size of monumental architecture, the lavishness of a feast, the quality and rarity of gifts, all serve to help chiefs size up their potential allies or foes.

Chiefs, like any leaders, have children. However, since the leaders in a chiefdom have increased access to food and other resources, they tend to have more surviving children than common folk. This situation leads invariably to more people of "chiefly" status than can actually become chief. Consequently, there will be constant competition and intrigue among the potential chiefs about who actually gets to be chief. This problem, as well as some administrative problems, is partially solved by having different levels of chief. Most chiefdom-level societies did not consist of lots of commoners and a single chief. Instead, there was a "chiefly class" of people with the various chiefs of the group ranked in status. Not all chiefs were equal, but certainly all wanted to be top dog.

When I lived in Samoa in the 1960s, the country still functioned very much as a traditional chiefdom. My village had almost a thousand people and about thirty chiefs. A chief and his wife, and to some extent their children, were given special treatment at social occasions, which were almost all organized and run by the chiefs. They also met in a special house to settle local disputes. Each chief had a well-determined place in the chiefly pecking order, demonstrated by who got served in which order at feasts and ceremonies, and how high the roofs of their houses could be built. About thirty people who were related, sometimes fictively, to the chief farmed his land and did other work for him. If any of these "relatives" earned income from an outside job, their chief got the pay. In return he provided housing, food, clothing, and all else to the entire lot. The organization was like a minicorporation, and he was the CEO. Even more important, chiefs could call upon the lesser chiefs in their district to provide food and labor for larger undertakings. In the past, these projects might have involved building forts or war canoes; today, the groups often communally build churches. Each nonchief was linked to a chief, each chief to a more important chief, and so on until, at the top of the hierarchy, four or five chiefs competed to be the paramount chief of the islands, a goal rarely attained.

In a typical chiefdom, it was not easy for a chief to live to old age. Many were murdered or defeated in war and lost their power—and usually their lives. There was never a shortage of people ready to take on the role of the most powerful chief. Warfare would be an integral part of this highly competitive, contentious environment.

States are even more complex than chiefdoms. Of particular interest are the first ancient states, often referred to as "pristine states," because these societies did not come into existence as a response to other nearby states but evolved on their own. These initial state-level organizations were small by today's standards but much larger than most chiefdoms. Few paramount chiefs controlled more than ten thousand people, while state-level societies could be ten times or even one hundred times larger. Early states began around 3000 B.C. in the Middle East, almost a thousand years later in China, and another thousand years or so later again in Mesoamerica and Peru. In all these areas, the first states were ultimately followed by much larger and more complex states, culminating in the Roman Empire and the famous dynasty states of China. At slightly smaller scales were such later states as the Aztec Empire in Mesoamerica and the Inca Empire in the Andes.

In these ancient states, leadership was hereditary, and there were even more and grander monumental building efforts, the pinnacle of these state-level monuments being the great pyramids of Egypt. Besides the larger numbers of people involved, what really set states apart from chiefdoms was the bureaucracy. A group of intermediaries existed to enforce and deliver the will of the state's leaders. These bureaucrats had an "in-between" social status and were not necessarily related to the ruling elite. In order to keep things functioning and to keep the bureaucrats from exceeding their authority, rules within a state became codified. The Laws of Hammurabi, written in 1750 B.C. in Mesopotamia, are a famous early example of these codified rules. Taxation, which was managed by these bureaucrats, was the mechanism that gave the state its real power, but it could lead to internal unrest and revolution. Taxing 50 percent of the harvest while people were starving during a famine was far from uncommon among early states.[2]

Another important part of the tapestry of early states was writing. The ability to record their own history and affairs has contributed to much of our knowledge about many such recent states as Greece and Rome. A written language does not seem to be an essential ingredient for "statedom," however. Virtually all ancient states had cities of some sort, but these could be relatively small, say, ten thousand people or so, as in Egypt or Peru. In some states there was an acknowledged or de facto separation of leadership into the secular and the religious. One primary function of the secular leadership was managing warfare and diplomatic relations with other states. Succession of leadership, as with chiefdoms, might have been codified at the state level, but orderly succession at the state level often failed to function that way in practice, leading to civil wars or wars of succession.

Classic states include the city-states and empires of ancient Mesopotamia, for example Ur, with its ziggurats, temples, great encircling wall, cuneiform writing, and elaborate burials of kings, which included quantities of valuable items plus sacrificed humans and animals—and, of course, ancient Egypt. The Minoan and Mycenaean cultures of the Aegean were right on the cusp between chiefdoms and states. The great palace of Knossos on Crete, with its famous frescoes of youths jumping bulls, looks like the residence of a state-level Minoan king. The later Mycenaeans, the actors in the Trojan War who took over Knossos, had hilltop palaces surrounded by massive walls, but only small towns. Yet they did have writing, elaborate burials, and craft specialists, who made the kind of beautiful armor of Achilles that Homer described.

Despite the differences between chiefdoms and early states, the two share characteristics of social organization, such as professional warriors and

MAIDEN CASTLE   16.10.37 7.95

Chiefdoms maintained hilltop fortresses the world over. This site, called Maiden Castle, is the largest such fort in England. Ringed with ramparts and moats, the fort was used from the Bronze Age (ca.2000–700 BC) into the Iron Age (700–100 BC). Chiefdoms used alliances, often shifting, to survive what were perpetual states of war.

more organized warfare, extraction of tribute or taxes, and the ability of the elite to "control" the lower classes. What is of interest is how effectively these better-organized, larger groups controlled their populations and affected their environments. While all the popular myths of the "noble savage" involve anthropologically "less complex" societies, the more complex societies are rarely considered to be capable of pulling off any form of ecological "bliss." In fact, it's probably no great surprise to many of us today that the Sumerians of Mesopotamia destroyed their fields through overirrigation, even though they invented writing and had the first cities. The ancient Maya radically changed their landscape, the Vikings denuded Iceland, and the ancient Greeks, the descendants of the Trojans, overgrazed their hillsides. In all, ancient history reveals that complex societies deserve no reputation for living in ecological balance, even though it might be expected. One might anticipate that societies with a strong central leader or government should have been able to "lay down the law" and exert more environmental and population control over the commoners.

In egalitarian societies, the ability of group members to sanction one another is limited. The view of the individual within these less complexly organized groups is parochial. There is no one leader or bureaucrat in a position to see the ecological "big picture." With more complex societies, the leadership would be in a much better position to perceive whether or not the entire system was in trouble. The government might receive complaints of hunger from some quarters before others, or have trouble extracting tribute in some regions. Such rulers, or their minions, could travel to see the downstream silt and the upstream forest clearing. Most important, once this information had been gathered, the chiefs and state-level leadership would have the authority to make people change their behavior before things got out of hand.

The trouble is, few among us accept this scenario. We tend to be confident in the ability of bands and tribes to work out these challenging issues of population control and environmental renewability yet have no faith in the abilities of complex societies to tackle the same issues. After all, we live in complex societies and we know better.

Increased social complexity has not led to ecological balance—if anything, it has made things worse. Complex societies result in more people and more specialists, which result in more technology. More people with more technology can make a much bigger environmental mess. No attitudes need to change for greater impact; people can have great reverence for nature and remain out of ecological balance. I see no evidence that the people of South Asia—in particular India—had (or have) any less of an attitude about living in harmony with nature than the native North Americans did (or do). When Europeans came on the scene in India in the 1500s and 1600s, the ecological situation—denuded landscapes, recurrent famines—was far worse than it was in North America when Europeans first arrived there around the same time. India's high densities of farmers, with domesticated animals and iron tools, had been around a much longer time and was a much more complex technology and so had much more of an impact on the environment than North America's low-density and more recent corn farmers and foragers. Yet the attitudes those two distinct cultures had toward nature and the environment were probably not all that dissimilar.

When societies become more complex, several things change. The changes are not simultaneous, and they can affect certain groups more than others, but some of these changes apply to all complex societies. For example, all such groups have the ability to improve productivity by building dams, canals, farming terraces, windmills, and the like. The leadership in a complex society has more control over rates of population increase. A new form of social control over growth exists. For example, rules can be passed and enforced restricting marriage to people with enough wealth to set up a household, as was the case in England, or by not allowing the men of certain age-grade groups to marry until the leader announced it was appropriate, as with various Bantu chiefdoms.

Finally, when the members of a complex society run out of resources, they may receive some relief from distant regions or markets, or from centralized granaries or other state resources. Conversely, they could be forced by the leadership to starve, or almost starve, rather than resort to conflict to alleviate the situation. The possibility of complex societies achieving a greater balance between population size and carrying capacity could exist, but such an outcome just does not exist in the record. In spite of rules and possibilities for control, wide swings in growth and intense and deadly warfare seem to characterize chiefdoms and states everywhere scholars have studied them.

Complex societies are noted not just for monumental architecture but also for major public works. Irrigation systems and terracing of hillsides are common for both chiefdoms and states, but other examples of major public works projects exist. In Hawaii today, gigantic prehistoric fish traps are still visible. These traps consist of rock walls that look like contemporary breakwaters constructed in lagoons and often are hundreds of yards on a side, enclosing many acres of water. Small fish can swim through the rocks into the enclosure, but as they grow larger they are afraid to swim back out. These traps become giant fish-raising pens, devoid of predators, except for the human fish farmers. While living in Samoa, I once asked my chief, Sila, why the Samoans didn't build such fish traps. His answer was that the chiefs did not have enough authority to amass that amount of labor. Indeed, it's true that nowhere in Samoa are there public works of the magnitude of the terraces, fish traps, and temples found in Hawaii, which had a much stronger form of elite control. While there may have been ecological reasons why stone fish traps would not work in Samoa, overall the great difference in the scale of public works between Samoa and Hawaii cannot be explained by ecology but must relate to social differences.

As impressive as such public works projects appear today, they were a one-time event. Irrigation canals might raise the carrying capacity many times over in a particular locale, the farming terraces in Southeast Asia and the Andes might have dramatically increased the productivity of the hillsides, but the ensuing growth in population made possible by the increase in productivity would "eat up" these innovations almost as fast as they were built. Such public works raised the carrying capacity and consequently the population in complex societies but did not result in a higher standard of living. Wherever such facilities existed, the result was more mouths to feed and, if anything, people were then living even closer to the edge. Many of these facilities were built and used by small groups; probably the chief's role was to support the builders by supplying them with food. After millennia of land reclamation projects and irrigation systems in Egypt, famine was still common. Among the Maya, physical stature and health declined, even though they built thousands of acres of special farmlands, called raised fields. There is no correlation between the existence of productive public works and improved standards of living.

Another hallmark of complex societies is the inequality of their people: The elites in a chiefdom or state had more of everything—resources and power—than the non-elites, as seen in their grander houses, their burials filled with rare and valuable objects, and even their larger physical stature and better health. Societies with a controlling elite could enforce peace on members of the social group, and they could attempt population control. Though relative peace could be mandated, the efforts at population control almost never worked.

When Marie Antoinette allegedly said, "Let them eat cake," she meant, "Let the peasants starve." As societies became more complex, it was increasingly possible for the elite to let a portion of the population starve and prevent them from trying to fight for their own survival. Armies and police could, and did, put down riots and rebellions with great regularity. Today, the elite could push this only so far before the possibility of revolt and riots could turn against them—as in Marie Antoinette's case with the French Revolution. Within bounds, the linkage between the carrying capacity and conflict that had been a part of human existence for millennia was broken with the advent of more complexly organized societies. There was still a linkage between carrying capacity and population growth, but by forcing some people in the group to starve, there was no reason for one complex society to fight to increase its carrying capacity at the expense of other, neighboring groups. If the elite deemed it inadvisable to fight, they did not go to war, regardless of the well-being of the commoners. This doesn't mean they didn't often choose to fight, just that conflict was not as dictated by resource stress at the state and chiefdom level as it was in bands and tribes.

The practice of "starving" part of the population within a complex society was subtle. If certain segments were subsisting on a bare minimum of food and other resources, they wouldn't die immediately. There would be higher infant mortality and lower birth rates, and people would be more likely to die from disease. Actual famine with direct deaths also occurred, and still does today. All these factors are better attested to among more recent states, where there are good statistics, than for chiefdoms. However, the net result is the same. The population growth is held down to a degree, because people are dying from lack of food, either directly or indirectly. Complex societies can enforce an indirect form of population control by forcing people to live on inadequate diets.

A chiefdom's ability to enforce subadequate diets, controlled starvation, was probably much more limited than a state's. In chiefdom-level societies, if certain portions of the population were under resource stress, they could ally themselves with a different chief, revolt, or fight internally. Consequently, warfare as a means of solving the provisioning problem was much more prevalent among chiefdoms, which is probably why both ethnographers and archaeologists see much more evidence of warfare at the chiefdom level.

Complex societies not only fought among themselves but also attempted to expand into the territories of less complexly organized peoples—foragers and bands. This leads to a different, but no less deadly, form of war—guerrilla warfare. The concept of guerrilla warfare or "little war" is a familiar one: small, armed groups employing hit-and-run tactics, no massed armies, and with no centers or territories for the central government to conquer. Guerrilla warfare occurs when complex societies are confronted by tribally organized people using tribal tactics of war. This type of warfare has been going on for a long time and does not always consist of peasants hiding out in jungles—our common perception of guerrilla warfare. The Indian wars of North America, the mujahideen resistance to the Soviet invasion of Afghanistan, and the Scots' attacks on the Romans of England were also guerrilla wars. State societies traditionally employ several methods to deal with these nonstate societies they cannot conquer by defeating the leadership. The states either wall off the belligerent groups—as with Hadrian's Wall in England and the Great Wall in China—or push the tribes (and sometimes chiefdoms) into marginal geographic areas that are of little use to the state. Alternatively, states also try to exterminate or so thoroughly defeat the tribes—the American Indians, the hill tribes of Southeast Asia— or come close enough to exterminating them that the remainder can be put into marginal areas ("reservations" for Native Americans or "homelands" for South African Bantu). Overall, it has been very hard for states to deal with nonstate guerrilla warfare except by attempted extermination or ultimately by assimilation.

To see this from another perspective, states (and to a lesser extent chiefdoms) have fought other states and chiefdoms as their main adversaries.

Strong chiefdoms could amass large labor forces. The Tongans of the South Pacific had a massive fleet of war canoes, some more than 100 feet in length, and used them to dominate nearby islands. In spite of the ability of the leaders of chiefdom-level societies to conduct more intensive war, such complex societies actually have fewer battle deaths than do foragers and tribal farmers.

They don't fight foragers and tribes except at the margins of their worlds. The tribal Zulu were able to defend their territory against small contingents of British soldiers, even when dramatically outgunned, but they were quickly subjugated when the empire got serious and sent in a large army against them. A state can deploy an army and destroy the ability of the less complexly organized society to fight, just as the state would respond to a threat from a similarly organized, more complex society. This is true for the Soviets in Afghanistan, or the British and the Zulu. However, even though a tribal (or chiefdom) society is subjugated and its political centers captured and leadership dispersed, it can still launch guerrilla warfare for which the states have little effective response. In these cases, walls no longer work, nor does simply holding and controlling the population centers.

To cast this into the present day, such antistate guerrilla conflicts must be seen as involving very different social organizations. To resolve them, modern complex societies must do several things. One approach is to bring the traditional peoples, whose daily lives are those of tribal peoples, fully into the more complex society. Of course, these tribally organized people may not want to give up their traditions, their very way of perceiving the world—and why should they, or why should we feel we have the right to make them? But if they can be positively integrated, then the clash of two fundamentally different ways of life is reduced.

A second, and perhaps more fundamental, approach states could assume with nonstate societies to eliminate conflict is to bring the less complexly organized people back from the edge of survival, back from the edge of the carrying capacity. This is ultimately the real answer. Getting the resources back in balance with the population—making it possible to feed a family, even making it possible to marry and *have* a family—will produce the real seeds of peace, because underlying all the other reasons for warfare is almost always this fundamental imbalance of resource stress and population growth. Then give the traditional people a couple of generations to forget the hatreds, to get rid of the institutions and social rewards for war, and peace will come as it has again and again where these conditions have been met. This is a tall order and requires a lot of foresight and time. It is certainly not attainable everywhere in our lifetimes, but then again, neither will we solve global warming in our lifetimes. That's no reason not to start tackling the problem.

Whether or not there was (or is) conflict with neighboring complex societies, or with less complexly organized peoples living on a state's geographic fringes, a major problem for all complex societies was their direct impact on the environment. The effects of larger numbers of people devoting proportionally less land to buffering zones between polities, plus the construction of public works, all hurt the environment. Since early complex societies could afford to support specialists, archaeologists over time begin to see evidence of metallurgy (which necessitated the burning of charcoal for smelting) and other such behaviors that further stressed the environment. Most damaging, however, was the increasing use of domestic animals resulting in overgrazing and overirrigation that resulted in the salting of fields. Even now, vast areas of present-day Iraq are unfarmable because of ancient salt buildup. Pollen and sediment studies show that the silting of bays and estuaries, and the denuding of hillsides—especially in the Middle East and in Europe—is thousands of years old.

Anthropologists have observed that throughout the world, farmers in highly populated regions farm in ways different from horticulturists working in areas with fewer people. The optimal method of farming over much of the world is to sow a field for a year or two, let the land lie fallow for perhaps ten to twenty years to allow the wild vegetation to regenerate, then come back and clear and farm it again. This results in minimal effort for the food produced but requires a great deal of land per capita. In regions with too many people, this method does not work. Crop rotation—in which one crop helps fertilize the land after a previously different crop was harvested—replaces the long fallow periods. Finally, in areas of high demand and dense populations, crops are grown every year and the fields are fertilized.[3] This results in the greatest environmental impact. To put it simply, the greater the social complexity, the greater the number of people that can be supported per acre. Tribe-level societies may stay in a long-fallow-periods farming mode, while states often are in an every-year-with-fertilizer mode. Complex societies are more likely to cause erosion, silt up rivers, denude hillsides, overgraze, and eliminate wild animal and plants.

Another apparent "benefit" of complex societies is actually a detriment in regard to environmental impact. Both chiefdoms and states were able to take food from one place and move it to another—thanks to improvements in technologies and organizational structure as well as the ability to specialize. Although draft animals and large boats played a part in this coping mechanism—for example, ships loaded with grain from distant parts of the Mediterranean fed Rome—the ability of the strong central leadership to insist that farmers give up a large portion of their harvests was key. Some of this transport involved moving food from the producers to the elite, who used it for themselves, their retainers, and specialists. This ability to move edibles around could also help to feed the population in regions where there was a local shortage.

To the extent that this system of food transport worked, the chiefdom's or state's overall population would increase, because the local population need not starve if crops failed. However, this seemingly beneficial mechanism in fact backfires. In state-level and chiefdom-level societies, actual declines in diet have been discovered, as well as declines in forestation from overharvesting and declines in soil fertility because of salt buildup and lack of adequate fallow times. The large population densities made possible by complex societies pushed them inexorably closer to the absolute limits of the carrying capacity and brought about faster declines in the local ecology. Though this phenomenon is observable throughout the world, the case of Easter Island is perhaps the most graphic known.

Easter Island is one of the most isolated spots on the planet. Now part of Chile, it is located in the South Pacific, more than twenty-two hundred miles from South America and more than eleven hundred miles from Pitcairn Island, which itself is in the middle of nowhere. Measuring only eleven miles long and encompassing sixty-two square miles, Easter Island was first colonized by Polynesians (probably originating near Tahiti) sometime around A.D. 100 or 200. Even though the island was probably initially populated by just a few boatloads of settlers, they had a tradition of chiefdom society. Based on a considerable amount of archaeology undertaken on the island and oral histories obtained from the few surviving inhabitants, we know that the population soon grew and a traditional Polynesian chiefdom organization prevailed—with temples and elite residences. The monumental architecture the Easter Islanders built are the world-famous giant stone statues, termed moai.

During the first few hundred years of settlement, early Easter Island had an adequate agricultural potential, and the sea provided additional resources. Pigs had not survived the first settlers' voyage, and animal protein was available only from chickens, sea bird eggs, and fish. Over the years the population grew to a possible peak of twelve thousand people, and, as expected, along with that growth negative ecological impact followed. The island's resources were overexploited. All the trees on the once significantly forested island were chopped down, as known from the remains of ancient peat. Then the tailspin started. With the trees gone, there was no wood to make fishing boats. Without boats, the people couldn't fish, which reduced the sea as a source of food—not very good for an island surrounded by thousands of miles of water.[4] Even more significantly, clearing the land subjected it to erosion, moisture was not retained, and the wind was not blocked, resulting in reduced yields.

The population of Easter Island must have become extremely stressed and warfare must have been intense. Early European visitors relate how obsidian spear points littered the ground, and the remains of cannibalism have been found archaeologically. Archaeology and oral histories reveal that the social order collapsed, the great statues were deliberately knocked down, massacres occurred, and the population stabilized at a much lower level, to perhaps to about 25 percent of the peak.[5] After the ecological stress and resulting conflict, the population numbers were so small on Easter Island that the social group was not really organized as a chiefdom anymore. By the time Jacob Roggeveen arrived, on Easter Sunday 1722, the islanders no longer built monumental statues and were described as a war-torn and debilitated society. Or, to put it differently, Easter Island as originally found had the ecological potential to support a large population that could be organized as a chiefdom. Yet the inability to keep the population at an appropriate long-term sustainable level resulted in environmental degradation, causing a sharp decline in the population to levels that could be sustained by the then stressed environment. The lower population levels could support only more tribelike organization.

Similar sequences have been repeated in a number of other places around the world, many of them on islands, which are confined environments. It's much easier to cause extinction of a species on islands because they are relatively small and offer a much reduced likelihood of refugia where small pockets of endangered animals can survive, as the buffalo did in North America. Dwarf elephants were extincted on Santa Rosa Island off the coast of California, and dwarf hippos, elephant, and deer were extincted on the Mediterranean islands of Cyprus, Crete, Malta, and Sardinia. Most of the extinctions on islands were the result of farmers, but some were caused by foragers and others were due to the behaviors of complex societies, so all types of societies were capable of such severe ecological impact.

Even on larger islands, like New Zealand, such behavior occurred. When the Maori landed in A.D. 800, there were at least eleven species of moa and fifteen other flightless bird species, including a giant rail, ducks, geese, and crows—the largest being the moa that stood fifteen feet tall.[6] The remains of the butchering and cooking of moa, piles of thousands of bones, are common archaeological finds in New Zealand, and the bones carbon-date to the times soon after the Polynesian chiefdom societies arrived. These huge birds were so intensely slaughtered by the Maori that soon, probably in a couple of centuries, all were extinct. This elimination of a species occurred so rapidly that the Maori must have been aware of what was happening. Clearly, no successful effort was made to prevent it.

There have been numerous other extinctions, particularly of animals, in the recent past in which the people killing the last wild specimens realized they were doing it, or at least knew that the population was nearing extinction when they killed the last animal. Such recent extinctions include the quagga (a type of zebra), the Atlantic gray whale, the dodo, and the Japanese sea lion. For the extinction of the great auk, we even know it was the fishermen Jon Brandsson and Siguror Islefsson who killed the last two birds and smashed their single egg off the coast of Iceland on June 3, 1844. The Merriam's elk, native to the Mogollon Mountains of southwestern New Mexico, was known to have been very rare for at least a decade when in 1890 Spense Hill was proud to have killed the last cow ever seen. It is amazing to us today that any humans would do this, but it has happened repeatedly.

Another good example of the rising threat to the environment as societies became more complex is the Bronze Age in the Aegean. New crops, olives and grapes, and new technology, bronze, resulted in population growth and rising social complexity, a process that began by at least 5000

The chiefs of Hawaii built great stone-walled enclosure ponds to raise mullet. In spite of the apparently boundless ocean, these massive constructions were needed to feed an ever-increasing population. Isolated islands provide a test of human ability to live in peaceful ecological balance. Surrounded by unlimited ocean and ruled by leaders that could enforce population control, such islands might be predicted to have been sites of peaceful societies living in a bountiful "Garden of Eden." Instead, the inability of even these very powerful chiefs to control population growth eventually led to large-scale warfare on the islands.

B.C. Prior to 3000 B.C. there is little archaeological evidence of warfare or social stratification in the Aegean. Apparently, for a while, things went well in the region. For many hundreds of years, the new crops and technology were able to support the growing population. Then, beginning with the Bronze Age, things changed.

The Minoan civilization, centered on Crete and famous for its great palace of Knossos, held sway over the Cyclades Islands of the Aegean, from 2100 to around 1500 B.C. Though I do not believe the Minoans were completely peaceful, neither were they holed up in incredible fortresses with warfare as a dominant theme in their art or leadership. Some sites were fortified and bronze daggers were in use, and some Minoan murals show armed men. The Minoans were replaced (some scholars say conquered) by the Mycenaeans from mainland Greece around 1450 B.C. The Mycenaeans *did* live in fortified strongholds—for example Mycenae, Tiryns, the Acrop-

olis in Athens, etc.—and are best known from the Trojan War. Their fortified palaces had walls built of stones so large that later legend claimed they
were constructed by Cyclops, not men. The largest fortress, Gla, had almost
two miles of such walls. Some of these walls were twenty feet wide at the
base, and some, including those on the Acropolis, are still standing twenty-
five feet high. Their elite tombs were filled with men decked out in armor
and weapons. Clearly, the Mycenaeans were a war-leader-dominated society
if there ever was one.

Archaeologically, the Aegean region appears to be a picture of fairly
good ecological balance for a time, but around 1450 B.C. we begin to see
the good times run out, and fortified cities and warfare become the dominant form of social organization. During this long history, the Aegean Sea
region became ecologically devastated. The once green islands and mainland Greece and Turkey were turned into barren rocks, and vegetation was
cut down or eaten away by sheep and goats. Finally, over a period of about
fifty years, between 1250 and 1200 B.C., fortifications were improved, but
the palaces were soon all destroyed, some by catastrophic fires, and the
entire Aegean was plunged into a "dark age." While scholars have proposed many different explanations for these events, from this distance it
looks like a classic case of overexploitation of the region, coupled with considerable population growth, followed by an increase in warfare, then system collapse.

The list of complex societies that flourished, exceeded the carrying
capacity, and then crashed is long; humans are supremely capable of fouling
up their environments. This examination explains how the rise of complex
societies made things worse, not better, from an environmental viewpoint.
This ecological overtaxing occurred despite the greater ability of societies
with central governments and strong leaders to perceive the problems and
despite the governments' and leaders' increased power to control such problems. Examples of "maxed-out" complex societies are found over the entire
world and are hardly restricted to Western societies.

Another piece of evidence about ancient states illustrates just how frag-
ile they were. Had these very complex social organizations been able to control population and stay well below the carrying capacity, I would expect
them to have been able to cope with climatic events much better than less
complex societies, because of their ability to store great quantities of food
and distribute it in times of need. But this is not the case. Archaeologist
Brian Fagan has recently summarized some very convincing ideas about
how past El Niño events could have worldwide impacts and that they
brought down various states, including those of Egypt, the Classic Maya,

and the Moche of Peru. El Niños are not the only form of climate change, and shifts from warm to cool have been implicated in the demise of the Greenland Vikings, the collapse of the northern portion of the Roman Empire, and others.[7]

The incapability of complex societies to live in long-term ecological balance is, once again, inextricably tied to a group's inability to control its population growth. Larger, more intricately organized societies have all the same population issues as tribal farmers and bands of foragers—with the addition of the central authority trying to impose its will upon the situation. The significant difference involves the social complexity itself. With states come cities that have a major demographic impact on the organization as a whole; different regions within these large societies are linked together and resources can move around; there are new technologies that allow for much of this ability to transport food, build cities, and so forth; and there are also much greater disparities in the amount of food different segments of the society get than ever before. All these factors greatly compound a chiefdom's or state's ability to affect population growth. The elite has new tools to use to control growth, but the complexity of the problem, and their inability to recognize the problem, severely limits that control.

A few additional factors often came into play, including infanticide. With chiefdoms, the practice of deliberately killing or abandoning babies seems to be similar to tribes and bands. Infanticide was a socially acceptable practice that the larger society essentially stayed out of.[8] Infanticide was not always common, because additional children were sometimes very valuable in chiefdoms. In many situations there was a limit to the number of children a family could support, given that land was limited, and one sex or the other was preferred.

With the evolution of state-level societies, as always, things got more complicated. Infanticide was practiced in the ancient states of Rome and Greece and in more recent times in Europe, as well as China, Japan, and India, with estimates of 10 to 25 percent of all births being affected from various countries. As discussed earlier, this level of infanticide is a continuation of that found among foragers and tribal farmers, where even very small-scale societies, such as the Australian Aborigines or Eskimos, had equivalent rates to those found in many states. Some states officially outlawed the practice of infanticide, but it continued under disguised forms. In England prior to the establishment of the previously mentioned foundling hospitals in the mid-1700s, many abandoned infants were raised in workhouses. In the thirty years after 1728, of five hundred thousand abandoned infants in England, less than 40 percent survived to age two.

These numbers do not include the thousands killed by being given drugs, like the opiate laudanum, being "overlain," or being abandoned outdoors. In spite of these shockingly high numbers of deliberate infant deaths, in Europe from 1750 to 1850 the population doubled. A similar official concern with infanticide, which was in contradiction with actual practice, existed in the Tokugawa era (1603–1868) in Japan.[9] Evidence for female infanticide, or the undernourishment of female infants, at the state and chiefdom level is widespread. When the census data record three hundred to four hundred boys for every one hundred girls under one year of age, as was known for parts of India, female infanticide was taking place. Skewed sex ratios are also known for China and Japan. When the proportion of boys continues to grow after the first year, undernourishing female children can be assumed. It is hard to tell how much of male and female infanticide was being employed, because these statistics record only how much *more* female infanticide took place than male infanticide, not how much combined.[10]

In addition to tacitly condoning the elimination of some infants, many complex societies dealt with their overall population problems with enforced starvation. Once I began delving into life within some of these groups, I was surprised to learn how large a portion of the population lived at a basic subsistence level. Even in European states, the most minor changes in food availability often led to starvation and death for many. People in Europe from the Middle Ages on, unlike foragers, who might starve because of failure to find food in a short period of time, were living so close to the edge of starvation that their mortality rates can be tracked by the price of wheat. In complex societies, the elite have much better diets than most of the population. This is observed from skeletal remains, as well as historical and anthropological information. In Polynesia, the elite had a tradition of being obese and consumed great quantities of food. Though the commoners in Polynesia did not subsist on marginal diets, they consumed considerably less. The differences between the social classes were so pervasive in Europe, for example, that the elite had average life spans almost twice those of poor people, and they were of significantly larger physical stature. The malnourished adolescent poor of late eighteenth-century London were so short that only two societies in the world, the exceedingly impoverished Lumi and Bundi of New Guinea, were shorter.[11]

A complex society's "central authority" could exert influence in the matter of marriage and the formation of households. In some cases, such rules were deliberate acts intended to slow the population's growth rate. In Europe, records from the eighteenth and nineteenth centuries indicate that some marriages were occurring when women were older than normal, greatly reducing the possible number of children each could bear in her life-time. Elite women at this time were married by age twenty, while the poor, when they did marry, averaged closer to age twenty-five or twenty-six. Even a five- to six-year delay would have a significant effect. The ultimate form of such a social rule, or a common consequence of it, was that a significant portion of the society might never marry. Domestic servants and nunneries for women, and the army and navy for men, became mechanisms by which this was accomplished. In France in the late 1700s, only 40 percent of men ever started families, and 30 to 40 percent of childbearing-age women were unmarried. On the other hand, the elite might encourage population growth in order to have more men for the army.[12]

The persecution of witches in Europe in the 1500s and 1600s had sig-nificant demographic impact on the population growth of the day. It has been estimated that more than half a million people were killed as witches during this time, almost all of them women, which accentuated the demo-graphic impact. Marvin Harris and Eric Ross argue that this sudden attack on women, sanctioned by the state, occurred during a period of famines, which correlated with the cold of the Little Ice Age.[13]

Another significant difference found among complex societies is birth rates. Individuals' circumstances vary much more in complex cultures, and, consequently, the desire for children is more varied. For subsistence farmers in complex societies, the benefits of children are every bit as high as they are for farmers living in tribes. Children in state-level societies can work in factories or cottage industries. Family size in rural Ireland, for example, was very sensitive to the availability of work other than farming.

The city is almost *the* defining characteristic of that most complex of societies, "civilization." Cities are demographically unique. For most of human history, cities were demographic sinks—they lost population. This was true in the Old World and New and for many different countries.[14] Urban residents had few children, and lack of sanitation and crowding encouraged the spread of disease on an unprecedented scale. In the seven-teenth, eighteenth, and early nineteenth centuries, London had a death rate twice as high as its birth rate and existed as a city only because tens of thou-sands of people annually migrated in from the countryside. In fact, states can almost be considered nothing more than cities surrounded by farmers, with the farms providing the food and people necessary to maintain the cities. This is almost a self-perpetuating cycle: As the city folk make tools and improve the technologies that make the farming more efficient, more people can live in the city instead of farming, and the cities grow. To some

The site of Cahokia in Illinois was the largest town in North America in A.D. 1100, and contained the fourth-largest pyramid in the Americas, the top of which probably served as the residence of the ruling chief. The core of the town was surrounded by a massive fortification wall studded with defensive bastions. In spite of its great size, the town had been attacked and parts of the wall burned, requiring its rebuilding.

degree, this process solves the resource/population pressure found among farmers.

In cities, children are a burden. Space is expensive, food is expensive, and productive jobs for children can be limited. There are more productive jobs for women in cities, so having children costs them the lost opportunity of that work. The result is that, on average, families are smaller in cities. The Industrial Revolution accelerated this process, leading to a "reproductive revolution," when individual families began choosing to have fewer children.

Perhaps no example of recent population growth and subsequent decline in a complex society has been more intensively studied than the Irish potato famine of the nineteenth century. The theories about what actually happened are almost as numerous as the scholars who have studied the tragedy. Rather than redissecting this catastrophic event in detail here, I will make a few key points relevant to this discussion.[15] The arrival of the potato in Europe from the Americas in the late 1500s had a great impact on the food supply. In the right climate, as in Ireland, a family could subsist on much less land by growing potatoes rather than cereal grains. This new diet was not all that healthy, but it was nourishing and led to rapid population growth. Ireland's population numbered just over two million people in 1627, three million a hundred years later, and almost seven million people by 1821, not counting emigration. In short, Ireland's population more than tripled in fewer than two hundred years.

Regardless of just why the population grew so fast, by the 1800s most of the Irish were on the margin of survival in terms of diet and wealth. Then, the potato crop was hit by a fungus, the potato blight, that destroyed the crops in 1845 and 1846. More than one million people in Ireland starved to death and another million emigrated. At the same time, the English continued to import great quantities of cattle, pigs, and wheat from Ireland. In other words, the British elite let the Irish peasants starve. The blight also hit other parts of Europe and England, such as Cornwall, also with devastating impact.

Actually, the population growth in Ireland was a particularly dramatic example of what was happening all over Europe. With the introduction of potatoes in the north of Europe and corn in the south, the peasantry all over the continent was able to expand. During the one hundred years between 1750 and 1850, the European population grew from 140 million to 265 million. Though some of this increase was due to better medicine and sanitation, and perhaps better transport of foods between regions, certainly new, more productive foods—an increase in the carrying capacity—resulted in a great increase in people. However, a large proportion of them were living at a bare survival level.[16] Since the European peasants must have been at the subsistence level initially, increasing the carrying capacity did nothing to eliminate the problem over the long term. The Irish or other peasants could not fight each other for food, nor could they fight the elites. Similar famines, accompanied by major population declines, took place in other states around the world and in other times, with the state preventing the peasants from competing for resources.[17]

Such curtailment was far from perfect. In feudal Japan, for example, between 1603 and 1868 (the Tokugawa era) more than one thousand eight hundred peasant uprisings are recorded. Some were small, involving only a few peasants, but many involved twenty thousand or more peasants, and one uprising engaged two hundred thousand. At least some of these incidents correlate with famines, including those of the years 1783–1787 and 1833–1837, at the same time taxation extracted a large proportion of the harvest. The Japanese population grew very slowly, from twenty-six to thirty million over more than a century, and ever more marginal land was being brought into production. This implies that a significant portion of the Japanese peasantry was at the nutritional margin for survival, and it is not surprising that uprisings were common, but the elite was never really threatened by them. In Europe, there were five hundred insurrections in Aquitaine between 1590 and 1715. In Lyons, one out of three years had a "disturbance," which was generally unsuccessful and often violent. Similar uprisings can be found in many other states—but, with the arguable exception of the French Revolution, the elites were not deposed. From all this evidence, it is clear that state- and chiefdom-level societies tried to impose rules slowing growth. They condoned infanticide, had large cities that functioned as population sinks, and enforced starvation. Yet they were unable to achieve ecological balance more effectively than less complexly organized societies. With the rise of the complex societies come new social mechanisms but no practical success.

Complex societies were hardly peaceful—now or ever—and, once again, ecological imbalance leads to conflict and warfare. One clue to understanding complex-society warfare involves how such groups became complex in the first place. At the core of this complexity is the uneven balance of power found within all chiefdoms and states. The supreme chief, pharaoh, or city council—whatever the central leader or government is called in a complex society—has the power to exert control over the masses, and at some point, force becomes involved. What has to be considered is why people are willing to surrender individual status and power to a single leader or elite group in the first place.

Social mechanisms undertaken to keep large societies together might be perceived as good for all involved, bringing rapid benefit to many people, once put in place. These mechanisms include systems or procedures to settle land disputes; organizations to put on large, entertaining public displays; or mandates to ensure the gods will intervene or be placated. Once an individual is born into such a society, he or she has little choice than to go along with such an unequal situation. But that still doesn't explain why people who are roughly equal to each other—people who live in tribes—knowingly give up that equality and turn their lives over to others, the chiefs and state leaders. I believe the answer revolves around homeland security. Members of complex societies trade their power as individuals for group protection. By giving an individual member of the group strong authority, he (or she) can be a much more effective wartime leader than one who must lead by consensus building. Once given such power, the leader may well try and maintain the power and pass it to his children, thereby institutionalizing the power. What may begin as emergency power can be converted into full-time, hereditary power. What started as an egalitarian society may, after needing to appoint a strong war leader, become a complex society with chiefs whose power extends into all domains. An essential component of the evolution from egalitarian to complex societies was fallout from competition over scarce resources.

Imagine several societies situated in the same region. Each is a tribe with weak central authority and leaders who have very limited ability to make the people around them do anything. Now imagine these groups in conflict with each other, as they invariably would be most of the time. In tribal-level societies, warriors tend to be rewarded (and perhaps feared) by the members of their own group; in this case assume that one warrior in the tribe is feared enough that he is able to force some level of real obedience to him from the rest of his social group. In a time of crisis, a combination of fear of this warrior and fear of losing the conflict may well bring about such a shift. If the group gets behind a clever and experienced warrior, this may well give the tribe the edge and it might defeat its neighbors or even a couple of neighboring groups.

Now, since for well over 99 percent of human history societies were organized as bands and tribes (more egalitarian societies), most of the time once the fighting was over, or once this leader tried to take advantage of his war-leader position in other ways, his leadership role would be taken away or diminished. However, if conditions were right (for example, if there were enough people who feared a continued threat from still other groups, or if a war leader had a very strong or charismatic personality), the leadership role could "stick"—at least long enough for the population in general to experience the immediate benefits such a central individual might create. For instance, one benefit might be that the unused no-man's-lands that separated the small competing polities would, under central leadership, be available for farming, providing an instant increase in the carrying capacity. If these benefits lasted long enough, and people perceived that these benefits derived from the existence of this particular individual, the new leader could begin to institute an ideology for inheritance and the sanctioned right to lead (and to gain benefit from being a leader).

This scenario illustrates how warfare, under the right circumstances, could lead to leadership taking on a new social-organizational level. And once in place, it's very hard for any group to revert to egalitarian organization, especially if, in the process, its neighbors also developed social complexity. In that case, any group that shifted back to a tribal society would be greatly disadvantaged and most likely quickly conquered and incorporated into the larger chiefdom, once the transformation to the more complex chiefdom-level social order takes place and "sticks." There are a few places where archaeology provides a hint of just such scenarios really happening. One of these is the most famous of all the ancient civilizations.

Africa's Nile River flows out of the highlands of Ethiopia and Sudan into the vast Sahara. This was not a region in the Old World where plants and animals were initially domesticated, but rather a place where early farmers eventually became established, using the classic crops and animals: wheat, barley, goats, sheep, and cattle. The Nile floods annually, adding both silt and water to the land, then it recedes, allowing time to sow and harvest before it floods again. The flooding is predictable, although it does vary from year to year. This is an optimal regimen in which to farm. By 5000 B.C., the banks of the Nile were lined with farming villages. By 3600 B.C., some of these villages became walled towns, and not much later these were consolidated into clusters of towns with empty zones between them. The archaeology shows that these polities were organized as chiefdoms. At this time, we begin to see some of the iconography of Egyptian leadership that was used for millennia in murals and stone sculpture, including a ruler depicted smiting enemies or sitting on a throne under an awning. Over time, what appear to have been tribally organized villages became consolidated into a string of chiefdoms along the Nile. The process probably involved conquests of villages by groups with increasingly strong leadership.

This situation of independent polities, situated along a stretch of river and encompassing a number of villages or towns, each with a political center, must have been stable for some time because it appears they were the basis of the forty-two nomes, or administrative provinces, of pharaonic Egypt that lasted more than two thousand years. In Upper Egypt, an area of more limited potential for expansion than Lower Egypt's exceptionally fertile Nile Delta, warfare among the nomes led to one group gaining dominance over all the others. The process probably involved dominance over one adjacent nome, then another, and so forth, but our collective knowledge is too scanty to see the process in detail.

Exactly what was happening in the much more fertile region of the Nile Delta also is not clear, whether the groups consolidated into one polity, or remained divided into several. Either way, the Upper Nile polity defeated Lower Egypt's Nile Delta, either at once or piecemeal, and for the first time, around 3050 B.C., there was one leader of the entire Nile. This process of Upper Egypt taking over Lower Egypt is well recorded in artifacts dating from near that point in time. The famous Narmer palette, a slab of slate more than two feet tall with scenes carved in relief, shows the leader of Upper Egypt dispatching an individual from Lower Egypt with his mace. He is also shown reviewing the bodies of the defeated, who, incidentally, have been decapitated. Another fragmentary palette of the same age shows a series of walled towns being attacked by a coalition of forces, but whether this represents the conquest of the north by the south, or an earlier stage in the process of consolidation, is not clear.[18]

We do know that by a series of steps, villages were consolidated into chiefdoms, then consolidated into a large polity, which finally assumed control over the entire reach of the Nile. Once under single rule, no threat from outside the immediate region could take on the entire Nile Valley. External peace prevailed and the Old Kingdom was ushered in, at around 2680 B.C. The role of pharaoh was defined, and deified, and not long afterward the pyramids were built. One can envision the great social benefits of this consolidation: the use of previously unavailable no-man's-lands for agriculture, the reclamation of marshes for additional fields by means of mass labor, the ability to move food supplies, and the ability to store food in case of bad harvests. These accomplishments must all have resulted in unprecedented improvements in the lives of the ancient Egyptians.

Unfortunately, there is no direct evidence on demographic growth at the time, although it has been estimated that Egypt's population grew by a million people during the next few centuries. As expected, things eventually soured in the Old Kingdom. According to a tomb inscription of Ankhtifi, a governor in Upper Egypt, ca. 1250 B.C., "All of Upper Egypt was dying of hunger, to such a degree that everyone had come to eating his children...."[19]

After about five hundred years, the Old Kingdom collapsed with strife, civil war, famine, and plundering. Consolidation worked wonders, but a stable situation was not developed. Within Egypt at this time (2134–2040 B.C.), and even much later in the New Kingdom (1550–1070), the archaeology shows that there were forts or fortlike constructions in Egypt proper. Some are clearly forts, while others, such as Meninet Habu at Thebes, have been termed palaces, but they have high walls and well-defended gates, and some have bastions. We do not know whether these strongholds were constructed to guard against peasant revolts or perhaps against internal nome-leader-led power grabs. Egyptian civilization seems to have been born through conquest. Ecological balance was not maintained, and periodic internal strife and political disintegration were part of the historical pattern.

In Mesoamerica, an almost identical series of events occurred, but on a much smaller scale, between 1000 B.C. and A.D. 200. Thanks to extensive long-term research in the area by archaeologists Kent Flannery, Joyce Marcus, and their colleagues, a great deal is known about the development of

This 1700s etching of a chief in the Southeastern United States being carried in a litter is typical for chiefdom social organization. In chiefdoms, hereditary elites had power of life and death but were never able to control population growth.

social complexity in Oaxaca.[20] The valley of Oaxaca is situated within the mountains formed by the coalescing of two long mountain chains some 250 miles south of Mexico City. It consists of three long valley "arms," each with fertile bottomlands and each the locus of some of the earliest farming villages in Mesoamerica (dating to 1700 B.C.). Over time, these villages grew in size, and some became regional centers with temples and large, elaborate houses for the elite. The once tribal Oaxacan farmers evolved into chiefdom-like societies, and there is evidence of warfare among the different polities in the valley. Just as in Egypt, each arm of the valley was slowly incorporated into larger polities, until finally it appears there were no more than three political entities, all in competition with each other. All three were separated by their own no-man's-lands, which must have been unusable because no sites are found in them. One must assume that crops were being destroyed, and the general strife was a drag on farm productivity.

Sometime around 300 B.C., one polity stole a march on its competitors. Abandoning its villages in one arm of the valley bottom, this group resettled on the hill now called Monte Alban. This large new community, perched on an eminence rising some one thousand three hundred feet from the valley floor where the three arms of the valley come together, was terraced with house sites and became home to more than five thousand people. A portion of the hill was fortified with a wall almost two miles long. Since the entire society's population lived in one place, they were too numerous to be attacked successfully by any other community in the valley and more major fortifications were not needed. The residents of Monte Alban had the military advantage. They could attack any other smaller community with impunity until they had conquered the entire valley. Soon after, around A.D. 200, the consolidated polity with strong leadership, now known as the Zapotec civilization, began to expand out of the Oaxacan Valley and conquered or dominated much of the southern highlands of today's Mexico.

Although the Egyptian and Oaxacan consolidations did not occur in a vacuum—some charismatic and effective leaders were probably required to pull off these conquests—it's easy to see how similar the process and the benefits would be. Once the entire Oaxacan Valley was under the control of a single polity, there would have been no need for no-man's-lands, no need to suffer the periodic destruction of crops. In addition, the expansion of the state into new areas would have allowed for the migration of people and the removal of still more no-man's-lands. For some period, perhaps even a couple hundred years, there certainly would have been great benefits to consolidation for the society as a whole. From archaeology, we know that the Zapotec elite did attain a status of kingship and that the great ceremonial center of Monte Alban continued to be expanded over many centuries.

As the many early written accounts of ancient conflicts and heroism on the battlefield clearly show, the rise of social complexity results in more organized and intense warfare. Even though the strong central authority of a chiefdom or state can force people to starve and keep them from fighting in times of stress, competition between leaders and warfare itself can be a major avenue to increased status, resources, and power, giving the leaders of these much larger social groups new motivation to make war. Consequently, chiefdom warfare tends to be much more episodic than conflict among bands and tribes. Once chiefdom-level societies are organized, very large groups—for the first time what can legitimately be called armies—are engaged, and warfare becomes much more intense. The most notable differences between the warfare staged by these three levels of societies is found in the amount of labor chiefdoms put into defenses and the ability to achieve real conquest. Tribal farmers would defend their homes by constructing wooden palisades, or by building their dwellings next to each other to make a defensive wall with the exterior walls. With chiefdoms, the magnitude of these fortifications becomes impressive. The hill forts of Europe, New Zealand, and Peru, and the massive earthen walls built around towns in China, are the most striking examples of such major warfare-related public works.

With band- and tribal-level warfare, one group will replace another over time, and/or small amounts of land will change hands. Rarely are the vanquished incorporated into the conquering polity at that social level; the defeated are killed or displaced. And the pace of band- and tribal-level warfare is slow. It may take many generations for replacement of one people by another over even a few dozen square miles. All this changes with chiefdom-level warfare. The vanquished are not necessarily eliminated; instead they are incorporated into the conquering polity. In fact, the polity size grows as a consequence of chiefdom-level warfare, as in the rise of pharaonic Egypt.

There is also an evolution of attitudes toward war and enemies as tribes and states evolve. Tribes do not take prisoners, and war is very personal. A member of a foraging band or a tribal farmer considers the enemy his personal adversaries. The competing group has more than likely killed a relative or close neighbor, and you likely saw them do it. This is what makes it so very personal. Moreover, you know that if you are victorious and capture them or let them live—in short, do not kill them—they will sooner or later regroup and try to kill you. While among tribes, enemy women and some children might be taken captive and allowed to live, very rarely are men ever taken captive—except to be publicly killed later, often including torture.

This personalization of tribal-level conflict contrasts sharply with state-level warfare. Most state fighting is conducted by conscripts, and the opposition is usually perceived to be other conscripts who need to be defeated, not personal enemies who must be killed at all costs. Although certainly state-level conflict can sometimes get very personal, more commonly it is perceived as state versus state, and the actual fighters on both sides are considered to be "just doing their jobs." Therefore, states take prisoners and do not kill the leaders of the defeated side. While there are war crimes trials in state-level conflicts, these proceedings are most often held for individuals who broke the conventions (sometimes horribly) of warfare, especially for those who deliberately killed civilians. Such trials are not held for vanquished fighters just because they lost.

However, there is no concept among tribal farmers, foragers, or even most chiefdoms of letting the defeated enemy just go home. Even with all the viciousness and hatred generated by the Second World War, most of the German and Japanese generals simply returned home afterward. As civilized as those of us who live in state-level societies consider this practice to be, it can be totally misunderstood by people coming from a tribal or chiefdom tradition of warfare. Letting defeated enemies like the Taliban or Saddam Hussein simply go home (and sometimes remain in power) must strike them as bizarre. They must think they fought people who did not consider war very real, or lacked an understanding of how real warfare is fought.

One unexpected consequence of chiefdom-level conflict is that warfare becomes less of a controller of population. Though warfare may seem more terrible as a group's social and technological complexity develops, the opposite is actually true. As societies become more complexly organized, the "common" people—or those of the lowest status—become pawns of the social elites. Increasingly often, those of lowly status are more valuable when they are alive and adding to the chiefdom's economy, than dead. The tribal warfare of attrition becomes replaced at the chiefdom level by episodic pitched battles, with many men, but few women, being killed, and incorporation rather than extermination a result of defeat. With chiefdoms, the total deaths due to warfare actually decline. Single battles can kill large numbers of participants: For example, Maori or Zulu battles could result in 10 to 15 percent casualties for the victors and 20 to 40 percent for the losers. Yet estimates of per-capita annual battle deaths among these more complex groups are around half of those suffered by the New Guinea high-land tribes in their conflicts.[21]

Even after successful war at the chiefdom level, there may still be subsistence stress for some percentage of the population, but this stress is unevenly distributed. The vanquished group or groups will fare the worst in the new balance of power. Those of the lowest classes, but who rank within the victorious group, will perhaps come out of the conflict a bit better off, but not necessarily much. The victorious chiefs, by incorporating the defeated into their own social groups, will have even more people to draw upon for food and services, better cementing their chiefly position and power.

A few well-understood examples, drawn from archaeology, ethnography, and early historical accounts, provide the flavor of complex-society warfare. Polynesia, for instance, was not influenced by Europeans until the 1700s, and it provides excellent evidence of chiefdom warfare. Other early chief-doms developed in sub-Saharan Africa and in Southeast Asia. In these areas contact with state-level societies, both European and Chinese, occurred for a long time before detailed accounts of these chiefdoms were written, so the nature of indigenous warfare is difficult to interpret. We do know that prior to European impact most of the South Pacific islands had large forts often perched on high ridges, and actual battles occurred involving armies numbering in the hundreds if not thousands. On some islands, the Marquesas, for example, the topography consisted of deep, easily defended valleys radiating from the central mountains, making it difficult for a chief to control more than a single valley, and the edges of each small territory were heavily defended. On the other hand, where the topography was flatter, as in Tahiti or Hawaii, once one chief had more territory than the others, he could slowly but surely defeat the smaller chiefdoms and then control an entire island. One leader rarely controlled a large archipelago, like the Hawaiian chain, because he lacked the ability to move a large army over water.

There is an exception to this pattern. In Tonga, located deep into the South Pacific not far from New Zealand, the high chiefs of one island were able to conquer their entire island group, and a unified kingdom or chiefdom emerged. The leaders then built fleets of great war canoes, actually catamarans, that could carry up to 150 men each and were propelled by sails and paddles. These large catamarans were so fast that they could sail circles around European ships under full sail. Individual Tongan canoes were named and some became famous, very much like the battleships of state-level societies. With these fleets, the Tongans took command of the seas and had the ability to move large numbers of men to key locations. For example, they conquered Samoa, which had a much larger landmass and population, and also held sway over the outlying islands of Fiji.

No one knows exactly why the Tongans were better at creating a navy than their competition. The canoe builders were part of the high chief's group of experts. Since Tonga was long controlled by one ruling family, this may have aided their ability to amass resources for the development and construction of these great vessels. The consequences of these Tongan naval campaigns represent a great change from tribal warfare. When the Tongans conquered Samoa, they did not slaughter the population or drive them out as tribes would have. Instead, they made the Samoans pay tribute, in the form of food and rare and valuable items, to the Tongan high chief.

The Americas present additional information on chiefdom warfare. The people of North America's Northwest Coast, including such groups as the Tlingit, Kwakiutl, and Nootka; the people of the Southeast, such as the Creeks, Cherokees, Natchez, and Choctaw; and the people of Central America, the Caribbean, and northern South America were all organized as chiefdoms. All these groups had forts and defended towns—and the ability to amass large armies.

The Spaniard Hernando De Soto's account of his 1540 expedition into North America is a particularly rich source for evidence of early chiefdom warfare in the region. After his party landed in Florida and traversed the South, eventually crossing the Mississippi River, De Soto's army encountered great palisaded towns that were variously allied and warring with each other. The Spaniards found buffer zones between these polities that no one was able to live in and reported that the chiefs were able to amass hundreds, if not thousands, of men to fight. Much of the same is known from early accounts of chiefdom-level warfare in Colombia and other Central and South American areas, including early accounts of the Cauca and the Tairona of Colombia, and the chiefdoms of Panama. In particular, the Cauca amassed twenty thousand combatants, led by war leaders decked out in gold, to meet the Spanish invaders. When the Cauca were fighting each other, they employed palisaded villages and hilltop forts, and kept great stockpiles of weapons and food in preparation for military campaigns. They waged battles that lasted several days, they burned towns when they were successful, and the victors displayed trophy body parts and skulls on stakes.[22]

Similar aspects of chiefly warfare can be observed at the great site of Cahokia, located just to the east of present-day St. Louis, Missouri. The largest archaeological site in the Americas north of central Mexico, Cahokia was part of what is now termed the Mississippian Culture. This society populated the eastern United States, spanning the regions of Illinois, Tennessee, Alabama, Mississippi, Arkansas, and parts of other states. In addition to Cahokia, numerous Mississippian ceremonial/political centers dotted the landscape from around A.D. 1000 until the coming of the Europeans, although the period from 1000 to 1200 was the peak of the numbers and sizes of these settlements and polities. Although many Mississippian towns had significant ceremonial centers composed of large pyramids that were usually well defended, Cahokia was the greatest town; indeed, some archaeologists consider it a city. Today a state park preserves this early American culture.

A dense population of at least ten thousand people populated the immediate area around Cahokia, which featured the largest pyramid north of the Temple of the Sun in Teotihuacán, Mexico, the fourth largest pyramid in all the Americas. There were more than one hundred other pyramids within the city core, some used as burial chambers and others as platforms for the houses of the chiefs. Scholars know Cahokia from more than fifty years of scientific excavations by a variety of university and government archaeologists, including a number of digs resulting from the encroachment of roads and recent urbanization.[23] Mississippian leadership was strong. The elite lived on the tops of the pyramids, and they were buried sumptuously, some with sacrificed retainers and bushels of valuable objects. Less than ten miles away from Cahokia, under what is present-day St. Louis, and farther downriver, were similar but smaller towns. The great public works, precincts for the elite, and the lavish burials show a chiefdom, which fits with the De Soto–Spanish accounts from the 1500s of similar towns encountered in Mississippi and Alabama.

The center of Cahokia was surrounded by a palisade with bastions jutting from massive walls, built with large posts and then plastered. The palisade was rebuilt at least three times and destroyed by fire at least once. High densities of arrowheads near the walls confirm at least one major attack. The other nearby large towns also had palisades. Even the greatest chiefdom of North America was not immune to attack, presumably by other nearby chiefdoms, who must have formed alliances against Cahokia in order to produce such a large army.

There were probably so many thriving chiefdoms in the Americas because chiefdoms are hard for states to conquer. When a state conquers a state, it is relatively easy to replace one bureaucracy with another, even when the social groups involved are radically different. For example, when the Spaniards conquered the Aztecs or Incas (one state-level society overpowering other state-level organizations), they were able to replace the bureaucracy and exploit the lower classes. With chiefdoms, the political organization is too closely tied to the social system itself to be taken over intact. When the state imposes itself on the chiefdom, the social system often collapses and with it the ability to manage the people. In places like Fiji or Hawaii, the chiefdoms continued to compete with each other after European incursions, but using Western weapons. The result was population decimation and a collapse of the overall structure of the social systems, and the replacement of the indigenous population, not its subjugation. This is what happened in the Caribbean with Columbus, the Southeastern and Northwest Coasts of the United States, and the Philippines. When the previous social systems were left more intact by the conquerors and exploitation was more indirect, the chiefdoms survived longer, as in parts of Polynesia, Africa, and Southeast Asia. Thus, colonial-indigenous warfare took on various forms depending on the circumstances and was different from the indigenous chiefdom warfare.

Though palisades were a common form of defense among chiefdoms, the hill fort, like the one I climbed to in Peru, is the most dramatic and obvious. Archaeologist Tim Earle has coined the term "hilltop chiefdoms" to describe the global cases of chiefdoms whose settlements focused on hilltop fortresses because of intense warfare. In the small Santa Valley of Peru, archaeologist David Wilson found sixty-two prehistoric forts in an area of only 275 square miles, most on hilltops.[24] Along the northwest coast of the United States, hilltop and promontory forts become common around A.D. 1300. In Europe, the Iron Age chiefs built them with multiple earthen walls and ditches, the most famous being Maiden Castle in England. I was unaware of just how common such fortresses were until I began doing research for this book and discovered that there are more different types of forts in Samoa than in almost any other Polynesian society. I was never shown one of these forts while I lived there, nor did I hear anyone talk about them. The Samoans seem to have "forgotten" about this aspect of their past.

With chiefdom-level warfare, conflicts evolved from encounters in which almost all adult males were fighting into military events involving specialized warriors. What might be considered "armies" in modern times are found at chiefdom-level warfare, and people, as opposed to land, become the spoils of war; massacres are few. The chiefs may change, but the communities continue and chiefdom-level conflicts result in some elites being replaced by other elites. At this social-organizational level, wars are being fought for the benefit of the elite, rather than the people as a whole. Warfare does not disappear with the advent of chiefdom society; it intensifies—and it changes form.

State-level war continues these trends. Since most state-level societies had writing, the conflicts that immediately come to mind are those that are most eloquently recorded: Greek versus Greek in the Peloponnesian War, or Greek versus Persian in the Persian wars of Darius and Xerxes, Roman versus Gaul in France, even the Aztec conquest of much of Mexico and the Inca conquest of Peru. Even more closer to the present day are the incessant wars of Europe of the last few centuries, the Napoleonic wars being one of the best-known examples.

Warfare at this social level consisted of massive building efforts, from fortified cities, some still in use during the Napoleonic wars, and huge protective walls, to huge fleets of boats, chariots, and cannon. Massive walled cities date back to ancient Mesopotamia. The recent British consumed great quantities of the empire's resources building and maintaining a large fleet, as did the Romans and Greeks. The Chinese not only built miles of walls to defend their state borders against outsiders, but when China was not under complete central control, many large cities were fortified, just as in Europe, Mesoamerica, India, and the Middle East. In China, walls were constructed by pouring wet adobe into wooden forms, much like we pour concrete today, then pounding the adobe to force out the water and make it rock hard. The forms would be raised and the process repeated for the next course of the wall. The resultant walls surrounding a city were wide enough for chariots to be ridden on top.

Almost all ancient states were involved in enough warfare to be recognized archeologically, including the many states of China, the Middle East, Mesoamerica, and Peru. Of all these ancient states, only two have ever been proposed as major exceptions to this universality of state warfare: the Classic Maya and the Harappan society of Pakistan. Although fortifications were known from Maya cities, most archaeologists ignored them and saw the Maya elite as peaceful priests. During the last two decades, scholars began to decode the Mayan glyphs, discovering that they are all about wars, conquest, and the bloody sacrifice of defeated leaders. Renewed efforts by archaeologists have found much more evidence of fortifications, sacked cities, and the like among the Mayas. History now has one less "peaceful" state.[25]

The Harappan civilization of the Indus Valley, the heart of present-day Pakistan, which dates to 2500–2000 B.C., is much more difficult to figure out. Archaeologists have uncovered a significant amount of evidence that, to my way of thinking, belies a peaceful situation. For example, we do know that some pre-Harappan sites were fortified, contained burned layers, and seem to have been replaced abruptly by the Harappan culture.[26] The two largest cities of the Harappan civilization, Mohenjo-Daro and Harappa, had citadels with massive walls of fired brick, bastions, towers, defended gates, and parapets. The stronghold at Harappa was 1,300 by 650 feet in area with a wall height of thirty-five feet, and some exterior defensive walls have been found. Other Harappan sites also had defensive walls or citadels. Recovered copper and bronze weapons include spears, swords, arrowheads, possible battleaxes and mace heads, and many additional recovered mace heads are made of stone. Clay sling missiles are common, and a large pile was found on the citadel parapet at the site of Mohenjo-Daro. A number of bodies that were not properly buried but lying in jumbles were found in a dozen different places in the topmost layer of the site.

The Harappan society ended abruptly, possibly due to environmental degradation.[27] Pollen studies and other evidence indicate that over time more and more of the area's riverine forest was cut for farmland and to fire the millions of bricks used in construction. Intense grazing also denuded the landscape. When the land was denuded, there was less vegetation to control the Indus River floods, which led to building flood works, which, in turn, required more bricks and more wood to fire them. This looks like a classic case of population growth and environmental degradation. As chronicled in the *Rigveda* and other Vedic literature, the millennium just following the demise of the Harappan civilization was marked by considerable warfare. The above evidence undercuts the notion that the Harappan civilization was formed in a peaceful way, or existed as a peaceful state, or declined in a peaceful way. It was no more immune to the problems of increased population and its impact than any other state. The Ganges civilization that ultimately followed the Harappan civilization in the Iron Age consisted of at least sixteen competing kingdoms. Many of these city-states were centered on fortified cities having massive stone or mud-brick fortifications, and one city is known to have been surrounded by a fortified wall measuring more than three miles in circumference. South Asia was not spared state-level warfare.

State-level warfare requires that much larger amounts of resources be devoted to the overall effort. In terms of the fighting forces alone, there is a shift from every available man, and some women, joining the fray, accompanied by minimal labor investment devoted to fabricating weapons and mounting fortifications, to an entire class of people working to build forts or ships, cast cannon, fashion suits of armor, or maintain fighting horses, with relatively few men actually fighting on the battlefield. The state-level armies of medieval Europe, approximately thirty thousand men, were no larger than the Egyptian state armies of two thousand years earlier. Such an army, when drawn from a state's population of even a few million, was actually minuscule when compared with a tribe fielding more than 20 percent of its total population for battle. The Inca conquered the entire Andes region with an army of fewer than fifty thousand men. It was not their numbers, but their organization, that enabled them in A.D. 1450 to take the Peruvian hilltop towns like the one I climbed into thin air to reach.

From all accounts, the fatalities suffered in battle were a relatively minor factor in most state-level warfare. A few thousand deaths at Agincourt were insignificant on a total population basis. Certainly 25 percent of fighting-age men never died from warfare in state societies—never was as much as 25 percent of the population engaged in state-level warfare.[28] Even in the most violent epochs in Western Europe or Aztec Mexico, less than 5 percent of the population died from warfare, but more and more of the "civilian" population was indirectly affected by warfare between states.

During the Napoleonic wars (1799–1815), for example, battlefield deaths were still relatively small. At Waterloo, probably the most lethal battle, 48,500 men were killed or wounded out of almost 200,000 soldiers engaged. Less than one-tenth of 1 percent of the adult males of Europe were killed at Waterloo. Nevertheless, over the course of his fifteen-year campaign, Napoleon Bonaparte was responsible for the deaths of more than three million people—including those who died from starvation or disease due to his scorched-earth policies or societal disruption. Even three million fatalities is a relatively small number, compared to the two hundred million humans living in Europe at the time, especially when the deaths occurred over a period of more than a decade. In spite of the enormous numbers of people killed in the First and Second World Wars, the proportions killed, when compared to the overall populations of the countries involved, were still much smaller than the percentage of combat fatalities suffered by many tribes. The twenty million Russians, including combatants and civilians, and the five million Poles killed during the Second World War began to reach levels associated with the 10–20 percent warfare deaths found in tribal-level societies, but no other countries came close to these losses of about fifty-five million people killed out of a combined population of over a billion people involved in the war. While the deaths in Russia and Poland were very high for a six-year period, they were followed by a generation of very low warfare deaths, so on a generational basis the war deaths are a fraction of those known for many tribes.

This evidence from many time periods and locations around the globe points to a distinct pattern as societies gradually became more and more complex. Beginning around seven thousand to eight thousand years ago in the Middle East, and soon thereafter in other places, as social groups grew larger, strong hereditary leaders emerged and chiefdoms came into being. Specialist military personnel and equipment, as well as particularly powerful or charismatic warriors who evolved into paramount leaders, became more common. The transition from tribe to chiefdom was probably the result of war leaders taking permanent power. Later, these chiefdoms transformed themselves into state societies—civilizations—with warfare as a major component of the process. This led to the famous early civilizations of Teotihuacán in Mexico, dynastic Egypt, the Shang Dynasty of China, and the city-states of Mesopotamia.

Conflict waged by complex societies resulted in a new twist. Warfare was controlled by the elite, and wealth and prestige began to play a role. The commoners became valuable as a means to supply wealth to the elite, so warfare began to include conquest instead of annihilation as a goal. Plenty of people were killed in conflicts among chiefdoms and states, but the proportion of the population directly involved in fighting, and the proportions killed, was greatly reduced.

In contrast to what was actually taking place through time, the changing nature of warfare influenced our attitudes toward modern wars, making us

The ceremonial center of Cerro Sechín on the Peruvian coast was one of the earliest large complexes in South America dating around 1500 B.C. A procession of hundreds of victorious warriors and their captives carved in bas-relief lined the walls of the major precinct. This captive has been disemboweled, with his intestines falling out. Elites all over the world recorded their power and conquests so that their subjects, allies, and potential enemies all were reminded of their military prowess.

perceive them as being more deadly than they were in the past. Part of this confusion is a result of differences of time scale and the frequency and intensity of military clashes. Tribal and chiefdom wars were short affairs. No side had the capability of sustained and continuous military operations. There were certainly long periods of conflict—tribes were usually under threat of conflict, and even Europe had its Thirty Years War. However, these wars were all episodic in nature. Battles might be fought only at certain times of the year, last a few days at best, and several years might go by between clashes. Wars in the past were not like the experience of the English or the Germans during the Second World War where there were six years of continuous conflict involving much of the societies' resources. Moreover, nation-state wars can be so protracted and involve so many people and countries that their residual effects can be long-lasting. Some argue that the Second World War was a continuation of the First, and the ongoing conflict in the Middle East is a result of the breakup of the Ottoman Empire after the First World War and the Holocaust of the Second. The present political instability of Afghanistan is the result of the Russian-instigated Cold War conflict there.

This long duration of "modern" warfare need not be universal. After the overwhelming experience of the First and Second World Wars, modern states went back to the more episodic warfare found in the past. In another hundred years, I think the perception of the Cold War will be that it was a forty-year-long episodic conflict, with long periods of positioning and maneuvering punctuated by intense fighting. Because of atomic weapons, the situation was too dangerous for either state to confront the other directly, so the conflicts were localized. Today, we identify them as individual wars—the Korean War, the Vietnam War, the war in Afghanistan—but these engagements are better seen as massive multiyear battles, and the Berlin Airlift and the Cuban Missile Crisis as skirmishes, probing for weak points—all within the Cold War.

Far more profound than the changing nature of modern conflict are new human-ecological relationships. Up until the last century or so, even though more of the world became incorporated into nation-states, and overall this process of increasing social complexity changed the nature of the relationship among population growth, carrying capacity, and warfare, it did not eliminate the problems humans faced. Members of complex societies had the same need to live in ecological balance as did the inhabitants of egalitarian societies. Although the elites in chiefdoms and states may have tried to control population growth and build public works to increase the carrying capacity, nothing was effective for long. The greater technological ability resulting from more people and more specialists led to increased environmental degradation. Despite the additional means complex societies had to control growth—whether by design or by accident—it never seemed to happen.

Until the twentieth century, no complex society, either chiefdom or state, was able to stabilize its growth at a level that allowed it to weather minor food-provisioning problems without some segment of the population suffering death. The population would always grow, something would go wrong, and the chiefdom or state would crash, then recover, and so on. With tribes, these swings in population seem to be minor and more regular. With more complex societies, bad times seemed to be of a greater magnitude and are spaced further apart. This phenomenon probably occurred because bigger societies result in bigger, slower swings. Complex societies had, and continue to have, the ability to recover from population declines. Chiefdoms or states, in which most of the population were farmers, tended to grow whenever the chance became available.

With chiefdoms and states, societal control became great enough that subsistence stress, either chronic or episodic famine, did not lead automatically to competition between people within the large polities. Disease, malnutrition, and starvation began to play an increasing role in dampening population growth among these larger societies. The development of cities, which were population sinks, was another factor that slowed growth, but such factors failed. Environmental degradation was even more pronounced with states, due to greater numbers and improved technology. Consequently, continued growth and environmental impact resulted in significant segments of the complex societies' populations living on the subsistence edge, followed by high death rates. Any negative changes in climate only aggravated the problem.[29]

Basically, complex societies are ecological disaster areas and are unable to control their population sizes with respect to resources. That being the case, one would expect horrific warfare to be the result, as one state or chiefdom tried to take resources from another. However, this is not what we find. High levels of conflict are observed among most chiefdoms, but warfare among states actually is less intense and less demographically relevant than for foragers and tribes. There are a number of explanations for this phenomenon, but one is simply that people living in states will starve before they fight because the government won't allow them to fight. Moreover, such great crises as famines and other disasters knock the state's population back down to a sustainable level, so the problem is periodically—though only temporarily—solved.

Finally, there is the problem of definition. Peasant uprisings or feuding can be seen as warfare within a state. Looking only at warfare that occurs between states could miss this point. Yet a person living in a state-level society had much less chance of dying from riots, feuds, or external war than an individual living in most tribes, forager bands, or chiefdoms. As

violent as states are, part of the inherent violence is removed—or "cush-
ioned"—by chronic undernourishment and the consequent deaths among
some portion of the state's population. The average commoner in a state-
level society was far more likely to die of malnutrition or outright starvation than expire on the battlefield. Even though modern state-level military
encounters may seem more frequent, in the perspective of history, they are
much less frequent.

By the eve of the Industrial Revolution, most of the world's population
was living in complex societies. A few foragers still were residing in very
marginal places, and most of those who had previously been tribal farmers
had been incorporated into nation-states. Similarly, by the 1800s, almost
all the chiefdoms had been swept away. Warfare had become highly profes-
sionalized, and pre–Industrial Revolution state-level warfare, instead of
becoming intense and devastating conflicts, was actually having a much
smaller impact on the overall society than ever before in human history.
The rise of complex societies began to change the six-million-year-old
equation of population growth, resource stress, and warfare. This change
still resulted in much suffering, but the formula had indeed been altered.
The Industrial Revolution once again changed the equation, ushering in the
most dramatic transformation in the last twelve thousand years—and perhaps in all history. In the next chapter I consider whether this new equation
finally provides a formula for peace and ecological balance.

chapter eight

WAR OR PEACE FOR
THE FUTURE?

Today's world is hardly peaceful. Almost daily we are confronted by the prospect of terrorist attacks, civil wars, and the threat of major clashes among states—including the horrible possibility of nuclear warfare. Millions of people have been killed during multiyear clashes in the last century, civilians have been massacred, and genocides carried out behind the clouds of war. Many assume that war has never been more prevalent or more deadly than it is today. Yet much of our perception of present-day war—or even the notion of why we *have* wars—fails to see warfare in proper perspective. Many "modern" civil wars are actually old tribal wars that never ceased and have just been resurrected in a nation-state context. Sad to say, the act of massacring civilians is as ancient as war itself. A study of warfare and coming to grips with past encounters, however unpleasant, can do more than simply illustrate where modern conflicts fit along a continuum. The past can help us to understand the basic nature of warfare as well as to put the present and future war in perspective. One important observation about the present and the recent past is that pockets of peacefulness have been identified throughout the world. Understanding these peaceful societies provides insight into why humans do and do not have warfare.

My most recent archaeological work in the American Southwest has involved studying prehistoric murals and painted pottery created by the ancestors of northern Arizona's Hopi. Many of the murals I'm studying came from ceremonial rooms at the great prehistoric town of Awatovi, which was occupied from the A.D. 1200s to 1700, situated on Antelope Mesa just east of the present-day Hopi community. The modern Hopi probably live the most traditional lifestyle of all the North American Indians, and many continue to live in stone houses perched on top of mesas overlooking vast expanses of the Arizona desert. They still actively practice their traditional religion, which involves the men of the community partic-ipating in ceremonies in underground rooms, called kivas. Organized into societies, Hopi men also perform public ceremonies in the town plazas, the famous Hopi kachina dances. The kachinas are best thought of as spirits of the deceased and are central to the Hopi religion. They come to the towns to bring rain and benevolence, and are impersonated by the men in the kachina societies, who wear masks and garments depicting the different kachinas in a variety of ceremonies and observances held throughout the year. This tradition goes back hundreds of years, and elements of it are clearly depicted in the Awatovi murals.

This current research project is collaborative, and I work closely with a number of Hopi colleagues. We often talk about the present as well as the past. When these conversations take place on the mesa and we're sitting around the kitchen table in a stone house that could be hundreds of years old, eating mutton stew and paperlike corn *piki* bread, I feel as if I've been transported to a totally different time period. At times like these, my Hopi colleagues, who are fully aware of my interest in past warfare, seize the opportunity to point out how peaceful the Hopi are. They often remind me that the very word *Hopi* means "peaceful people." And they are absolutely correct: The Hopi are incredibly peaceful!

For example, in the late 1800s, the people of the Hopi town of Oraibi got into a serious dispute, in large part instigated by the behavior of the U.S. government, and the community split into two factions. There was a great deal of tension, people were extremely upset, and it was decided that one faction would have to leave the village permanently. Deciding which group should go and which should stay was a terrible dilemma. Leaving their mother village is probably one of the hardest things a Hopi would ever willingly do, because the ancestral home of each lineage and clan has strong religious and emotional ties. If there was ever likely to be a time of violence among the community, this was certainly the occasion. The decision was made—not as the result of a bloody brawl but by a tug-of-war! This is a concept of peacefulness rarely seen in the world.[1]

Remember, though, this peaceful resolution to a very contentious situa-tion occurred relatively recently, not in ancient times. Many of the scenes in the prehistoric Hopi murals I'm studying at Awatovi depict weapons, war-riors, and the resultant dead. The same Hopi who explained what the word *Hopi* means also tells of violent episodes in the past when entire villages were destroyed. According to their vivid oral traditions, many generations ago massacres and raids were launched on the neighboring Navajo—and even on the Hopis' now close friends, the Zuni. In fact, Hopi oral history recounts how the Hopi town of Awatovi was destroyed by other Hopi in the winter of 1700.

I see no contradiction between what the modern Hopi know and what their oral traditions and legends portray. The Hopi of eight hundred or five hundred or even three hundred years ago were actively engaged in serious and deadly warfare as known from archaeological and historical accounts. Great warriors were respected and given special privileges. For the most part, the Hopi were successful. They defeated neighboring people and were not conquered or forced to flee their homeland—during prehistory or in the historic period. Yet the Hopi for the last 150 years have been peaceful. This apparent paradox raises the broader question of whether any peaceful societies ever *did* exist in the past. If, as I've set out to show, our past was riddled with continuous warfare, the prospect of finding some peaceful societies somewhere would provide a ray of hope that humans are not obsessed by or somehow programmed to attack their neighbors and take over their land. If any noncontentious social groups can be identified, the question is how they were able to live without conflict while most others were not.

This also raises the specific question of why the Hopi changed from a society with warfare to one so peaceful. The Hopis' transformation from a group that engaged in regular and deadly warfare into a peaceful and peace-loving society is interesting but is not very instructive as an example of why societies become peaceful. The transformation occurred in an impacted environment. From the mid-1800s on, the United States Army enforced peace in the Southwest. From that time, the Hopi were not allowed to, nor did they need to, engage in intense warfare to survive. By the late 1800s, this was the case over all of North America.

Other especially intriguing examples of peaceful societies have been identified from various parts of the world. In fact, anthropologists have searched for peaceful societies much like Diogenes looked for an honest man.[2] They have tried to find a pattern in why some groups are peaceful. They have questioned whether some types of social organizations or certain kinds of resource bases lead to peacefulness. In spite of the presumption that most societies were peaceful in the past, anthropologists have had a lot of trouble finding ethnographically known peaceful people. Despite all the effort that has been devoted to the search, the number of what can be considered classic cases of peaceful societies is quite small, including the Copper Eskimo, the closely related Ingalik Eskimo, the Gebusi of lowland New Guinea, the African !Kung Bushmen, the Mbuti Pygmies of Central Africa, the Semang of peninsular Malaysia, the South American Sirionó of

Amazonia, the Yahgan of Tierra del Fuego, the Warrau (Warao) of the Orinoco Delta of eastern Venezuela, and the Aborigines who lived along the west coast of Tasmania. Actually, some of these same "peaceful" societies have extremely high homicide rates. Among the Copper Eskimo and the New Guinea Gebusi, for example, a third of all adult deaths were from homicide. This might be explained by the fact that among small societies almost everyone is a relative, albeit a distant one. Naturally, this raises some perplexing questions: Who is a member of the group and who is an outsider? Which killing is considered a homicide and which killing is an act of warfare? Such questions and answers become somewhat fuzzy. So some of this so-called peacefulness is more dependent on the definition of homicide and warfare than on reality. In fact, some of these societies did have warfare, but it has usually been considered to be minor and insignificant.

At one level, the particular examples of peaceful societies on this list and their subtleties are irrelevant. Anthropologists have studied more than a thousand societies throughout the world. Even if every one of this handful of groups was actually peaceful, the numbers would not be very encouraging. However, the *reasons* these groups might be considered peaceful can reveal a great deal about why societies in general are—and are not—peaceful.

This short list of so-called peaceful societies does not represent evidence that human social groups have been able to live peacefully for any extended period in the past, because most of them became "peaceful" only relatively recently. In the majority of cases, either the group's population had been decimated and the survivors were then living far below the carrying capacity, or they had received such useful technology that the carrying capacity grew markedly. As was often the case, both factors occurred at the same time. So, consequently there was plenty of food and no reason to compete for it. In a few other situations, a modern state imposed peace upon a group, as in parts of highland New Guinea, or the "pacifist" society was really part of a larger social group, and this larger group was the entity that did the fighting, as with the Mbuti and Efe Pygmies of equatorial Africa. What is known about these "peaceful societies" is almost always the same: The societies that are considered peaceful today were not peaceful in the past, and they have almost all undergone the same transformation in their lifestyle.[3]

The Siriono are a good example of a social group whose numbers were so decimated by the time they were studied in 1940 that they were living well below the carrying capacity of their Amazon environment. They were so peaceful, anthropologists noted, that when threatened, the Siriono moved away from their enemies. Yet this extraordinary coping mechanism must be examined more closely. First, a group has to have a lot of land at its disposal to be able to isolate itself in this way. Evidence shows that many people in the Amazon were decimated initially in the 1600s and 1700s by European disease, and then again in the 1900s by intertribal warfare when some groups in the area obtained shotguns while others could not. The fact that the Siriono group studied by anthropologist Allan Homberg numbered only a few hundred people in 1940 points to such a situation: Their own reduced numbers were at that point living in a depopulated area, free of most human competitors, because all the neighboring social groups' populations had also been depleted. The Siriono existed well below the carrying capacity, and I would expect to see little conflict in their recent past, which is exactly what was found by the anthropologists.[4]

The Warrau of Venezuela are a good example of new technology altering the carrying capacity. The Warrau appear to have been pushed into very marginal swamp areas by their notoriously expansive and aggressive neighbors, the Caribs and Arawaks. The arrival of the Spaniards altered the equation. The Warrau, who previously had to eke out a precarious living in these marginal areas, obtained metal tools, especially axes. This made creating dugout canoes and fishing much more productive. The Warraus' vegetal staple was the pith of a palm tree, which involved cutting down and splitting open entire trees, chopping out the pith, and processing it. Steel tools must have made this task much easier. The vast swampland of the Orinoco Delta suddenly became a productive place, and the Warrau were well below capacity when described in the late 1700s and 1800s.[5]

An interesting group of peaceful societies that became that way only because the traditional human-resource balance had abruptly changed is found in the Plateau region of North America. The anthropological literature considers this area—centered on present-day eastern Washington and Oregon, and parts of Idaho and British Columbia—to be a good example of a region without warfare in the past. Scholars have considerable detail about the history and prehistory of societies in the Plateau and in particular several adjacent groups that occupied the Southern Columbia River–Frazer Plateau. There are accounts dating to the early 1800s and careful, detailed ethnographies of the related but politically independent groups the Sanpoil, Okanogan, Wenatchee, and Chelan. These accounts describe people without war or enemies, with ample food, living a life marred only by the coming of the European settlers: "The Sanpoil, at the geographic center of the Plateau, emphasize no other value in life more than pacifism. . . . Warfare is virtually unknown to them and has been since time immemorial. No living man can recount an instance of conflict even from traditional history."[6]

The land in this region is not lush, and subsistence for the foragers dating to the 1700s and early 1800s was based on gathering roots and hunting, with some fishing supplementing the diet. There is no reason why the Plateau people should always have been peaceful, based on their way of life or their environment—or the social groups living around them. Those groups, including the salmon fishers of the Northwest Coast and the Plains buffalo hunters to the east, were certainly not peaceful in the 1700s and 1800s.[7] What possible set of circumstances would have allowed the "peaceful" foragers of the Plateau to remain that way, living as they did between such contentious neighboring groups as the Spokane, Coeur d'Alene, and Nez Perce to the east and the Coastal Salish to the west? Archaeology provides key information in resolving this dilemma. Although the amount of archaeology undertaken in the Plateau area is far less than for other parts of the United States, the evidence for prehistoric warfare is unmistakable.[8]

In one study, sixteen prehistoric burials in the Plateau were carefully examined for evidence of violent death, and the remains included men, women, and children. Three-quarters of the bodies showed evidence of violent deaths, including mass graves; eight victims had projectile wounds or arrows found within the body cavity, and some remains had previous wounds the individuals had survived.[9] Equally relevant are the archaeological discoveries of defensive sites, constructed of low rock walls on mesa tops, that are at least two thousand years old. Archaeologists have found evidence of Plateau settlements situated on high places with steep sides that are made further defensible by walls. These sites are prehistoric and fit patterns of what defensive sites look like in other parts of the world. From an archaeological point of view, I would never reach the conclusion that the Plateau was a uniquely peaceful part of the world.

This evidence of a violent prehistoric past can be reconciled with the Plateau's peaceful historic period by noting the consequences of the direct, as well as the indirect, impact of Europeans on North America. Neighboring native groups on both sides obtained metal tools, guns, and horses. The Plains Indians—the Blackfoot, for example—received tools and guns from the French and later from English and American fur trappers, while groups on the Pacific coast, including the Coastal Salish, received them from whaling and fur-collecting ships from the eastern United States and Russia. These groups began to encroach upon the Plateau area. As seen in many parts of the world, European diseases and depopulation reached the Plateau long before the accounts of the 1800s were written. The new tools and means of obtaining food eventually reached the declining Plateau people, effectively increasing their productivity and the land's carrying capacity.

When all the evidence is examined, it shows an initial prehistoric pattern of warfare extending from the Pacific coast to the interior desert, incorporating the vast Plateau region. When the population in the Plateau declined in the early historic period, and carrying capacity increased due to the introduction of horses and metal, warfare declined. This occurred so early on that by the time ethnographic accounts of the Plateau people were recorded in the 1800s, there was little if any memory of the true aboriginal situation.

The sequence of events on the Plateau illustrates how the lack of evidence for warfare in the ethnographic record is not necessarily an indicator that intergroup conflict was insignificant in the past. More important, it's easy to see how a region that had experienced considerable warfare in the past could quickly turn peaceful. The area's inhabitants, like the Hopi, would perceive themselves as having "always" been peaceful. Among the Plateau people, once the survival needs of warfare had disappeared, there was no inherent desire to kill outsiders, and no religious beliefs or social institutions existed that caused them to be perpetually warlike. Warfare was necessary for survival early on, but when conflict was no longer needed for survival, it ended.

More evidence that conflict can end among people who have had a long history of intense warfare comes from social groups that have had peace imposed on them by an outside force. In New Guinea, for example, the transition from intense endemic warfare to enforced peace was extremely rapid. The young boy in the 1960 anthropological documentary film *Dead Birds* lived in the highlands where warfare was deadly and a daily way of life. In fact, his young playmate was killed in an ambush while the film was being made. As a grown man today, he is probably living in the same region but driving a four-wheel-drive Toyota and raising coffee for the world market. Right after peace was forced on them by colonial governments in the 1960s, the New Guinean people were very happy. Ethnographic studies showed how much they had been terrified by their conflict-riddled way of life and hated the constant, endemic war that had surrounded them. With new technology, new crops, and the like, the carrying capacity was raised, the need for war was eliminated in most places, and the people of New Guinea were able to be peaceful. The groups' previous need to kill for revenge and to appease the ancestors was quickly replaced by the recognized overwhelming benefits of peace.[10]

And look at the Yanomama, the "fierce people" of the Amazon rain forest, famous for their violence and deadly warfare. Their villages were always fortified, they left large empty zones between competing groups, and raiding, ambush, and treachery were part of daily life. Today, the presence of missionaries often brings an end to fighting in localized areas, and the Yanomama are happy to stop fighting. They hate war. Given the opportunity—elimination of threat and adequate food—the Yanomama stop fighting right away.[11] When they get guns, utensils, and steel tools, it increases the carrying capacity, as does the ability to trade for food. If no social institutions necessitate warfare, old animosities and needs for revenge are ignored.

Another case of "peaceful" conversion is the Vikings. Beginning sometime around A.D. 800, Scandinavians underwent a great population explosion and began to spread over much of Northern Europe and to raid and plunder as far south as the Mediterranean. The scourge of the Norsemen was deeply imprinted on the English, but the Vikings also captured Normandy and parts of Eastern Europe, all in the most violent manner. Battleaxe-wielding Vikings in their horned helmets are still a common mental image of violent, pillaging, war-loving men. Such violent behavior is no longer displayed among today's Swedes, Danes, and Norwegians—the Vikings' direct descendants. What happened to that Nordic love of war? What happened to the Scandinavian social values and approbation given to successful, violent warriors?

The answer is the same as for the Hopi or the New Guinea highlanders: Just about everything changed over time. Beginning in the 1300s, the Black Death and the Little Ice Age decimated the population of Europe. At the same time, new technologies, like windmills and waterwheels, that increased productivity became increasingly common and widespread. A New World was discovered that was able to siphon off much excess population that did develop and that generated new, productive crops. As with the other examples, Scandinavia's population declined and technology increased the carrying capacity. This was not necessarily a pleasant process, but it did result in a better balance between population and resources.

There are definitely societies around the world that do not have warfare. Many of these groups seem to have switched from war to peace very rapidly—and in many cases willingly made the transition. This transformation need not be an instant process. The Vikings did not become peaceful Swedes in a weekend, and the Hopi didn't translate into the "peaceful people" overnight. Even a couple of hundred years is quick in the overall scheme of things. The anthropological record shows that few societies kept fighting for even that long after the real ecological reasons for warfare ended. This list of so-called peaceful societies includes examples of all the major types of human societies. The Bushmen, the Plateau people of North America, and the Warrau are foragers, while the Hopi and the highland New Guinea groups are tribal farmers. And this same process of transitioning to peace was observed among the chiefdoms of Polynesia and the Vikings. There is no change in the ability to shift to peacefulness as social complexity evolves. Rather, the shift occurs when the ecological relationships suddenly change, regardless of the type of social organization affected.

These "peaceful" societies did not get that way because of new social organizations, new social rules, or new ideas about the goodness or value of peace, or even because of newly devised abilities to live in ecological balance. In all known cases in which ecological balance was rapidly attained, this balance came about from external factors, not from the society's developing mechanisms to adjust the balance. Changes in population have all been due to declines from disease or deadly exploitation by outsiders. Changes in carrying capacity have been the result of new foods, tools, or technology brought in by another society. Even changes in climate have altered carrying capacity. Changes in social behaviors worked out by the societies themselves never seem to be the reasons for the transition to peacefulness.

In spite of the different types of social institutions, new social rules, and new religious ideas that have evolved over the millennia, the societies that developed these innovations continued to have warfare. Such social developments were never able to get and keep groups well within the carrying capacity. Alterations in a society's attitudes toward warfare, ecological behavior, and/or population growth may have occurred under many different types of social systems and many different circumstances, but as far as I can see, based on the archaeology and ethnography, they never resulted in long-term peace.

Although I have explored many of the reasons why warfare has existed for much of human history, I have not discussed the motivations for warfare. Although there is boundless evidence for the existence and centrality of warfare in human life, this could be because intergroup conflict is an automatic human behavior that would exist regardless of the circumstances involved, or because constant warfare is a result of competition brought on by human failure to live in ecological balance. Though some warfare might be the result of survival needs, most warfare might be the result of genetic predisposition, culturally transmitted values that warfare is good, or rewards to great war leaders that have nothing to do with actual survival needs. Many people intuitively assume that some societies are warlike, some individuals like war, and humans or some humans may be predisposed to warfare, and that it is these and not survival needs that are the real motivations behind most human warfare. If this were true, then most of what I have said is irrelevant. If warfare is not caused by competition over scarce resources, then whether or not humans have always been confronted by such scarcity, they would have had warfare anyway. I believe the evidence refutes such ideas. First, if warfare was automatic, conflict would not stop so quickly when factors of population and ecology change. When social complexity increased, warfare would not change in nature. Second, ingrained social behaviors that promote warfare are better seen as the consequences of warfare, not its ultimate cause.

Examining some other possible reasons for warfare helps to clarify the cause-and-effect connection. When social groups have been studied by anthropologists or described in historical accounts, resource competition is rarely the reason given for much warfare—either today or in the recent past. A classic common explanation for warfare is that in forager and farmer social groups, the conflict involved men fighting over women. Closer inspection reveals that this type of warfare actually has a food basis as well. When food is in short supply, as it has been for most of human history, female infanticide is common and usually soon results in a shortage of adult women. Men fight for access to women, raiding and capturing them from an adjacent group being common among foragers and farmers. Fighting over women is easily seen as a consequence of an overall food shortage, when the shortage of food translates into a shortage of women. Though such fighting might appear to be a consequence of males inherently fighting over females, such fighting is related to how plentiful women are. In reality the fighting for women is a consequence of food shortages, for it is then that there are shortages of women.

Other explanations as to why social groups fight often involve revenge, hatred, and the need for men to gain status from warfare. Most people accept these as the common reasons for intergroup conflict—they are reasons often cited by anthropologists, historians, and even reporters. I believe that these explanations are actually societies' responses to needing a will and ability to fight, and should be seen in a larger context, namely, as the consequence of warfare. When warfare becomes endemic, societies that reward and encourage good fighters are more likely to survive than those that do not have some sort of reward mechanism in place. Revenge, hatred of the enemy, rewarding good fighters with prestige or women, and other such behaviors can become institutionalized. The better they are institutionalized, the more effective the society's war potential becomes, along with the group's survival. Social institutions cannot be turned off in an instant—that's the whole point of social institutions in the first place. Even if they could be dropped quickly, it would be dangerous to do so. Just because people have ample food today does not mean they will tomorrow. Whether it's a foraging band or state, dismantling the group's warfare capability because no one happens to be hungry at the moment is obviously a dangerous long-term approach. Several generations of any new situation might go by before such social mechanisms would be gradually and fully dismantled. Since turning off the mechanisms of warfare when they are no longer needed takes time, warfare should continue to happen even if it is no longer "rational" for several generations. Such warfare is perceived—correctly—as "senseless." Its costs to the society are high and the benefits minimal or even nonexistent. Yet the warfare that set up the social and cultural behaviors that cause this "senseless" fighting need not have been senseless in the past.

Such issues have come to a head in the Middle East. Agriculture actually began in the area that is today part of Israel, Jordan, and Syria and the region has been farmed continuously for more than ten thousand years. The invention of horticulture has also been accompanied by thousands of years of competition over land that has become less and less productive. Even today, when agriculture is less important economically than in the past, the population in the Middle East exceeds the long-term availability of water, and there may be an economic component to this ongoing conflict that is not openly acknowledged. Resources have long been inadequate in the region, and still are. Looking at it from a purely resource–population growth standpoint, a long tradition of conflict in the area would be expected and for that reason makes sense.

Yet today the level of hatred and fear on both sides exceeds anything that can be considered rational from a resource competition perspective. The economic value of the land being fought over is minimal compared with the economic cost of the conflict, much less the lives lost. Moreover, these are societies noted for their business acumen and willingness to work hard. If peace prevailed, in today's global economy the entire Middle East could become an economic powerhouse. The fact that the hills are overgrazed and the land incapable of supporting the population is irrelevant. A conflict that may have been deeply rooted in the need to compete for and hold what land one could has now become one based on ideology, not resources. But most of the world is emotionally very involved in the Middle East, and it is hard to put that conflict in perspective. Turning back to history, there are other cases of warfare that started out resource driven and evolved into ideologically driven warfare.

One carefully worked out example of such a lag between changed circumstances and contentious behavior involves an 1857 battle between the Yumans of the Lower Colorado River and the Maricopas, who were living some 150 miles away, not far from present-day Phoenix. Eyewitness historical accounts and the Yumans' own oral histories described a force of more than one hundred Yumans, joined by a number of allies, that set out to attack their traditional enemies, the Maricopas. They marched this considerable distance on foot and caught the Maricopas by surprise. Most of the Yuman allies had abandoned the effort by the time the war party arrived. Due to poor reconnaissance, the invading force did not realize that the Maricopas were living next to a large, powerful group of Pima. The Yumans began killing and burning the Maricopa village, but the Pima soon swept in, overwhelmed the Yumans, and slaughtered them almost to the man as they fled. The Yumans' poor decision making and weak control over their forces are classic aspects of much farmer warfare, but that is not the point here.[12]

An analysis of this encounter begins with the fact that the Maricopas and Yumans lived too far apart to be in legitimate conflict over anything. The Yumans risked, and actually lost, a large portion of the men of their entire community over a fight with "traditional enemies." Oral histories and linguistic analysis show that for the preceding hundred or two hundred years, the Yumans had been engaged in a process of taking over more and more of the Lower Colorado River Valley at the expense of their neighbors. By the early 1800s, they had become militarily dominant in the region, and not long before they had driven the Maricopas from the valley and pushed other groups away from prime farming areas. The Yumans had successfully competed over scarce farmland. By the 1850s, new technology and population decline had probably eliminated the need for such territorial expansion, just as observed for other Native American societies affected by westward expansion.

As an aside, this example points out the importance of no-man's-lands as a means of survival. Though the empty spaces between polities were relatively unproductive, the separation did allow societies to avoid being constantly in conflict. Today, such buffer zones are almost impossible to maintain. In the Middle East or the Balkans, given the military technology, rockets, mortars, and other long-distance weapons, no-man's-lands would need to be far wider than the twenty miles or so typically found for noncomplex societies, or the more than one hundred miles found between the Yumans and Maricopas. Instead, modern adversaries are, at best, only a few miles apart. On a global scale, with today's rapid transportation you can fly across a country in less time than a tribal farmer would need to transit a prehistoric buffer zone. Without workable buffer zones, conflict can become so continuous that the fabric of daily life disintegrates, a situation that cannot long continue.

The important lesson to be learned from this episode between the Yumans and the Maricopas is that it can be understood only in historical context. The Yumans could not have been expected to extinguish all their long-held, highly successful social mechanisms that encouraged and rewarded warfare just because things had recently changed. They embarked upon what appears, in hindsight, to have been a "senseless" military campaign. Surely, many other cases of warfare that do not seem to have logical explanations probably took place before there was enough time for one or the other social group or groups involved to have dismantled such internal social institutions. Apparently "senseless" warfare can have an underlying cause related to past disputes over scarce resources.

When I was in Turkey doing fieldwork thirty years ago, we hired local men to help us dig, as well as wash the broken pottery fragments we found. At one point we had twenty men working, each paid a dollar a day. Toward the end of the field season, it became obvious that after a few more days of washing the last pottery sherds, the workmen would no longer be needed. I still remember the sinking feeling I experienced when I saw the look on one man's face when he learned there was no more work. He was trying to support his family any way he could. It was clear he had no other options, and he slowly, sadly walked away. I wonder about what his children are doing today, having been raised in a land that was overgrazed, overfarmed, and overpopulated. There is nothing to keep them from fighting, and they have nothing to lose.

A study by Canadian social scientists Christian Mesquia and Neil Wiener has shown that the greater the proportion of a society is composed of unmarried young men, the greater the likelihood of war.[13] Why would there be such a correlation? The answer hinges on *why* the young men are not married. The reason is usually that they are too poor to support a wife and family. The idea that poverty breeds war is far from original. However, the reason poverty exists has remained the same since the beginning of time: Humans invariably overexploit their resources and overreproduce, and a segment of the population always winds up on the very margins of existence.

There is plenty of resource-competition warfare today, especially in Africa, but other areas of the world have wars that we presume to be driven by ideology rather than a lack of resources. Yet many of these places have very long histories of degraded or depleted natural resources. Ideologies that promote a "them versus us" attitude are much more likely to take hold in regions where there has been a long history of ecological stress and degradation. The Balkans have had agriculture longer than any other area of Europe, and the Middle East has been farming longer than anywhere else in the world. Chiapas, Mexico, the scene of antigovernment conflict by the Indian population, is an area of early domestication in the Americas. The Shining Light terrorists in Peru have been able to find supporters in a landscape that had also been the scene of very early agriculture.

All these geographic locations have been heavily impacted by farmers for thousands of years—they are all used up. The places where humans have had the greatest amount of time to "foul their nest" will almost always have many more people and a degraded resource base. In today's societies, competition over lack of resources translates into despair and a "nothing to lose" mentality. It should be no surprise that guerrilla warfare and terrorism find support in the regions where poverty is prevalent and warfare and conflict common.

That warfare in the past may have ultimately been driven by a rational response to diminishing resources does not mean that such conflict did not—and does not now—have an emotional component. Even chimpanzees observed in the wild get very excited during an attack and also show clear sorrow when their own are killed. Since killing and dying bring out some of the strongest human emotions, warfare would be expected to be emotionally charged. There is plenty of evidence that in less complex societies emotions over warfare were tempered by reality. Accounts of war councils from people as diverse as those from the mountains of Montenegro to highland New Guinea show that members of these smaller-scale societies assess their chances of success and try to fight only when they think they will win.[14] Just because warfare is emotional does not mean past conflict was not also rational.

In considering the wars of the last few centuries, one might wonder if those conflicts could possibly be driven by ecological imbalance, or be based upon a careful assessment of potential gain versus the consequences of losing. First, many of the "modern" wars around the world are clearly fought over resources and occur in and between the poorest nations, not the richest. The richest nations surely have had horrific wars too. This warfare between modern state-level societies is perhaps the most difficult to explain. It's one thing to see how the 3000 B.C. city-states of Mesopotamia would have had to fight or be wiped out by other city-states—and that growing populations and the salting of fields would have led to food crises, even if peace did prevail in the region for some period of time. It is quite another to see any economic rationale for the First and Second World Wars with their ultimate costs in lives and resources.

Historically, the scarce resource was land, but today that is not true. Just as it is often claimed that the generals fight the last war, the politicians in the twentieth century fought wars for old, no longer relevant reasons. Modern economies are not based on land. Think of the economic success of Singapore or Hong Kong, Japan or Taiwan. If land were the most scarce and valuable resource, a country as small as Japan would never be such an economic powerhouse. Yet Germany was after more land in its invasion of Russia in the Second World War, and Japan felt it needed to control the land of Southeast Asia at the same time. In both cases, the rationale for war was based on an agrarian mentality. In today's world, it's clear that without the land they coveted, both Germany and Japan are economically strong. As we understand today, what they really needed in the 1930s and '40s was markets for what they made—but instead they were killing off their potential customers. These deep-rooted attitudes toward land as the scarce resource continue to today. The Middle East will never feed itself, and the economic future of the Balkans does not rest with who owns the farmland. Yet in both regions, old adversaries are fighting as if it was two hundred years ago and adequate farmland was the key to survival.

Modern complex societies have become so complex, and the perceptions of the leaders and the average person living in these modern states are so divergent, that the explanation and understanding of what occurs in "modern" warfare are quite different than from earlier, less complex social organizations. Yet even modern states have some of the same problems foragers, farmers, and chiefdoms have: Who are our allies? What are our true long-term interests? And just how good is our assessment of our enemy's ability to fight? Every type of society must regularly make these judgments, and they often get them wrong. An Eskimo village can be massacred because the men left without properly assessing the likelihood the community might be attacked in their absence. The Yumans horribly misjudged the military alliance that existed between the Maricopas and neighboring Pima. Social groups in highland New Guinea were constantly trying to assess the reliability of their allies and frequently shifted their alliances. One can easily view the First and Second World Wars as colossal miscalculations of the warmaking capability of potential enemies, of the value of particular allies, and of the long-term natural alliances and shared interests that actually existed around the world at the time. If not the major reasons for these modern wars, such faulty judgments were certainly big contributors.

Assessing the social factors relating to warfare turns out to be increasingly difficult as societies become more complex—and as they do, serious misjudgments become more likely to arise. Since warfare among foragers and farmers was more frequent, those social groups were actually able to assess the overall situation almost continuously. As states began to have less warfare and as the clashes became more intense, the information levels declined and the consequences of judgmental error increased. As groups grow larger and more complexly organized, it becomes progressively easier for warfare to be considered "irrational," based on flawed judgments at the leadership level.

This disarticulation of the populace from the war leadership is probably the greatest structural difference between state war and forager, farmer, or even chiefdom war. Today, not only do a small number of people make the decision to go to war (although in some states there does need to be popular acceptance), but a small number of people can manage the war in almost total isolation from reality. In the past, any chief, or especially any tribal war leader, was an active participant in battle and carefully judged his men for their willingness to participate. There were no mechanisms to coerce participation. Failure to be sensitive to the limitations of your authority was likely to get you deposed, if not killed by your own side.

Also, front-rank fighting leaders existed in many ancient states. Alexander the Great fought at the head of his army and as a consequence had men who were willing to follow him, literally, to what appeared to be, at the time, the ends of the earth. Even in the American Civil War, generals were at the front and often got killed or wounded in battle. These leaders understood the attitudes of their men, and when they made tactical mistakes in battle they died like their men. Over time, war has become much more complex. By the time of the First World War, generals stayed far behind the front and ignored reality, while tens of thousands were killed because of poor leadership. This probably culminated with Stalin and his senior generals and their ruthless and almost total disregard for casualties. This aspect of modern state warfare is hard to comprehend, and it is not a characteristic of most human warfare. In the past, not only did you try hard not to be killed, but you also tried hard not to have anyone on your side killed. The warriors fighting next to you were your relatives and neighbors. Past warfare was not impersonal; it did not appear irrational. It was necessary for survival.

Among foragers and tribal farmers, everyone in a group has access to the same information about the group's strength—and that of the enemy—and this information is assessed collectively. Certainly, errors in these assessments are made, as the Yumans' disastrous attack on the Maricopas shows, but most of the time the frequency of contentious encounters ensures that information about one's enemies and the group's own capabilities was reasonably accurate. And leaders were frequently tested; bad leaders were soon eliminated. In most forager and tribal societies, if the men did not have confidence in the leader, they simply did not participate. Poor leaders were quickly relegated back to the ranks. This changes with state-level warfare. Contrast tribal warfare with Saddam Hussein, the master of miscalculation. Saddam had no ability to assess U.S. and world response to his invasion of Kuwait. There was no consensus building among his army: A handful of men made a phenomenally bad assessment. Invading Kuwait was his second mistake. Saddam had not been weeded out for his earlier, equally disastrous invasion of Iran. No foragers or tribal farmers would have let their leaders behave that way. This disengagement of the decision making from the people who actually do the fighting is what makes modern warfare so terrifying. At the same time that the proportional number of deaths and frequency of clashes have diminished, the ability to act "rationally" has also declined.

The societies that compete are now so complex that it is almost impossible to predict their political reactions to acts of aggression. Political uncertainty, coupled with an inability of the leadership to grasp the technical changes that swirl around us at a faster pace, makes this all even more unpredictable. For example, if Adolf Hitler had waited to wage war until after 1939 and been able to grasp the revolution in physics, the rest of the world might have faced the Nazis with atomic bombs. Now, it is true that both Hitler and Saddam Hussein were and are not sane in some fundamental way, but that only emphasizes the point that the selective process for military leadership has become badly distorted by the nature of modern societies.

Sometimes the failure to comprehend the opposition's political will and new technology works against modern adversaries. Although Osama bin Laden and Al Qaeda may have been a small group of fanatics for whom personal survival held little meaning, that was not true for the Taliban government in Afghanistan. The willingness of that Islamic fundamentalist regime to aid and abet bin Laden was a phenomenal miscalculation. "We defeated the Russians, we don't need to fear the United States," was probably the Taliban's mantra of the day—but they were very wrong. The U.S.-

led allies had a political will the Taliban never anticipated—plus new, sophisticated war technology, and its use was devastatingly effective. The leaders of the Taliban were using the warmaking tactics of tribal farmers and chiefdoms without the traditionally rational and careful decision making accompanied by knowledge of their enemies or the potential consequences of their own acts. Based on these few, sketchy examples of "modern" warfare, one might say that we humans have not lost an inherent peacefulness, but rather have lost, to a considerable degree, a societal-based ability to assess warfare rationally.

Miscalculation is certainly an important component of modern war and why we perceive it to be so irrational, but we are also faced with a hybrid world, a world those of us living in industrial states do not fully understand. Though the current world order appears to be a collection of nation-states, it is not. All parts of the globe have been put into one nation-state or another, but this is a recent and artificial construct in many places. Millions of people are still living in chiefdoms and even tribes, and there is much modern warfare that does make sense when examined from the context of tribes and chiefdoms. These social groups may not look like the chiefdoms or tribes of old, yet they still function much like them. In the past, chiefdoms were organized around strong leaders whose important role was defense against other chiefdoms, and that is what we find today.

Most of the chiefs are referred to as "warlords" in the media, which misses the point. These social units invariably translate into segments of society that have little allegiance to a central government. Instead, these segments focus around a regional or ethnic group that has existed for hundreds, if not thousands, of years. Such societies within societies are led by a group of hierarchically structured "chiefs," the top chief being the "warlord." The warlords do not just conduct war—that is simply the role an outsider sees. They are "the government": In their regions, they settle land disputes, organize public works, and collect taxes or tribute. In Afghanistan, for example, there were media reports that food packets dropped by American airplanes to feed the "starving peasants" were not consumed by the finders but gathered up and turned in to their local warlords. In Somalia, the warlords essentially taxed the distribution of humanitarian relief food in their territories. Everything—all transactions and exchanges—is very personal; there are no bureaucrats. Usually relatives help carry out the orders of the chiefs (warlords). In such "nation-states," the central government usually controls only the large cities and leaves these warlords alone. Lacking any kind of strong central authority out in the hinterlands, these local chiefs embedded in weakly organized nation-states—

Afghanistan, Somalia, or China a hundred years ago—are warlords by necessity. All chiefs compete, they always have, and there is no reason we should expect this to change.

So warlords are really chiefdom-level social organizations embedded in quasi states. Almost always the state was set up by outside powers and is not a fully functional state. The result is a hybrid mess, because such states contain some aspects of more complex social organizations, including bureaucrats and courts of law—but these institutions don't always apply to all parts of the quasi state. The chiefs can ignore the laws and restrict the reach of the bureaucrats. It's no wonder that chiefdoms, and even some tribally organized peoples, that have been arbitrarily lumped into nation-states do not work very well. The buffer zones are removed between competing groups by setting up national governments that presumably provide security, which encourages the buffer zones to become occupied. Sometimes this works and a viable state emerges: India is a state formed from a series of independent polities. Sometimes it almost works: Indonesia is a recently formed state where there are strong separatist movements and regional conflicts, East Timor being the best-known example. For the most part Indonesia is a coherent nation-state. Sometimes, these arbitrary nation-states do not work at all: Yugoslavia and Rwanda had preexisting polities that were incapable of forming viable states. In Yugoslavia, the original political units were strong enough that more realistic states could be structured, resulting in its disintegration and reconstitution into Slovenia, Croatia, Bosnia, and Herzegovina, Serbia, and probably Kosovo and Montenegro. Over time, one can predict that the incorporation of these new states into the European economic sphere will change the centuries of conflict over resources into peaceful interactions in spite of the long-held animosities.

It is not surprising that imposed nation-states work best when the chiefdoms were very complex and when there were already some state functions in place, as in India. In places like Africa, where the organizations were tribal or not very complex chiefdoms, the nation-state has often been unable to provide the security necessary to occupy the buffer zones. When warfare breaks out, it can be severe, as seen in much of Central Africa.

Another aspect of modern conflict is the fact that the basic perceptions of what's valuable and worth fighting over have changed over time. As land recedes as the critical resource and economic interaction becomes vital, conflict will not provide the needed resources—it will diminish them, because much of the present "economic resource" is political stability, rule of law, social infrastructure, and the like. War harms all these. In some parts of the world where poverty is greater and the previous social organization was much less statelike, what is valuable has not changed and the critical resource remains productive land. We should expect warfare in such areas to continue as it has for millennia.

When the industrial world gets tangled up in these quasi nation-states, trouble usually follows. Outsiders tend to want the flimsy central government to take control of the hinterlands, but it cannot, and the rural, more traditional societies are not able to be organized into the state. Control over the hinterlands in such cases has been successful only in places like Pacific Islands, where colonial administrators have let the chiefdoms continue to function. This is how Samoa worked when I was living there, and it was working well. There was no state government in the sense we think of it. The highest-ranked chief was the prime minister, and the "bureaucracy" was the lesser chiefs. New names, traditional system, but it worked fine. In nearby Fiji, the traditional social structure did not remain intact, and the recent political instability is the consequence.

If we look at today's "hot spots," whether Rwanda, Somalia, Sudan, Afghanistan, or even parts of the Balkans, we find chiefdoms, and in some cases even tribal farmers, scooped up into a state but not really part of it. In such regions, traditional, often long-running conflicts already exist, and these disputes are exacerbated by outside influences, often in the form of money and weapons flowing to one chiefdom to the detriment of another, which upsets the old balances of power that have existed for centuries. Any good chief will take advantage of such a situation; that is his job. We don't think it is a nice job—killing your enemies if you can—but if your enemies will kill you as soon as they get the chance, it is rational behavior for the chiefs and their followers. This does not mean that the members of these societies like these situations. They no more like war than the Yanomama do—or we do, for that matter. Yet under the circumstances, when the central government is weak, the safest thing for them to do is to be part of a strong chiefdom. People will fully participate in a true state only when they become convinced it is safe.

Also, remember that tribal and chiefdom societies are not geared for rapid change. When international politics and economics—often oil and drug money—suddenly show up, traditions get out of whack and chaos begins. If the causes of the warfare between the traditional societies still exist, then the ensuing "modern" chaos is an opportunity to begin conflict again.

What can the industrialized states do in these situations? Not much, I'm afraid. Getting rid of the underlying causes—poverty, distrust, and long-term animosity—is a slow process at best. It is probably realistic to accept the social systems for what they are—and that does not mean they are nice or fair—and try and maintain the traditional balances and leadership structure while trying to keep one side from getting an advantage. Simply telling chiefs to behave like politicians of "proper" states is a waste of time.

This simplified analysis of quasi nation-states does not imply that all third world states are tribes and chiefdoms embedded in weak central governments. Many areas of the world, including China, India, Mexico, and Peru, have had social systems that were states for a very long time. Though these countries may have internal conflicts, they are of the kind many states have had, in which the marginalized peasants are close to starving and react with riots or attempts to take resources from other peasants. The conflicts do not arise from local warlords, chiefdom-level leaders, competing with each other. Though true wars between states do happen today, and certainly are a real threat, much of today's violence is actually conflict between warlords, or is a case of peasants fighting peasants in regions where the states cannot control the conflict. These encounters are often described in terms of religious or ideological differences. Those social differences need not be the cause of the warfare, but can be the consequence of centuries of conflict that have polarized the people who define themselves by religion or religious ideology.

Yet ideology is certainly a component of warfare, and in many ways ideological warfare is even harder for us to understand, much less reconcile as rational, than war that results from miscalculation or that derives from social systems that are foreign to modern industrial societies. Ideological warfare is pervasive, and most warfare, regardless of the antagonists, has involved some component of ideological difference. When ideology becomes so intense and dominant, we often fear that nothing can ever restrain or eliminate such feelings and consequent behavior. The beliefs under dispute, whether religious or other attitudes, can be so strong that resources, rationality, and even long-term survival seem to become irrelevant. There is no question of the force such beliefs can have on all sides involved. The question here is whether such passionate reactions evolve from external circumstances or from some deep-seated needs within all of us. These incredibly angry ideologies could have developed as a means to cope with real problems of survival, or they could have developed because humans have become programmed to want to hate and kill.

Considering the length of time humans have been warring and the intensity of this conflict again and again, one has to consider the possibility that humans might be genetically predisposed to warfare. If warfare has been part of the human condition for more than a million years (or six million years, depending on the start date), we just might be selected for behaviors that make us warlike. Six million years of intergroup conflict might result in a human genetic predisposition for love of war. This is a classic "nature versus nurture" problem: How much of our behavior is learned and how much has a genetic basis? Just as an increased understanding of the past—and of our closest ape relatives—can help in grappling with this issue, so does the accelerating unraveling of the human genome sequence. Ultimately, the combination of these lines of evidence will make short work of this question. Since science is not there yet, I will go out on a limb to address it. Not being a geneticist, I am not really qualified to express an opinion. I'll venture out only a bit.

I suspect that there must have been selection among humans for aggressive behavior during the last million years or so. I don't see a genetic selection for making war or for killing people. I do see a genetic selection for more generalized aggressive behavior. This is the argument that primatologist Richard Wrangham makes for chimpanzees. His research has shown that there has been selection for male-dominant behavior among chimps. One aspect of such behavior is the killing of males from other chimp groups, but this chimp "warfare" is carried out by clear and calculated thinking, not by instinct.

Similarly, for humans I would initially assume that males have been selected for aggressive behavior—but genetic selection does not work that way. The issue is not nearly this simple. Genes for aggression might not all be male-specific; both human sexes may have been somewhat selected for aggressive behavior. Such selection would be for many different genes, some perhaps male-specific and some not. In this case males might have been selected for aggression more than females.

Humans have been selected for many different things, and we have instinctive behaviors that may or may not be useful or appropriate in today's world. On the biological side, for example, males have blood chemistry that differs from that of females. Males seem to be adapted to great spurts of excited effort, adrenaline-like behavior, while female blood chemistry is adapted to much more efficient use of energy and more conservation of iron. Since women of childbearing age lose some iron regularly during menstruation, this seems logical. Today, this male blood chemistry is maladaptive. After all, men don't get into fights with cave bears anymore, or engage in hand-to-hand combat too often. A blood chemistry adapted to moments of great physical effort is, in large part, why men have more heart attacks than women. This does not mean that men are doomed by their heritage. By taking aspirin each day, a man can mitigate most of the blood chemistry differences between the sexes. Once understood, the maladaptive blood chemistry can be dealt with by behavior and chemistry. Understanding the differences in blood between men and women and finding a way to deal with them is better than pretending that such differences do not exist.

The same approach holds true for potential genetic aggressive behavior. All humans, especially males, must learn to deal with genetic predispositions that may derive, in part, from millennia of warfare or other causes. For example, humans are probably genetically conditioned to be uncomfortable around strangers, who in the past were very likely enemies and would probably try to kill us, but we learn to deal with this behavior. We are probably genetically conditioned to be afraid of snakes, an important predator of primates, yet there are lots of snake lovers among us. And many of us (especially males) are certainly genetically predisposed to want sex. Yet the overwhelming majority of us are able to deal with this instinct in a socially acceptable manner.

In addition, there appears to have been selection for many other human traits that seem to "cancel out" or blunt overly aggressive behavior. Concern for children or those less fortunate, for example, is quite strong in humans. Hearing a baby crying upsets us. In fact, crying itself has been selected for. Chimpanzees don't cry. Crying and a response to it are intertwined in our genetic makeup. Other uniquely human behaviors are sharing and altruism. Sharing of food—bringing edibles back to the band, especially males bringing meat—was a critical human trait and another that separates us from chimpanzees. There must have been as much genetic selection for sharing, and the ability to cooperate it implies, as there was for aggression. Altruistic behavior in general can be seen as a strong human trait. Impulsively jumping into a body of water to save another—even a total stranger—is a strong human response. Think of firefighters who rush into burning buildings every day. This powerful urge to help or save others must be as inherently human as aggressive behavior. Aggressive human tendencies are often mitigated by other human tendencies.

In any given situation there is no reason to believe that aggressive behavior will be the only response elicited. Furthermore, there is no reason to assume that a learned response cannot override such a possible genetically induced behavioral response. A scantily clad young woman entering a room does not trigger a response from all nearby males to tear off their clothes (or hers). It may cross their minds, but they stay dressed in most instances. Similarly, an undesirable action by a neighbor usually doesn't cause us to rush next door and set his house afire, or commit murder, although such thoughts might dominate more rational solutions when a loud party continues at two A.M.

I see no reason to believe that selection for aggressive behavior has made modern humans unable to function in nonaggressive ways. The very fact that warfare was so patterned in the past strongly argues against this. If humans were innately programmed to fight all the time, we would fight all the time. But humans do not do this. When there is no reason to fight, we are capable of ending the conflict. Repeatedly in the past, when populations declined or new tools and technologies made acquiring food easier, scholars see a decline in or cessation of warfare. There were "peaceful Pueblo people" in A.D. 1900 living right where archaeologists find evidence of warfare dating to 1300. The Hopi really do perceive themselves as inherently peaceful people. I do not believe they are any more inherently peaceful than any others on Earth, but they certainly are peaceful. The Vikings were once the scourge of Europe, but not today. Those same Polynesian Islands that were sites of so much warfare in the past are now tranquil tourist spots. !Kung are so peaceful today that the anthropologists who studied them forty years ago were unable to see that their past was hardly peaceful. If warfare was genetically built into humans and not outweighed by other inherent human tendencies, none of this could be true.

Intergroup conflict—warfare—is far more likely to be controlled than individual acts of aggression. It is one thing to get angry and pick a fight, to melt down in a case of "road rage," or to lash out at a spouse, but it is quite another to start a war. Wars are group activities. The uncontrolled aggression of one or a few individuals will not result in warfare—maybe a barroom brawl, but not war. The larger group must sanction aggression in the case of war.[15] Warfare, of all human aggressive behavior, is probably the least likely to be driven by genetically induced behaviors unmodified or uncontrolled by cultural behaviors. Chimpanzee males are aggressive on an unregulated basis in their own groups. Undoubtedly some of this behavior involves unplanned knee-jerk aggressive reactions to random events. Chimp warfare, on the other hand, is carefully calculated. Aggressive groups retreat when the odds are not overwhelmingly in their favor. No "hothead" rushes forth and attacks when the odds of success are poor. Among chimps, as well as humans, warfare is the least impetuous aggressive behavior, one act that is most moderated by group decision making and cold, hard calculation of the risks involved.

Among humans, animosities can linger for a long time, and it may indeed take generations for true peace to come to the Balkans or the Middle East or large portions of Africa. Just because humans cannot make peace does not mean they have genes that preclude being peaceful. A history of warfare is something that should be accepted as reality. A good portion of the world's people go to bed hungry, and many starve. As long as resource scarcities continue in many parts of the world, I expect conflict based on competition over resources to continue, even if it is sometimes disguised as ideological. This does not doom us to a future of war any more than our past dooms us to a future of heart attacks.

A careful reading of the past shows that humans are not programmed for war. Perhaps even more surprising, the real history of warfare shows that it has declined over time, further evidence that warfare is not an inherently human behavior. As societies have become more and more complex, a decline in the proportion of the population involved in war, along with a concomitant increase in professional soldiers, can be observed. Among foragers and farmers, all adult males were expected to participate in warfare—not every man in every fight, but at some point in their lives all men would have been participants. As social complexity increased, specialists were trained for warfare and conflict became their full-time occupation, while far less of the population was directly involved. There has been a decline in actual war deaths, on a per capita basis, as societies become complexly organized. In 1294 B.C., Ramses II was able to field twenty thousand men at the battle of Kadesh in present-day Syria. With a population in the multimillions, this army represented only 2 percent of the able-bodied men of Egypt, and armies did not increase in size until the last two centuries. Only a small portion of the men in states ever were in battle.[16] Warfare in complex societies has increasingly had less of an impact on the population as a whole and has become less of a daily fact of life.

This has been true for people living in states for some time. While many societies engaged in psychological warfare in the past, it is more likely to work with states. Tribes may have hung up enemy skulls to unnerve their competitors, but states do it on massive scales. The early states of Mexico, Peru, and the Middle East all created public imagery of victorious armies and enemies being killed, sacrificed, and dismembered. The skull racks of the Aztecs, the largest holding one-hundred thousand human heads, were the culmination of a long tradition of psychological warfare.[17]

It sometimes works well in states because so much of the population is buffered from war. Terror loses its impact when it is commonplace. For example, if you fight with the neighboring groups constantly and know that you kill about as many of them as they do of you, the act of placing a skull on a post is likely to generate little fear on either side. However, in a society where there have been no battles on the home soil for six generations, the destruction of a structure like the World Trade Center can bring forth feelings of vulnerability that reach far beyond the probability of any individual within that society being killed by a terrorist. Today's threat of terrorism, and especially suicide bombings, has the potential of reverting us—at least psychologically—to what life was like in less complex societies. People living in those times and social groupings did worry every day about themselves and their loved ones being killed in attacks, often in ambush. For many of us living today, this type of fear has returned, and the potential for such psychological warfare can be far-reaching.

Over time, as social groupings became more and more complex, there has been a shift from constant battles to more infrequent major clashes. Intergroup conflict evolved from the multiple battles, raids, and massacres that were more than annual events for foragers and farmers, to the great militaristic encounters that last several years once a generation—or even once in a lifetime—of modern nation-states. The clashes of the complex societies are horrific and long remembered, but the constant battles of the past were every bit as feared by those who participated in them. The impact of the more frequent, constant warfare on the people involved—both demographically and on their daily lives—was far greater.

This evolution of conflict becomes clear when today's warfare is placed in perspective. It is estimated that one thousand people are killed daily in localized conflicts around the globe. Whether in the Balkans, Central Africa, Timor, or Sri Lanka, there is still a good deal of conflict in the modern world. With more than six billion people on the planet, a third of a million deaths per year (1,000 a day for 365 days)—as horrible as that is—is much less than the number of fatalities that occurred on a per capita basis in a highland New Guinea village forty years ago. As observed ethnographically in New Guinea, typically 25 percent of the men died from warfare in farmer and forager societies. If all six billion people on Earth today were involved in warfare like that experienced by most egalitarian farmers in the past, the fatality rate would be more than eight thousand deaths per day, or more than eight times what actually occurs.

With this in mind, let's examine the myths of a peaceful past and of humans living in ecological balance and contrast them with a careful assessment of reality that turns the more traditional view on its head. These myths assume that for long periods of time the earliest humans were simple foragers who lived in harmony with nature, had few wants, and were able to control their populations. When agriculture was developed, populations grew, but these farmers managed to remain inherent environmentalists and continued to avoid stressing the environment. Then finally, but not until the rise of complex societies, we humans lost our ability to live in ecological balance. At that point, the appealing story of millions of years of peaceful coexistence with nature turns ugly, and violent, environmentally threatened societies—in particular Western European society—command a starring role. As Western society spread or affected much of the planet, the myth continues, warfare and environmental degradation spread like an infectious disease, engulfing most of the world—except where vestigial remains of this peaceful, ecologically balanced existence survived among such groups as the !Kung, Australian Aborigines, Eskimos, Siriono, and the like. In other words, noble Cro-Magnon humans were replaced by warlike, modern imperialists.

Reality paints a different picture, one with many opportunities for peace and ecological harmony, but it is a portrait of opportunities lost. Looking back through history, several radical changes in human societies occurred, and each change provided, in theory, an opportunity to improve the population-ecological balance and usher in a new era of peace. Each time one of these dramatic changes took place, peace and ecological balance remained elusive.

The first of these transformations was becoming human. As proto-humans became fully human beings and gained superior intelligence, language, and cultural norms, these initial human foragers were hardly peaceful. Greater intelligence did not result in greater peacefulness. Although some ecologically benign behaviors did develop, they were never effective enough to regulate population growth and to establish a peaceful, stable system. Except in the harshest environments, forager populations grew, reached the carrying-capacity limit, and then competed for resources. For more than a million years, humans lived in a precarious balance between population growth and the limitations and variability of the environment. Periodic population increases that could not be sustained by an ever-changing resource base led to chronic starvation, infanticide, and warfare. These early people modified the environment by such means as fire and were no more "environmentalists" than their short-term goals dictated. Since their numbers were, by necessity, low, and their technology limited, the impact of the first foragers was relatively minor.

Beginning around ten thousand to twelve thousand years ago, people began to farm in the Middle East, China, and later in Africa and Central and South America. This new situation might have resulted in a peaceful world. Farmers were able to get far more food from an acre of land than had ever before been possible, and there was the potential for plenty for all—but the balance was not maintained. Farmers could reproduce at rates far beyond those of foragers, and they spread quickly over much of Earth. In spite of its potential, farming itself solved no problems. The benefits of every new plant domesticated, every new animal tamed, and every new technology invented were quickly consumed by the growing number of people such advances could additionally support. Horticulture and domestic animals caused environmental degradation that went way beyond the effects of just the higher population numbers. More people translated into more degradation. In any given region, in spite of efforts to control growth or to develop new foods and technologies, the population soon grew to stress the resources once again. Malnutrition, if not starvation, and even more intense and chronic warfare were common among the early farmers.

Once again, a major social transformation occurred. Complex societies developed. The leadership in these societies had the mechanisms and potential ability to control population growth and to force people to be more ecologically sensitive. Along with more complex societies came more complex technologies. The chiefdoms and early states had developed enough technology to harm the world's environment at levels and rates not seen before. The result was even more degradation of the environment. Although some efforts were made to control population growth, such mechanisms were always far from fully successful, and resource stress was as common as ever.

In chiefdoms especially, the elite were constantly competing, resulting in chronic warfare. When the large bureaucratic organizations—states—developed, the average person could be forced to starve, because the centralized government might not allow the lower classes to fight for survival. As societies became more complex, the level of human suffering did not diminish. In fact, the average person in a preindustrial state was malnourished, had a short life span, practiced infanticide, suffered from the highly communicable diseases that went along with living in urban areas, and engaged in feuds and peasant revolts—and sometimes got caught up in wars that killed millions of people. Despite the fact that the number of people killed in state-level warfare actually declined, the diet and health of the state's overall population also declined.

In spite of several dramatic changes in human social systems that might have led to very different human-ecological balances over the course of time, no such enduring balance was ever found. But the story is yet to be completed. One more dramatic change in the human social order took place, one that, again, provided the opportunity for ecological balance and peace. We live in this period today, and seeing it in its long-term perspective is especially important.

With the rise of complex societies, the increasing pace of new technological developments began to change the nature of human-ecological relationships. These changes ultimately produced a unique human condition. At first, these new technologies made things worse. Technology enabled humans to despoil the environment much more intensely than farmers and foragers ever could. Specialists developed new knowledge and technologies. At first, the positive impact of these trends was slow and probably outweighed the negatives. Then the world changed again. The Industrial Revolution altered the rate of technological change in a dramatic way. Beginning around 1800, change began to accelerate at a pace humans had never experienced, and this quickening had two particularly important impacts on population growth and ecological balance. The Industrial Revolution dramatically slowed growth rates and increased the world's carrying capacity.

Great suffering accompanied the Industrial Revolution as it changed societies rapidly and dramatically. It increased our ability to degrade the environment in unprecedented ways. At the same time, it laid the foundation for breaking the relationship between population growth and carrying-capacity stress, because industrialization enabled us to increase the world's carrying capacity immensely. Six thousand years ago, a Neolithic farmer was lucky to achieve yields of eight bushels of wheat per acre. In Kansas today, farmers get almost eighty bushels per acre.

The Industrial Revolution also caused the world's population to become more urban. Well over 90 percent of the U.S. population lives in a nonfarm situation. The cost-benefit of having children changed, as it did for earlier cities. Very large farm families have been replaced by a typical urban family with one or two children. The difference now is that in industrialized states, almost everyone lives in a city, so the number of children desired has declined measurably. It is staggering to discover that 160,000 people a day move to an urban environment around the world.[18] This, of course, has created its own problems, especially the rise of megacities such as São Paulo (18 million), Mexico City (18 million–plus), and Karachi and New Delhi (12 million each). Though the low birth rate found in urban environments is a pattern that has existed since the time of the earliest cities, as a greater and greater portion of the world's population lives in cities, the impact of low urban birth rates is ever more pronounced. Technology and science have provided effective birth control so that the desire for fewer children can actually be met. In combination, these changes are resulting in some societies around the world, including much of Europe, reaching stable population levels. Already, about 25 percent of the world's population on a country-by-country basis is either stable or slightly declining, and the rates of most of the high-growth areas like China, India, and South America are also declining. Such a transformation in demography has affected hundreds of millions of people. Though many more hundreds of millions have remained unaffected.

Today, just about two hundred years after the start of the Industrial Revolution, modern states have incredibly severe ecological problems, yet at the same time the greatest awareness and technological ability humans have ever had to amend or soften their impact on the world's environment exist. In spite of the pronounced impact industrialized states make on the environment, their technology and slow growth rates enable them to live well below the carrying capacity. The decline in warfare among those countries with stable or declining growth rates is incredibly strong. This is especially promising for the future and provides additional confirmation of the relationship between resource stress and warfare. Remove the one, and the other soon disappears.

The great irony is that we humans have not lost our ability to live healthily and peacefully within a pristine environment as a result of advancing industrialization. On the contrary, we never had any such ability. The Industrial Revolution is not another major sea change that denied us our ancestors' capabilities to live properly and prosperously in a warfare-free environment. Modern humans can't be denied an ecological balance nobody on Earth has ever enjoyed, nor be denied a peaceful way of life that has never existed. As difficult as the adjustment to the Industrial Revolution was—and continues to be for many of the world's societies—it did not cause an increase in warfare.

This transformation has not been as complete as the agricultural revolution that preceded it. We live in a world where the impact of the Industrial Revolution is spotty. Highly urban, low-growth regions, like Europe, have low levels of warfare and little malnutrition. Yet other parts of the world—South and Southeast Asia, much of Africa—are rural, high-growth regions and have great food shortages and internal strife not often considered warfare, which kill millions directly or indirectly. In addition, environmental degradation continues unabated everywhere.

There is no guarantee that the current low growth and resource abundance among the industrialized, or urbanized, states will continue over the long term. Just because the situation seems stabilized does not mean that a long-term balance has been developed. Remember Europe in the 1100s, when for a couple of hundred years resources were plentiful due to the good climate—but then the Little Ice Age hit. As the world becomes more connected, the continued population growth of the underdeveloped countries may well result in even more accelerated migration to the industrialized countries, leading to significant population increases again. The use rate of resources among the industrialized states does not appear to be sustainable for the world as a whole. If everyone on Earth used energy, seafood, trees, and a long list of other resources at the rate Americans do, resources would be depleted far faster than they could regenerate.

The Industrial Revolution has presented modern humans with an opportunity to live healthily and peacefully within a pristine environment—an opportunity we do not recognize for what it is. Humans can now actually monitor how we are affecting the environment and do something about it. The detection of the depletion of the ozone layer and the abandonment of production and use of fluorocarbons, its cause, is a milestone in our understanding of the complex ecology of the planet and a willingness to correct past behaviors. We are succeeding in monitoring and controlling overfishing in some places in the world while we continue to deplete the ocean in others. Modern humans are far from being able to stop degrading the planet, but we have shown we can sometimes succeed. In the past, humans did not succeed in this regard. Their failures simply resulted in less dramatic impacts.

The problems of the modern world are certainly bigger, but so are our capabilities. And these problems get solved only by big efforts. The war on cancer is a big effort and should pay off in our lifetimes. There is no comparable big effort to eliminate the underlying causes of warfare in most of the world—certainly nothing on the scale the problem demands. This is not an appeal for more foreign aid, or more lecturing from the haves to the have-nots about what to do. It is an appeal to accepting the true nature of the human condition and the real nature of the problem. With this realization, some new ideas will be taken seriously by the leadership of the developed world. We are on the right trajectory for world peace. We are moving in the right direction, but this process will not produce instant success any more than the war on cancer has.

The inability to evolve a worldwide ecological balance would not reflect a breach from the "noble savages" of the past. We have never had that heritage, or the opportunities we have today. For the first time in history, technology and science enable us to understand Earth's ecology and our impact on it, to control population growth, and to increase the carrying capacity in ways never before imagined. The opportunity for humans to live in long-term balance with nature is within our grasp if we do it right. It is a chance to break a million-year-old cycle of conflict and crisis.

Taking the long view of human history points to our controlling warfare just as medical science has made great strides to conquer heart disease. Everything in the past points to the reduction of warfare. In spite of the wars of the last century, in spite of the numerous wars taking place today, many characterized as civil wars, and the many victims of these wars, we are still making progress. Twenty-five percent of all the men alive today will not die from warfare, as men did for most of human history. Entire societies will not be swept away as they frequently were in the past. From a centuries-long perspective, we are making great improvement. A greater proportion of the world is at peace today than any time in the past.

Undoubtedly, humankind has a long way to go toward bringing peace on Earth and living in ecological balance. There are more people today who understand the impact the human race is having on the world's environments, and are prepared to take the steps needed to achieve ecological balance, than has ever been the case in the past. To think we have lost our "roots" or are somehow out of touch with our ancient ancestors—and have lost the ability to live in peace and in ecological balance—is a myth and a dangerous one. The myth implies that if we can just relearn how to think about nature and remember our ancient abilities to be one with the natural environment, warfare will stop and ecological balance will be regained.

If warfare has, in fact, been based on rational behavior for much of human history, then deciding that warfare is bad and should be stopped will not solve our problem. If, as I believe, warfare has ultimately been a constant battle over scarce resources throughout the ages, then only solving the problem of adequate resources will enable us to become better at ridding ourselves of conflict. For the first time in history, we have a real ability to provide adequate resources for everyone living on the planet. If we have reached a point at which we can live within Earth's carrying capacity, we can eliminate warfare in the same way we can eliminate infectious disease: not perfectly, not immediately, but slowly and surely.

NOTES

Chapter One: Warfare and Ecology: Myth and Reality

1. Watson, et al., "Aspects of Zuni Prehistory: Preliminary Report on Excavations and Survey in the El Morro Valley of New Mexico"; LeBlanc, "Warfare and Aggression in the El Morro Valley, New Mexico."
2. Scarre, *The Seventy Wonders of the Ancient World: The Great Monuments and How They Were Built*; Taylour, *The Mycenaeans*.
3. Leroi-Gourhan, *The Art of Prehistoric Man in Western Europe*.
4. Cooper, *Rousseau, Nature, and the Problem of the Good Life*; Cranston, *Rousseau: Selections*; Horowitz, *Rousseau, Nature, and History*.
5. While this belief has been widely held, it was the publication of *Man the Hunter* in 1968 that really pushed this model and it was widely picked up by nonanthropologists, such as Ehrlich, et al., *The Stork and the Plow: The Equity Answer to the Human Dilemma*.
6. Goble, *Crow Chief*.
7. Wheat, "The Olsen-Chubbuck Site: A Paleo-Indian Bison Kill"; Brink and Dawe, *Final Report of the 1985 and 1986 Field Seasons at Head-Smashed-In Buffalo Jump, Alberta*; Verbicky-Todd, *Communal Buffalo Hunting Among the Plains Indians: An Ethnographic and Historic Review*; Malouf and Conner, *Symposium on Buffalo Jumps*.
8. Krech, *The Ecological Indian: Myth and History*; Redman, *Human Impact on Ancient Environments*.
9. Rotha, "Nanook and the North"; Bilby, *Nanook of the North: The Story of an Eskimo Family*.
10. Washburn, "Seventeenth-Century Indian Wars."
11. Beyond the reality of the situation, there is also the perception of the situation. Certainly today, many "environmentally" sensitive people and many Native Americans do believe that the "noble savage" did live in peaceful harmony with nature. This has become a dogmatic position, not one that can be popularly questioned. And, as a consequence, there is little to be gained by getting in an argument about it. While I will show that this position is not and in fact could not possibly be true, the danger is that the idea that humans have never been an ecologically ideal species could be used as an excuse to continue present-day ecologically disastrous behavior.

Chapter Two: Was There Ever an Eden?

1. Models and ideas that come from human ecology include "optimal foraging" theory that argues that humans try to maximize short-term results while minimizing effort. Bettinger, *Hunter-Gatherers: Archaeological and Evolutionary Theory.*
2. Rappaport, *Pigs for Ancestors;* "Ecology, Adaptation, and the Ills of Functionalism."
3. Thomas, *Man's Role in Changing the Face of the Earth.*
4. Bettinger, *Hunter-Gatherers: Archaeology and Evolutionary Theory.*
5. Stiner, et al., "The Tortoise and the Hare: Small-Game Use, Broad-Spectrum Revolution, and Paleolithic Demography"; Glassow, *Purisimeno Chumash Prehistory: Maritime Adaptations Along the Southern California Coast;* Klein, "The Impact of Early People on the Environment: The Case of Large Mammal Extinctions."
6. Gopher, "Early Pottery-Bearing Groups in Israel—The Pottery Neolithic."
7. Alvard, "Testing the 'Ecologically Noble Savage' Hypothesis: Interspecific Prey Choice."
8. See Burney, "Tropical Islands as Paleoecological Laboratories: Gauging the Consequences of Human Arrival," for a recent summary of many of these examples.
9. Woodburn, "An Introduction to Hadza Ecology."
10. Dewar, "Environmental Productivity, Population Regulation, and Carrying Capacity"; Chapman, "Putting Pressures on Population: Social Alternatives to Malthus and Boserup."
11. Many of these are known only archaeologically and provide evidence for very intensive use of areas, such as parts of the Yucatán that are not densely populated today.
12. Boserup, *Conditions of Agricultural Growth: The Economics of Agrarian Change Under Population Pressure.*
13. Societies by nature are conservative, and such changes do not come easily or automatically. It is not that human societies cannot change and adapt—if anything, this is the hallmark of being human. The question is, can societies under threat make the necessary changes rapidly enough—and under enough different circumstances—to get around problems of exceeding the carrying capacity in the short run?
14. Lamb, *Weather, Climate, and Human Affairs,* and *Climate History, and the Modern World;* Berger, *Abrupt Climate Change;* Bryson and Murray, *Climates of Hunger: Mankind and the World's Changing Climate;* Ingram, et al., "Past Climates and Their Impact on Man: A Review"; Le Roy Ladurie, *Times of Feast, Times of Famine: A History of Climate Since the Year 1000;* Wigley, et al., *Climate and History: Studies in Past Climates and Their Impact on Man;* Galloway, "Longterm Fluctuations in Climate and Population in the Preindustrial Era"; Berger and Labeyrie, *Abrupt Climate Change.* There is a distinction between climate and weather. Climate is the long-term weather pattern of an area; weather is today's (or this week's) temperature and precipitation. For our purposes, the distinction does not always matter (and it rarely matters to the people being affected by it). What we care about is unpredictable change that occurs relatively rapidly and has significant impact on resource availability.
15. Sothers, "The Great Tambora Eruption of 1815 and Its Aftermath." The less-known Laki eruption in Iceland in 1783–1785 probably caused as much cooling. Krakatoa erupted in 1883 with less effect but may also have erupted in the sixth century with greater impact (Keys, *Catastrophe: An Investigation into the Origins of the Modern World*).

16. Le Roy Ladurie, *Times of Feast, Times of Famine: A History of Climate Since the Year 1000;* Galloway, "Longterm Fluctuations in Climate and Population in the Preindustrial Era"; Grove, *The Little Ice Age;* Lamb, *Climate History, and the Modern World.*

17. Grove, *The Little Ice Age.*

18. Wood, *Dynamics of Human Reproduction: Biology, Biometry, Demography.*

19. This is a much more complex topic than presented here. See Wood, *Dynamics of Human Reproduction: Biology, Biometry, Demography* for more details.

20. Hill and Hurtado, *Ache Life History: The Ecology and Demography of a Foraging People.*

21. The population of Ireland grew at over 1.5 percent per year between 1753 and 1821, not even adjusting for the high emigration at this time (Clarkson, *Irish Population Revisited, 1687–1821. Irish Population, Economy, and Society: Essays in Honour of the Late K. H. Connell*). Such a rate will double a population in fewer than fifty years.

22. Wrigley, *Population and History* and *The Population History of England 1571–1871: A Reconstruction.*

23. Stone, "Social Mobility in England, 1500–1700"; Langer, "Checks on Population Growth: 1750–1850" and "Infanticide: A Historical Survey"; Rose, *The Massacre of the Innocents: Infanticide in Britain 1800–1939.*

24. Langer, "Checks on Population Growth: 1750–1850"; but Hansen, "Overlaying in Nineteenth Century England: Infant Mortality or Infanticide?" presents a counterview.

25. General sources on infanticide include Harris and Ross, *Death, Sex, and Fertility: Population Regulation in Preindustrial and Developing Societies;* and Hausfater and Hrdy, *Infanticide: Comparative and Evolutionary Perspectives.* Specific ones include Balickci, "Female Infanticide on the Arctic Coast" (Eskimo); Hanley, "Marriage and Fertility in Japanese Villages" (Japan); Hassan, "Determination of the Size, Density, and Growth Rate of Hunting-Gathering Populations"; Cashdan, "Natural Fertility, Birth Spacing, and the 'First Demographic Transition'" (hunter-gatherers); Langer, "Checks on Population Growth: 1750–1850" and "Infanticide: A Historical Survey"; and Rose, *The Massacre of the Innocents: Infanticide in Britain 1800–1939* (Europe); Strangeland, *Pre-Malthusian Doctrine of Population: A Study in the History of Economic Theory;* and Wilkinson, *Classical Attitudes to Modern Issues* (ancient states); Cowlishaw, "Infanticide in Aboriginal Australia" (aboriginal Australia); Wagley, "Cultural Influences on Population: A Comparison of Two Tupi Tribes" (Amazonia).

26. The desire by Chinese to have at least one son has resulted in a very male-biased sex ratio, implying that infant girls were killed or abandoned. The orphanages are full of girls.

27. McNeil, *Plagues and Peoples;* Ramenofsky, *Vectors of Death: The Archaeology of European Contact;* Denevan, *The Native Population of the Americas in 1492.*

28. Many of these ideas were first put forth by Thomas Malthus (1766–1834), in particular in his famous *An Essay on the Principle of Population* written in 1798. Malthus argued that a portion of society will always live in misery because population growth will always outstrip the ability to increase production. The reader may feel that the position presented here is just Malthus warmed over. Wasn't Malthus wrong? It turns out, ironically, that Malthus was writing just at the beginning of the Industrial Revolution. For all but the last couple of centuries, Malthus was very right and very relevant for the entire world—and even today he is right and relevant for a good portion of it.

29. Firth, *We, the Tikopia; Social Change in Tikopia;* "History and Traditions of Tikopia"; Borrie et al., "The Population of Tikopia, 1929 and 1952"; and is summarized by Kirch, *The Evolution of Polynesian Chiefdoms.*
30. Borrie et al., "The Population of Tikopia, 1929 and 1952."

Chapter Three: Enter Conflict

1. Over the years some other archaeologists had also seen these locations as defensive; see LeBlanc, *Prehistoric Warfare in the American Southwest.*
2. In societies where social groups are fluid and people are related to people in many other groups, it is hard to determine where one group ends and the next begins. Determining what was intragroup homicide or an intergroup act of warfare is not easy, so I deliberately ignore a great deal of evidence for intragroup violence, but simply to be conservative.
3. Kidder and Guernsey, *Archaeological Explorations in Northeastern Arizona.*
4. Hurst and Turner, "Rediscovering the 'Great Discovery': Wetherill's First Cave 7 and its Record of Basketmaker Violence"; Cole, "Basketmaker Rock Art at the Green Mask Site, Southeastern Utah"; summarized in LeBlanc, *Prehistoric Warfare in the American Southwest.*
5. Brown, *The Ethnography of Cannibalism.*
6. Arsuaga, "The First Europeans: Spanish Caves Paint a New Picture of Evolution on the Continent"; Askenasy, *Cannibalism: From Sacrifice to Survival;* Brown and Tuzin, *The Ethnography of Cannibalism;* Dornstreich and Morren, "Does New Guineau Cannibalism Have Nutritional Value?"; Fernando-Jalvo, et al., "Human Cannibalism in the Early Pleistocene of Europe"; Heidenreich, "Huron"; Tannahill, *Flesh and Blood: A History of the Cannibal Complex.*
7. Marcus and Flannery, *Zapotec Civilization: How Urban Society Evolved in Mexico's Oaxaca Valley;* Anderson, *The Savannah River Chiefdoms: Political Change in the Late Prehistoric Southeast;* DePratter, *Late Prehistoric and Early Historic Chiefdoms in the Southeastern United States;* Kemp, *Ancient Egypt: Anatomy of a Civilization;* Wenke, "Egypt: Origins of Complex Societies."
8. See Marcus and Flannery, *Zapotec Civilization: How Urban Society Evolved in Mexico's Oaxaca Valley.*
9. Kirkbride, "Umm Dabaghiyah."
10. Catlin, *Letters and Notes on the Manners, Customs, and Conditions of the North American Indians.*
11. Unburied bodies are found all over the world, as are formal burial areas containing far fewer fighting-aged men than women, with the obvious presumption that the missing men died in battle and were buried where they fell rather than in their own community.
12. Sugiyama, "Burials Dedicated to the Old Temple of Quetzalcoatl at Teotihuacan, Mexico" and "Worldview Materialized in Teotihuacan, Mexico."
13. Malotki, *Hopi Ruin Legends.*
14. Burch, "Eskimo Warfare in Northwest Alaska."
15. Chagnon, "Yanomamo Social Organization and Warfare."
16. Kirch, *The Evolution of Polynesian Chiefdoms.*
17. The obvious exception is when new lands are first colonized, but this is a one-time and irrelevant event.

Chapter Four: Our Earliest Past

1. Wrangham and Peterson, *Demonic Males: Apes and the Origins of Human Violence.*
2. Darwin, *The Descent of Man* [1871] 1997; Wrangham, "The Evolution of Coalitionary Killing."
3. Wrangham and Pilbeam, *African Apes as Time Machines.*
4. Goodall, *Africa in My Blood: An Autobiography in Letters: The Early Years.*
5. Especially Chapman and Wrangham, "Rage Use of the Forest Chimpanzees on Kibale: Implications for the Understanding of Chimpanzee Social Organization"; Nishida, "Review of Recent Findings on Mahale Chimpanzees: Implications and Future Research Directions"; Boesch and Boesch, *The Chimpanzees of the Taï Forest: Behavioral Ecology and Evolution;* and enumerated in Wrangham, et al., *Chimpanzee Cultures.*
6. Wrangham and Peterson, *Demonic Males: Apes and the Origins of Human Violence,* based on actual field observations.
7. Manson and Wrangham, "Intergroup Aggression in Chimpanzees and Humans"; Hill et al., "Mortality Rates Among Wild Chimpanzees"; Keeley, *War Before Civilization.*
8. Wrangham and Peterson, *Demonic Males: Apes and the Origins of Human Violence;* Manson and Wrangham, "Intergroup Aggression in Chimpanzees and Humans."
9. Wrangham and Peterson, *Demonic Males: Apes and the Origins of Human Violence.*
10. Wrangham and Pilbeam, *African Apes as Time Machines.*
11. Stern and Susman, "The Locomotor Anatomy of Australopithecus Afarensis."
12. Issac, "The Sirionó of Eastern Bolivia: A Reexamination."
13. Dunsworth et al., *Throwing and Bipedalism: A New Look at an Old Idea.*
14. Topic, "The Ostra Site: The Earliest Fortified Site in the New World?"
15. Thieme, "Lower Paleolithic Hunting Spears from Germany."
16. Crabtree et al., *Early Animal Domestication and Its Cultural Context.*
17. Arsuaga, "The First Europeans: Spanish Caves Paint a New Picture of Evolution on the Continent."
18. White, "Cut Marks on the Bodo Cranium: A Case of Prehistoric Defleshing."
19. Harrold, "A Comparative Analysis of Eurasian Paleolithic Burials."
20. Berger and Trinkaus, "Patterns of Trauma Among the Neandertals"; Defleur, et al., "Neanderthal Cannibalism at Moula Guercy, Ardeche, France." Just as careful analysis supports the inference of cannibalism, so does it not, e.g., White and Toth, "The Question of Ritual Cannibalism at Grotta Guattari."
21. Villa, "Cannibalism in Prehistoric Europe."

Chapter Five: Warfare Among Foragers

1. Surovell, "Early Paleolithic Women, Children, Mobility, and Fertility"; Kelly, *The Foraging Spectrum: Diversity in Hunter-Gatherer Lifeways.*
2. Landcaster, et al., "The Evolution of Life History, Intelligence, and Diet Among Chimpanzees and Human Foragers"; Hill and Kaplan, "Life History Traits in Humans: Theory and Empirical Studies."

3. Binford, "Willow Smoke and Dog's Tails: Hunter-Gatherer Settlement Systems and Archaeological Site Formation."

4. There is a substantial literature on the strategies and organization of foragers and other hunter-gatherers. Classic works and recent syntheses include Service, *Primitive Social Organization: An Evolutionary Perspective*; Price and Brown, *Prehistoric Hunter-Gatherers: The Emergence of Cultural Complexity*; Price and Gebrauer, "The Spread of Farming into Europe North of the Alps"; and Kelly, *The Foraging Spectrum: Diversity in Hunter-Gatherer Lifeways*. More subtle and perhaps more useful terminology is successfully used by Johnson and Earle, *The Evolution of Human Societies from Foraging Group to Agrarian State*, but it has too many categories for our purposes here.

5. Much of this is summarized in Kelly, *The Foraging Spectrum: Diversity in Hunter-Gatherer Lifeways*. Additional summaries on most of the ethnographically known foragers are provided by Lee and Daly, *The Cambridge Encyclopedia of Hunters and Gatherers*.

6. This project ultimately involved a number of scholars and was headed by Lee and DeVore and headquartered at Harvard University. The project history is summarized in Lee and DeVore, *Kalahari Hunter-Gatherers: Studies of the !Kung San and Their Neighbors*, with publications and documentary movies too numerous to list.

7. Hill and Hurtado, *Ache Life History: The Ecology and Demography of a Foraging People*; Kelly, *The Foraging Spectrum: Diversity in Hunter-Gatherer Lifeways*.

8. Wilkie and Curran, "Historical Trends in Forager and Farmer Exchange in the Huri Rain Forest of Northeastern Zaire." The few true foragers in South America's rain forest are also heavily impacted by neighboring farmers, as apparently are all of those from Southeast Asia and India (Headland and Reid, "Holocene Foragers and Interethnic Trade: A Critique of the Myths of Isolated Independent Hunter-Gatherers").

9. Their speech includes a clicklike sound, represented by the !. It is acceptable not to try and say their name with a click.

10. This, technically, is not correct, but the terminology issues are complex and variously interpreted. See Gordon, "The !Kung in the Kalahari Exchange: An Ethnohistorical Perspective"; Parkington, "Soaqua and Bushmen: Hunters and Robbers"; Schapera, *The Khoisan Peoples of South Africa: Bushmen and Hottentots*; Schrire, "An Inquiry into the Evolutionary Status and Apparent Identity of San Hunter-Gatherers."

11. Godwin, "Bushmen: Last Stand for Southern Africa's First People."

12. Surovell, "Early Paleoindian Women, Children, Mobility, and Fertility."

13. Lee, *Subsistence Ecology of !Kung Bushmen*. See Kelly, *The Foraging Spectrum: Diversity in Hunter-Gatherer Lifeways* for detailed figures on foragers in general.

14. Denevan, *The Native Population of the Americas in 1492*.

15. Glassow, *Purisimeno Chumash Prehistory: Maritime Adaptations Along the Southern California Coast*; Stiner, et al., "The Tortoise and the Hare: Small-Game Use, Broad-Spectrum Revolution, and Paleolithic Demography"; Klein, "The Impact of Early People on the Environment: The Case of Large Mammal Extinctions."

16. Walker and Hewlett, "Dental Health, Diet, and Social Status Among Central African Foragers and Farmers."

17. These interpretations are summarized in Read and LeBlanc, "Population Growth, Carrying Capacity, and Conflict."

18. Cowlishaw, "Infanticide in Aboriginal Australia"; Edgerton, *Sick Societies: Challenging the Myth of Primitive Harmony*.

19. Balickci, "Female Infanticide in the Arctic Coast"; Cashdan, "Natural Fertility, Birth Spacing, and the 'First Demographic Transition'"; Freeman, "A Social and Ecological Analysis of Systematic Female Infanticide Among the Netsilik Eskimo"; Hill and Hurtado, *Ache Life History: The Ecology and Demography of a Foraging People.*

20. Benfer, "Holocene Coastal Adaptations: Changing Demography and Health at the Fog Oasis of Paloma, Peru, 5000–7800 B.P."

21. Morgan, *The Life and Adventures of William Buckley: Thirty-two Years a Wanderer Amongst the Aborigines.*

22. Quoted in Eibl-Eibesfeldt, "Aggression in the !Ko Bushmen."

23. Gordon, "The !Kung in the Kalahari Exchange: An Ethnohistorical Perspective."

24. Parkington, "Soaqua and Bushmen: Hunters and Robbers."

25. Gordon, "The !Kung in the Kalahari Exchange: An Ethnohistorical Perspective"; Eibl-Eibesfleldt, "Aggression in the !Ko-Bushmen."

26. Not all Arctic hunting was done with bows; harpoons and spears (thrown with spear-throwers especially used that way when seated in a kayak) were common hunting tools. However, bows could be used to take some animals, such as polar bears, so I don't argue that bows were exclusively a weapon for war.

27. Burch, "Eskimo Warfare in Northwest Alaska."

28. Melbye and Fairgreive, "A Massacre and Possible Cannibalism in the Canadian Arctic: New Evidence from the Saunaktuk Site"; Walker, *Appendix 5: Tool Marks on Human Bone from Saunaktuk.*

29. De Laguna, "Ahtna vs. Chugach Eskimos."

30. Diamond, *Guns, Germs, and Steel: The Fates of Human Societies;* also Lourandos, "Intensification and Australian Prehistory."

31. Palter, "Slinging Spears: Recent Evidence on Flexible Shaft Spear Throwers."

32. Taçon and Chippendale, "Australia's Ancient Warriors: Changing Depictions of Fighting in the Rock Art of Arnham Land, N.T."

33. Knuckey, "Patterns of Fracture upon Aboriginal Crania from the Recent Past."

34. Williams, "Complex Hunter-Gatherers: A View from Australia"; Lourandos, "Intensification and Australian Prehistory."

35. Morgan, *The Life and Adventures of William Buckley: Thirty-two Years a Wanderer Amongst the Aborigines.*

36. Warner, "Murngin Warfare."

37. Tabulated in Roper, "A Survey of the Evidence for Intrahuman Killing in the Pleistocene."

38. Giedion, *The Eternal Present: The Beginnings of Art;* Leroi-Gourhan, *The Art of Prehistoric Man in Western Europe.* See Clottes and Courtin, *The Cave Beneath the Sea: Paleolithic Images at Cosquer* for a nice summary of the evidence.

39. Wendorf, "Site 117: A Nubian Final Paleolithic Graveyard Near Jebel, Sahaba, Sudan"; Wendorf and Schild, "The Wadi Kubbaniya Skeleton: A Late Paleolithic Burial from Southern Egypt."

40. Frayer, "Ofnet: Evidence for a Mesolithic Massacre."

41. Frayer, "Ofnet: Evidence for a Mesolithic Massacre"; Vencl, "Interpretation des Blessures Causée par les Armes au Mésolithique"; Sandars, *Prehistoric Art in Europe.*

42. Chatters, "The Recovery and First Analysis of an Early Holocene Human Skeleton from Kennewick, Washington"; Jantz and Owsley, "Pathology, Taphonomy, and Cra-

nial Morphometrics of the Spirit Cave Mummy"; Owsley and Jantz, "Biography in the Bones."

43. Lambert, "Patterns of Violence in Prehistoric Hunter-Gatherer Societies of Coastal Southern California." We would expect that only a fraction of all deaths due to warfare would result in spear points still embedded in the skeleton. In the late prehistoric period, this number rose to more than 20 percent of all males with spear points in them. The spear could be pulled out to continue fighting and kinsmen would have removed some spears before the individual was buried. Only those points that broke off in the body were likely to be buried with the body.

Chapter Six: Conflict and Growth Among Tribal Farmers

1. Watson and LeBlanc, *Girikihaciyan: A Halaf Site in Southeastern Turkey.*
2. At least two other independent adoptions of agriculture took place: in the eastern United States and Africa, and most likely in highland New Guinea.
3. This growth potential can be unleashed in a variety of circumstances: farmers moving into new territories that were previously occupied only by foragers, or horticulturists moving into territories that were already occupied by farmers but where the initial farmers were decimated either by disease (as in much of the Americas) or by warfare (as in parts of South Africa), or were technologically much less well developed, or militarily weak (as in some of the invasions in Eurasia and parts of Africa during the Bantu expansion).
4. The archaeology of the Mimbres is summarized in LeBlanc, *The Mimbres People: Ancient Painters of the American Southwest*, Anyon and LeBlanc, *The Galaz Ruin: A Prehistoric Mimbres Village in Southwestern New Mexico.* The ecological story is presented in Minnis, *Social Adaptation to Food Stress: A Prehistoric Southwestern Example.* The survey data is in Blake, et al., "Changing Settlement Population in the Mimbres Valley, S.W. New Mexico." The Mimbres was not unique, and similar population cycles have been found in many places in the Southwest (Dean, "Demography, Environment, and Subsistence Stress"; Nelson, "Outposts of Mesoamerican Empire and Architectural Patterning at La Quemada, Zacatecas").
5. Redman, *Human Impact on Ancient Environments.*
6. Deliberately set forest fires probably had quite an impact on the vegetation of New England. But making the landscape more open was appealing both to the Indians, as it allowed for greater game populations and easier movement, and to the Europeans, as it was more like the open country they knew from Europe, which had been denuded by forest cutting and farming. Thus, while New England was not "natural" at first contact, it did not appear overexploited to the newly arrived Europeans as the Middle East did.
7. Bar-Yosef, "From Sedentary Foragers to Village Hierarchies: The Emergence of Social Institutions."
8. Cavalli-Sforza and Cavalli-Sforza, *The Great Human Diasporas: The History of Diversity and Evolution*; Renfrew, "Language Families and the Spread of Farming"; Bellwood, "An

Archaeologist's View of Language Microfamily Relationships" and "The Origins and Spread of Agriculture in the Indo-Pacific Region."

9. Bellwood, "Early Agriculturalist Population Diasporas? Farming, Languages, and Genes."

10. Bellwood, "An Archaeologist's View of Language Microfamily Relationships" and "The Origins and Spread of Agriculture in the Indo-Pacific Region"; Greenberg, *Language in the Americas.*

11. See Bellwood, "Early Agriculturalist Population Diasporas? Farming, Languages, and Genes," for a wonderfully worked out interpretation of this information.

12. Vayda, *Maori Warfare.*

13. Leahy, *Explorations into Highland New Guinea, 1930–1935.*

14. Meggitt, *Blood Is Their Argument,* provides a good example of this methodology.

15. Soltis, et al., "Can Group-Functional Behaviors Evolve by Cultural Group Selection? An Empirical Test."

16. Tierney, *Darkness in El Dorado;* Chagnon, "Yanomamo Social Organization and Warfare" and *Yanomamo: The Fierce People* and "Response to Ferguson" and "On Yanomamo Violence: Reply to Albert." Other early information in Peters, *Life Among the Yanomami;* and Ritchie, *Spirit of the Rainforest: A Yanomamo Shaman's Story.* There have been more scholarly disagreements with Chagnon; see Albert, "Yanomami 'Violence': Inclusive Fitness or Ethnographer's Representation"; Ferguson, "A Savage Encounter: Western Contact and the Yanomami War Complex" and *Yanomami Warfare: A Political History,* involving interpretation of the biological impacts of warfare.

17. Biocca, *The Yanoama: The Narrative of a White Girl Kidnapped by Amazonian Indians.*

18. Chagnon, *Studying the Yanomamo;* Early and Peters, *The Population Dynamics of the Mocajai Yanomamo,* give a somewhat lower estimate.

19. There is a substantial literature on the nature and causes of Yanomama warfare and its relationship to ecology, biology, changes in the density and nature of surrounding groups, etc. See Albert, "Yanomami 'Violence': Inclusive Fitness or Ethnographer's Representation"; Biocca, *The Yanomama: The Narrative of a White Girl Kidnapped by Amazonian Indians;* Chagnon, "Yanomamo Social Organization and Warfare" and "Is Reproductive Success Equal in Egalitarian Societies?" and "Life Histories, Blood Revenge, and Warfare in a Tribal Population" and "Response to Ferguson" and "On Yanomamo Violence: Reply to Albert" and "Reproduction and Somatic Conflicts of Interest: The Genesis of Violence and Warfare Among Tribesmen" and "Yanomamo: The Last Days of Eden"; Ferguson, "A Savage Encounter: Western Contact and the Yanomami War Complex" and *Yanomami Warfare: A Political History;* Harris, "The Yanomamo and the Causes of War in Band and Village Societies" and "Animal Capture and Yanomamo Warfare: Retrospect and New Evidence" and "A Cultural Materialist Theory of Band and Village Warfare: The Yanomamo Test"; Peters, *Life Among the Yanomami;* Ritchie, *Spirit of the Rainforest: A Yanomamo Shaman's Story;* Sponsel, "Yanomami: An Arena of Conflict and Aggression in the Amazon."

20. See Fagan, *Clash of Cultures,* for the impact of El Niños over history (but not this particular situation).

21. If we look at only males, where there was good skeletal preservation and the archaeologists did carefully recording, it jumps to about 30 percent of the sample.

22. Keeley, *War Before Civilization;* LeBlanc, *The Mimbres People: Ancient Painters of the American Southwest.*

Chapter Seven: Complex Societies

1. Earle et al., "Changing Settlement Patterns in the Upper Mantaro Valley, Peru."

2. Harris and Ross, *Death, Sex, and Fertility: Population Regulation in Preindustrial and Developing Societies;* Borton, *Peasant Uprisings in Japan of the Tokugawa Period.*

3. This process is described by Boserup, *Conditions of Agricultural Growth: The Economics of Agrarian Change Under Population Pressure.*

4. Being out of the tropics, the fish resources were not as substantial as other Polynesian islands, but they still existed.

5. Catton, "Carrying Capacity and the Death of a Culture: A Tale of Two Autopsies."

6. Martin and Klein, *Quarternary Extinctions: A Prehistoric Revolution.*

7. Fagan, *Clash of Cultures.*

8. I can find no case in which a chiefdom had rules for or against infanticide that were enforced by the elite.

9. Hansen, " 'Overlaying' in Nineteenth-Century England: Infant Mortality or Infanticide?"; Hrdy et al., "Infanticide: Let's Not Throw Out the Baby with the Bathwater"; Langer, "Checks on Population Growth: 1750–1850" and "Infanticide: A Historical Survey"; Rose, *The Massacre of the Innocents: Infanticide in Britain 1800–1939;* Hanley, "Marriage and Fertility in Japanese Villages."

10. Harris and Ross, *Death, Sex, and Fertility: Population Regulation in Preindustrial and Developing Societies.*

11. Fogel et al., "Secular Changes in American and British Stature and Nutrition."

12. Wilkinson, *Classical Attitudes to Modern Issues;* Strangeland, *Pre-Malthusian Doctrine of Population: A Study in the History of Economic Theory.*

13. Harris and Ross, *Death, Sex, and Fertility: Population Regulation in Preindustrial and Developing Societies.*

14. Polgar, "Population History and Population Policies from an Anthropological Perspective"; Wrigley, *Population and History;* Storey, "Estimates of Mortality in a Pre-Columbian Urban Population."

15. See Harris and Ross, *Death, Sex, and Fertility: Population Regulation in Preindustrial and Developing Societies,* for the complexities of the topic. See Langer, "Checks on Population Growth: 1750–1850," for a more general discussion of European population growth and constraints.

16. If population size remains stable for some time, and then rapidly increases when the food supply increases, this is evidence that the population was under considerable food stress initially and hence was at the carrying capacity.

17. Butzer and Freeman, *Early Hydraulic Civilization in Egypt.*

18. This interpretation is based on Kemp, *Ancient Egypt: Anatomy of a Civilization;* Scarre and Fagan, *Ancient Civilizations.* Other interpretations exist; see Wenke, "Egypt: Origins of Complex Societies" and "The Evolution of Early Egyptian Civilization: Issues and Evidence"; and Bard, "The Egyptian Predynastic: A Review of the Evidence" for overall summaries of the evidence and models.

19. Bell, "The Dark Ages in Ancient History: The First Dark Age in Egypt."

20. Marcus and Flannery, *Zapotec Civilization: How Urban Society Evolved in Mexico's Oaxaca Valley,* for an overview and other references.

21. Keeley, *War Before Civilization.*

22. Redmond, *Tribal and Chiefly Warfare in South America.*
23. Fowler, *The Cahokia Atlas: A Historical Atlas of Cahokia Archaeology;* Trubitt, "Mound Building and Prestige Goods Exchange: Changing Strategies in the Cahokia Chiefdom"; Demel and Hall, "The Mississippian Town Plan and Cultural Landscape of Cahokia, Illinois"; Anderson, "A Cahokia Palisade Sequence."
24. Wilson, "Reconstructing Patterns of Early Warfare in the Lower Santa Valley: New Data on the Role of Conflict in the Origins of Complex North Coast Society."
25. Webster, "Warfare and the Evolution of the State: A Reconsideration" and "Warfare and the Evolution of Maya Civilization" and "The Study of Maya Warfare: What It Tells Us About Maya Archaeology"; Schele and Miller, *The Blood of Kings: Dynasty and Ritual in Maya Art;* Demarest, "Interregional Conflict and 'Situational Ethics'" and "The Vanderbilt Petaxbatun Regional Archaeological Project 1989–1994: Overview, History, and Major Results of a Multidisciplinary Study of the Classic Maya Collapse."
26. Wheeler, *The Indus Civilization.*
27. The Indus flows from the Himalayas, a very active tectonic region. It is possible that uplift so changed the water flow regime that the society collapsed.
28. Keeley, *War Before Civilization.*
29. Fagan, *Floods, Famines, and Emperors: El Niño and the Fate of Civilizations.*

Chapter Eight: War or Peace for the Future?

1. Rushforth and Upham, *A Hopi Social History;* Titiev, *Old Orabi: A Study of the Hopi Indians of Third Mesa;* Whiteley, *Deliberate Acts: Changing Hopi Culture Through the Oraibi Split.*
2. A few studies summarize this hunt. David Fabbro, "Peaceful Societies: An Introduction," believed that he could find seven good cases of traditional peaceful societies— however, two of these (the Hutterites and the people of Tristan de Cunha) were really part of modern states and are not truly relevant. Bruce Knauft, "Melanesian Warfare: A Theoretical History" and "Violence and Sociality in Human Evolution," proposed another "peaceful" set of societies that consisted of very nearly the same groups, and on further reflection, Raymond Kelly, *Warless Societies and the Origin of War,* came up with three to eight examples of peaceful societies, depending on the criteria. (Does just a little warfare make you still peaceful?) For the most part, these three lists overlap, and a case has been made in the anthropological literature for only seven or so "peaceful" societies at best. See also Ember and Ember, "Resource Unpredictability, Mistrust, and War: A Cross-Cultural Study."
3. Some societies seem not to have warfare because life was so difficult. Examples include groups on the west coast of Tasmania, in the most desert areas of the Kalahari, and in central Australia, and the Copper Eskimo. Not all these societies were completely peaceful. For example, the Copper Eskimo claimed to be peaceful, but their neighbors to the east, the Neslilk Eskimo, said they fought with the Copper Eskimo who were considered treacherous. Moreover, the people neighboring these groups did have warfare, so the people of the west coast of Tasmania apparently did not have warfare, but the closely related people in other parts of Tasmania did. Similarly, the people of central Australia did not have as much conflict as those groups found along the more productive coasts, and those living in the middle of the Kalahari did not seem to have the level of conflict their relatives in other, better-watered places did.

4. Holmberg, *Nomads of the Long Bow: The Siriono of Eastern Bolivia;* Steward, *Handbook of South American Indians: Volume 3;* Isaac, "The Siriono of Eastern Bolivia." Edgerton, *Sick Societies: Challenging the Myth of Primitive Harmony,* claims the Siriono were hungry or starving most of the time. Another example might be the Tiwi of North Australia (Hart and Pilling, *The Tiwi of North Australia*). They are not noted for having warfare, but they were very capable of killing all foreigners before the mid-1800s. However, they had been subjected to slave raiding since the 1600s, and the acquisition of iron tools increased carrying capacity.

5. The Warrau were first described by Sir Walter Raleigh at the end of the sixteenth century, but really useful information came later; see Kirchoff, "The Warrau"; Wilbert, *Survivors of Eldorado: Four Indian Cultures of South America.*

6. Quoted in Ray, *The Sanpoil and Nespelem: Salishan Peoples of Northeastern Washington.* See also Teit, *The Middle Columbia Salish* and "The Salishan Tribes of the Western Plateaus"; Ross, *Adventures of the First Settlers on the Oregon or Columbia River, 1810–1813;* Miller, "Middle Columbia River Salishans."

7. There is considerable ethnographic and archaeological evidence for warfare among the social groups living on either side of the Plateau peoples, including the coastal people of western Washington, such as the Coast Salish, Makah, and Nootka. We find even more evidence for conflict, including forts, armor, population replacements, etc., among the somewhat more well known Kwakiutl, Haida, and Tlingit, who lived farther north along the coast (Moss and Erlandson, "Forts, Refuge Rocks, and Defensive Sites: The Antiquity of Warfare Along the North Pacific Coast of North America"). Maschner and Reedy-Maschner, "Raid, Retreat, Defend (Repeat): The Archaeology and Ethnohistory of Warfare on the North Pacific Rim." Just to the east of the Plateau, the very early account of a battle with hundreds of men involved was considered in Chapter 5. Even the Central Desert people to the south, such as the Paiute and the Shoshone, were not peaceful (D'Azevedo, *Handbook of North American Indians: Great Basin*).

8. A good summary of this information is provided by Chatters, "Pacifism and the Organization of Conflict on the Plateau of Northwestern North America," who although not the first to suggest the Plateau was not peaceful in the past, makes a really good case for it.

9. Another study also found evidence of violent death but problems with preservation did not allow for such detailed information. Even if these samples are somehow biased, this is a very high number of identifiable warfare deaths.

10. Edgerton, *Sick Societies: Challenging the Myth of Primitive Harmony,* discusses a number of cases of hatred of war and willingness for peace.

11. Again see Edgerton, *Sick Societies: Challenging the Myth of Primitive Harmony,* for a number of examples of peoples rapidly stopping warfare.

12. Kroeber and Fontana, *Massacre on the Gila.*

13. Mesquia and Wiener, "Human Collective Aggression: A Behavioral Ecology Perspective" and "Male Age Composition and Severity of Conflicts."

14. Boehm, Blood Revenge: *The Enactment and Management of Conflict in Montenegro and Other Nonliterate Societies* and "Emergency Decisions, Cultural-Selection Mechanics and Group Selection."

15. Examples of such deliberate decision making and control are presented or interpreted by Boehm, "Emergency Decisions, Cultural-Selection Mechanics and Group

Selection" for Montenegro; *Blood Revenge: The Enactment and Management of Conflict in Montenegro and Other Nonliterate Societies* for New Guinea and the East African Mursi.

16. It was not until the 1800s, with new technologies of food storage and better communications, that the size of armies grew much beyond what Ramses was able to do in the thirteenth century B.C.

17. Bernal Díaz and Andrés de Tápia, members of Cortés's army, methodically counted the skulls: "there were piles of human skulls so regularly arranged that one could count them, and I estimated them at more than a hundred thousand," and "The poles were separated from each other by a little less than a [yard], and were crowded with cross sticks from top to bottom, and on each cross stick were five skulls impaled through the temples: and the writer and a certain Gonzalo de Umbría, counted the cross sticks and multiplying by five heads per cross stick from pole to pole, as I said, we found that there were 136 thousand heads." *The True History of the Conquest of New Spain* written in 1568 by Bernal Diaz Del Castillo, and first published in 1632 and republished and translated numerous times.

18. United Nations Population Fund 2001.

LIST OF ILLUSTRATIONS

Dani people of Highland New Guinea. Copyright Film Study Center, Harvard
University. Courtesy of Robert Gardner   6

New Mexico's El Morro Valley. Photograph by Charles Lummis. Courtesy of the
Peabody Museum of Archaeology and Ethnology, Harvard University   11

Pile of bones from Iron Age fortified French town. Courtesy of Jean-Louis Brunaux   17

Highland New Guinea man on lookout tower. Copyright Film Study Center,
Harvard University. Courtesy of Robert Gardner   21

Samoan chief Sila and wife with grandchildren. Photograph by the author   27

Driving Herds of Buffalo over a Precipice, painted by Alfred Jacob Miller, 1867.
Courtesy of the National Archives of Canada (C-000403)   32

19th century engraving of Alpine Valley, artist unknown, c 1850   35

Bali rice terraces. Copyright Anthro-Photo File. Courtesy of Nancy S. DeVore   39

Woman twisting fiber "tube" containing ground manioc flour. Copyright
Anthro-Photo File. Courtesy of Nancy S. DeVore   44

Map of Troy. After Kraft, 1980   48

Posed attack upon a moa, Botanical Gardens, Dunedin. Courtesy of Alexander Turnbull
Library, Wellington, New Zealand (F-56038-1/2)   52

Map showing distribution of California Indian languages. Derived from
Moratto, 1984   58

Sling missiles. Photographs by the author, and Peabody Museum collections,
photograph by Hillel Burger. Copyright President and Fellows of Harvard
College. Courtesy of Peabody Museum of Archaeology and Ethnology,
Harvard University.   61

Skull bone from Krapina. Copyright David W. Frayer. Courtesy of David W. Frayer   65

Dani armor. Peabody Museum Collections, photograph by Hillel Burger.
Copyright President and Fellows of Harvard College. Courtesy of Peabody
Museum of Archaeology and Ethnology, Harvard University   70

Dead male chimpanzee. Copyright Martin N. Muller. Courtesy of
Martin N. Muller   88

!Kung woman and child. Copyright President and Fellows of Harvard College.
Courtesy of Marshall Collection, Peabody Museum of Archaeology and
Ethnology, Harvard University   103

Australian Aborigine cutting down tree. Anthro-Photo File. Courtesy of
Nancy S. Devore   108

Rock art battle scene. After Bleek, 1953   114

Wooden weapons. Peabody Museum Collections, photograph by Hillel Burger.
Copyright President and Fellows of Harvard College. Courtesy of Peabody
Museum of Archaeology and Ethnology, Harvard University.   120

Mimbres bowl. From LeBlanc, *Prehistoric Warfare in the American Southwest* 1999   130

Farming village of Ch'iang-chia. After Chang, 1963   133

Maori hilltop fort. Engraving by J. Newton, after Sydney Parkinson   136

Camel train passing Girikihaciyan, southeastern Turkey. Photograph by the author   140

Yanomama carrying spears. Anthro-Photo File. Courtesy of Nancy S. DeVore 144

Central Andes prehistoric hilltop site. Copyright Christine Hastorf. Courtesy of
Christine Hastorf   159

Maiden Castle. Courtesy of Asmolean Museum, University of Oxford   163

Tongan war canoes. Courtesy of Fiji Museum, Suva, Fiji Islands   168

Stone-walled enclosure ponds in Hawaii. Copyright Marshall Weisler. Courtesy
of Marshall Weisler   173

Cahokia Mounds State Historic Site, painting by William R. Iseminger. Courtesy
of William R. Iseminger   178

1700s etching of chief. From Le Page du Pratz, 1758   184

Cerro Sechin, Peru. Copyright Thomas B.F. Cummins. Courtesy of Thomas
Cummins   195

REFERENCES

Albert, B. 1989. Yanomami "Violence": Inclusive Fitness or Ethnographer's Representation. *Current Anthropology* 30:637–640.

Aleiss, A. 1999. Iron Eyes Cody: Wannabe Indian. *Cineaste* 25(1):31.

Alvard, M. S. 1993. Testing the "Ecologically Noble Savage" Hypothesis: Interspecific Prey Choice by Piro Hunters of Amazonian Peru. *Human Ecology* 21(4):355–387.

Anderson, D. G. 1994. *The Savannah River Chiefdoms: Political Change in the Late Prehistoric Southeast.* Tuscaloosa: University of Alabama Press.

Anderson, J. P. 1969. A Cahokia Palisade Sequence. In *Explorations into Cahokia Archaeology,* ed. M. L. Fowler, 89–99. Illinois Archaeological Survey, Inc., Bulletin No. 7. Urbana: University of Illinois Press.

Anyon, R., and S. A. LeBlanc. 1984. *The Galaz Ruin: A Prehistoric Mimbres Village in Southwestern New Mexico.* Albuquerque: University of New Mexico Press.

Arsuaga, J. L. 2000. The First Europeans: Spanish Caves Paint a New Picture of Evolution on the Continent. *Discovering Archaeology* 2(5):48–65.

Askenasy, H. 1994. *Cannibalism: From Sacrifice to Survival.* Amherst, N.Y.: Prometheus Books.

Balickci, A. 1967. Female Infanticide on the Arctic Coast. *Man* 2:615–625.

Bard, K. A. 1994. The Egyptian Predynastic: A Review of the Evidence. *Journal of Field Archaeology* 21:265–288.

Bar-Yosef, O. 2001. From Sedentary Foragers to Village Hierarchies: The Emergence of Social Institutions. *Proceedings of the British Academy* 110:1–38.

Bell, B. 1971. The Dark Ages in Ancient History: The First Dark Age in Egypt. *American Journal of Archaeology* 75:1–26.

Bellwood, P. 1994. An Archaeologist's View of Language Macrofamily Relationships. *Oceanic Linguistics* 33:391–406.

———. 1996. The Origins and Spread of Agriculture in the Indo-Pacific

Region. In *The Origins and Spread of Agriculture and Pastoralism in Eurasia*, ed. D. Harris, 465–498. London: UCL Press.

Bellwood, P. 2001. Early Agriculturalist Population Diasporas? Farming, Languages, and Genes. *Annual Review of Anthropology* 30:181–207.

Benfer, R. 1986. Holocene Coastal Adaptations: Changing Demography and Health at the Fog Oasis of Paloma, Peru, 5000–7800 B.P. In *Andean Archaeology: Papers in Memory of Clifford Evans*, ed. R. Matos M., S. A. Turpin, and H. H. Eling Jr. Monograph XXVII, 45–64. Los Angeles: Institute of Archaeology, University of California.

Berger, T. D., and E. Trinkaus. 1995. Patterns of Trauma Among the Neandertals. *Journal of Archaeological Science* 22:841–852.

Berger, W. H., and L. D. Labeyrie. 1987. *Abrupt Climate Change*. Boston: D. Reidel.

Bettinger, R. L. 1991. *Hunter-Gatherers: Archaeological and Evolutionary Theory*. New York: Plenum.

Bilby, J. W. 1926. *Nanook of the North: The Story of an Eskimo Family*. New York: Dodd, Mead and Company.

Binford, L. 1980. Willow Smoke and Dog's Tails: Hunter-Gatherer Settlement Systems and Archaeological Site Formation. *American Antiquity* 45:4–20.

Biocca, E. 1971. *The Yanoama: The Narrative of a White Girl Kidnapped by Amazonian Indians*. New York: Dutton.

Blake, M., S. A. Le Blanc, et al. 1986. Changing Settlement and Population in the Mimbres Valley, S.W. New Mexico. *Journal of Field Archaeology* 13(4):439–464.

Bleek, D. 1953. *Cave Artists of South Africa: 48 Unpublished Reproductions of Rock Paintings Collected by the Late Dorothea Bleek*. Capetown: A. A. Balkema.

Boehm, C. 1986. *Blood Revenge: The Enactment and Management of Conflict in Montenegro and Other Nonliterate Societies*. Philadelphia: University of Pennsylvania Press.

———. 1996. Emergency Decisions, Cultural-Selection Mechanics and Group Selection. *Current Anthropology* 17(5):763–793.

Boesch, C., and H. Boesch. 1999. *The Chimpanzees of the Taï Forest: Behavioral Ecology and Evolution*. New York: Oxford University Press.

Borrie, W. D., R. Firth, et al. 1957. The Population of Tikopia, 1929 and 1952. *Population Studies* 10:229–252.

Borton, H. 1968. *Peasant Uprisings in Japan of the Tokugawa Period*. New York: Paragon Book Reprint Corp.

Boserup, E. 1965. *Conditions of Agricultural Growth: The Economics of Agrarian Change Under Population Pressure*. Hawthorne, N.Y.: Aldine.

Brink, J., and B. Dawe. 1989. *Final Report of the 1985 and 1986 Field Seasons at Head-Smashed-In Buffalo Jump, Alberta.* Edmonton, Alberta, Canada: Archaeological Survey of Alberta, Alberta Culture and Multiculturalism, Historical Resources Division.

Brody, J. J. 1977. *Mimbres Painted Pottery.* Albuquerque: University of New Mexico Press.

Brody, J. J., C. J. Scott, et al. 1983. *Mimbres Pottery: Ancient Art of the American Southwest.* New York: Hudson Hills Press.

Brown, P., and D. Tuzin. 1983. *The Ethnography of Cannibalism.* Washington, D.C.: Society for Psychological Anthropology.

Browne, D. M., H. Silverman, et al. 1993. A Cache of 48 Nasca Trophy Heads from Cerro Carapo, Peru. *Latin American Antiquity* 4(3):274–294.

Brunaux, J.-L. 2001. Gallic Blood. *Archaeology* 54(2):54–56.

Bryson, R. A., and T. Murray. 1977. *Climates of Hunger: Mankind and the World's Changing Climate.* Madison: University of Wisconsin Press.

Burch, E. S., Jr. 1974. Eskimo Warfare in Northwest Alaska. *Anthropological Papers of the University of Alaska* 16(2):1–14.

Burney, D. A. 1997. Tropical Islands as Paleoecological Laboratories: Gauging the Consequences of Human Arrival. *Human Ecology* 25(3):437–457.

Butzer, K., and L. G. Freeman, eds. 1976. *Early Hydraulic Civilization in Egypt.* Chicago: University of Chicago Press.

Cashdan, E. A. 1985. Natural Fertility, Birth Spacing, and the "First Demographic Transition." *American Anthropologist* 87(3):650–653.

Catlin, G. 1973. *Letters and Notes on the Manners, Customs, and Conditions of the North American Indians.* New York: Dover.

Catton, W. R., Jr. 1993. Carrying Capacity and the Death of a Culture: A Tale of Two Autopsies. *Sociological Inquiry* 63(2):200–223.

Cavalli-Sforza, L. L., and F. Cavalli-Sforza. 1995. *The Great Human Diasporas: The History of Diversity and Evolution.* Reading, Mass.: Addison-Wesley.

Chagnon, N. A. 1968. Yanomamo Social Organization and Warfare. In *War: The Anthropology of Armed Conflict and Aggression,* ed. M. Fried, M. Harris, and R. Murphy, 109–159. New York: Natural History Press.

———. 1968. *Yanomamo: The Fierce People.* New York: Holt, Rinehart and Winston.

———. 1974. *Studying the Yanomamo.* New York: Holt, Rinehart and Winston.

———. 1979. Is Reproductive Success Equal in Egalitarian Societies? In *Evolutionary Biology and Human Social Behavior: An Anthropological Perspective,* ed. N. A. Chagnon and W. Irons, 86–132. North Scituate, Mass.: Duxbury Press.

Chagnon, N.A. 1988. Life Histories, Blood Revenge, and Warfare in a Tribal Population. *Science* 239:985–992.

———. 1989. Response to Ferguson. *American Ethnologist* 16:565–570.

———. 1990. On Yanomamö Violence: Reply to Albert. *Current Anthropology* 31:49–53.

———. 1990. Reproduction and Somatic Conflicts of Interest: The Genesis of Violence and Warfare Among Tribesmen. In *The Anthropology of War*, ed. J. Haas, 77–104. Cambridge: Cambridge University Press.

———. 1992. Yanomamö: The Last Days of Eden. New York: Harcourt Brace Jovanovich.

Chang, K.-c. 1986. *The Archaeology of Ancient China*. 4th ed. New Haven, Conn.: Yale University Press.

Chapman, C.A., and R.W. Wrangham. 1993. Range Use of the Forest Chimpanzees of Kibale: Implications for the Understanding of Chimpanzee Social Organization. *American Journal of Primatology* 31:263–273.

Chapman, J. 1988. Putting Pressures on Population: Social Alternatives to Malthus and Boserup. In *Conceptual Issues in Environmental Archaeology*, ed. J.L. Bintliff, D.A. Davidson, and E.G. Grant, 291–310. Edinburgh: Edinburgh University Press.

Chatters, J.C. 1989. Pacifism and the Organization of Conflict on the Plateau of Northwestern North America. In *Cultures in Conflict: Current Archaeological Perspectives*, ed. D.C. Tkaczuk and B.C. Vivian, 241–252. Proceedings of the Twentieth Annual Conference of the Archaeological Association of the University of Calgary.

———. 2000. The Recovery and First Analysis of an Early Holocene Human Skeleton from Kennewick, Washington. *American Antiquity* 65:291–316.

Clark, C. 1967. *Population Growth and Land Use*. New York: St. Martin's Press.

Clarkson, L.A. 1981. Irish Population Revisited, 1687–1821. In *Irish Population, Economy, and Society: Essays in Honour of the Late K. H. Connell*. Oxford: Clarendon Press.

Clottes, J., and J. Courtin. 1996. *The Cave Beneath the Sea: Paleolithic Images at Cosquer*. New York: H.N. Abrams.

Cole, S.J. 1993. Basketmaker Rock Art at the Green Mask Site, Southeastern Utah. In *Anasazi Basketmaker: Papers from the 1990 Wetherill–Grand Gulch Symposium*, ed. V.M. Atkins, 193–222. Salt Lake City: Bureau of Land Management.

Cooper, L.D. 1999. *Rousseau, Pasture, and the Problem of the Good Life*. University Park: Pennsylvania State University Press.

Cowlishaw, G. 1978. Infanticide in Aboriginal Australia. *Oceania* 48:262–263.

Crabtree, P. J., D. Campana, et al., eds. 1989. *Early Animal Domestication and Its Cultural Context*. Philadelphia: MASCA, the University Museum of Archaeology and Anthropology.

Cranston, M. 1988. *Rousseau: Selections*. New York: Macmillan.

Darwin, C. 1997 [1871]. *The Descent of Man*. Amherst, N.Y.: Prometheus Books.

D'Azevedo, W. L., ed. 1986. *Handbook of North American Indians: Great Basin*. Washington, D.C.: Smithsonian Institution.

Dean, J. S. 1996. Demography, Environment, and Subsistence Stress. In *Evolving Complexity and Environmental Risk in the Prehistoric Southwest*, ed. J. Tainter and B. B. Tainter, 25–26. Reading, Mass.: Addison-Wesley.

Defleur, A., T. White, et al. 1999. Neanderthal Cannibalism at Moula Guercy, Ardeche, France. *Science* 286:128–131.

De Laguna, F., and C. McClellan. 1981. Ahtna. In *Subarctic*, pp. 641–663. Vol. 6 of *Handbook of North American Indians*, ed. J. Helm. Washington, D.C.: Smithsonian Institution.

Demarest, A. A. 1978. Interregional Conflict and "Situational Ethics." In *Classic Maya Warfare. Codex Wauchope: Festschrift in Honor of Robert Wauchope*, ed. M. Giardino, B. Edmonson, and W. Creamer, 101–111. New Orleans: Tulane University.

———. 1997. The Vanderbilt Petexbatun Regional Archaeological Project 1989–1994: Overview, History, and Major Results of a Multidisciplinary Study of the Classic Maya Collapse. *Ancient Mesoamerica* 8(2):209–227.

Demarest, A. A., M. O'Mansky, et al. 1997. Classic Maya Defensive Systems and Warfare in the Petexbatun Region: Archaeological Evidence and Interpretations. *Ancient Mesoamerica* 8(2):229–253.

Demel, S. J., and R. L. Hall. 1998. The Mississippian Town Plan and Cultural Landscape of Cahokia, Illinois. In *Mississippian Towns and Sacred Places: Searching for an Architectural Grammar*, ed. R. B. Lewis and C. Stout, 200–226. Tuscaloosa and London: University of Alabama Press.

Denbow, J. R. 1984. Prehistoric Herders and Foragers of the Kalahari: The Evidence for 1500 Years of Interaction. In *Past and Present in Hunter Gatherer Studies*, ed. C. Schrire, 175–193. Orlando, Fla.: Academic Press.

Denevan, W. M. 1976. *The Native Population of the Americas in 1492*. Madison: University of Wisconsin Press.

———. 1992. The Pristine Myth: The Landscape of the Americas in 1492. In *The Americas Before and After Columbus: Current Geographical Research*, ed. K. W. Butzer.

DePratter, C. B. 1991. *Late Prehistoric and Early Historic Chiefdoms in the South-eastern United States*. New York: Garland Publishing.

Dewar, R. 1984. Environmental Productivity, Population Regulation, and Carrying Capacity. *American Anthropologist* 86(3):601–614.

Diamond, J. M. 1997. *Guns, Germs, and Steel: The Fates of Human Societies*. New York: W. W. Norton.

Donnan, C. B. 1976. *Moche Art and Iconography*. Los Angeles: UCLA Latin American Center, University of California.

Dornstreich, M. D., and G. E. B. Morren. 1974. Does New Guinea Cannibalism Have Nutritional Value? *Human Ecology* 2(1):1–11.

Dunsworth, H. M., J. H. Challis, et al. In press. *Throwing and Bipedalism: A New Look at an Old Idea*. Frankfurt: Courier Forschungsinstitut Senckenberg.

D'urville, M. D., 1835. *Voyage Pittoresque Autour du Monde: Resume General Des Voyages de Decouvertes*. Vol. 2. Paris: L. Tenré et H. Dupuy.

Earle, T. K., T. D'Altroy, et al. 1980. Changing Settlement Patterns in the Upper Mantaro Valley, Peru. *Journal of New World Archeology* 4(1):1–49.

Early, J., and J. Peters. 1990. *The Population Dynamics of the Mucajai Yanomamo*. New York: Academic Press.

Edgerton, R. B. 1992. *Sick Societies: Challenging the Myth of Primitive Harmony*. New York: Free Press.

Ehrlich, P. R., A. H. Ehrlich, et al. 1995. *The Stork and the Plow: The Equity Answer to the Human Dilemma*. New York: G. P. Putman's Sons.

Eibl-Eibesfeldt, I. 1975. Aggression in the !Ko-Bushmen. In *War: Its Causes and Correlates*, ed. M. A. Nettleship, R. D. Givens, and A. Nettleship, 281–296. The Hague: Mouton.

Ember, C. R., and M. Ember. 1992. Resource Unpredictability, Mistrust, and War: A Cross-Cultural Study. *Journal of Conflict Resolution* 36(2):242–262.

Fabbro, D. 1978. Peaceful Societies: An Introduction. *Journal of Peace Research* 15:67–83.

Fagan, B. M. 1998. *Clash of Cultures*. Walnut Creek, Calif.: Altamira Press.

———. 1999. *Floods, Famines, and Emperors: El Niño and the Fate of Civilizations*. New York: Basic Books.

Ferguson, R. B. 1992. A Savage Encounter: Western Contact and the Yanomami War Complex. In *War in the Tribal Zone: Expanding States and Indigenous Warfare*, ed. R. B. Ferguson and N. L. Whitehead, 199–227. Santa Fe: School of American Research Press.

———. 1995. *Yanomami Warfare: A Political History*. Santa Fe: School of American Research Press.

Fernandez-Jalvo, Y., J.C. Diez, et al. 1999. Human Cannibalism in the Early Pleistocene of Europe. *Journal of Human Evolution* 37:591–622.

Firth, R. 1936. *We, the Tikopia*. London: George Allen and Unwin.

———. 1959. *Social Change in Tikopia*. New York: Macmillan.

———. 1961. History and Traditions of Tikopia. *Polynesian Society Memoir 33*.

Fogel, R.W. et al. 1983. Secular Changes in American and British Stature and Nutrition. In *Hunger and History: The Impact of Changing Food Production and Consumption Patterns on Society*, ed. R.I. Rotberg and T.K. Rabb, 247–284. Cambridge: Cambridge University Press.

Fowler, M.L. 1997. *The Cahokia Atlas: A Historical Atlas of Cahokia Archaeology*. Urbana: Illinois Transportation Archaeological Research Program, University of Illinois.

Frayer, D.W. 1997. Ofnet: Evidence for a Mesolithic Massacre. In *Troubled Times: Violence and Warfare in the Past*, ed. D.L. Martin and D.W. Frayer, 181–216. Amsterdam: Gordon and Breach.

Freeman, M. 1971. A Social and Ecological Analysis of Systematic Female Infanticide Among the Netsilik Eskimo. *American Anthropologist* 73:1101–1118.

Galloway, P.R. 1986. Longterm Fluctuations in Climate and Population in the Preindustrial Era. *Population and Development Review* 12:1–24.

Giedion, S. 1962. *The Eternal Present: The Beginnings of Art*. New York: Pantheon Books.

Glassow, M.A. 1996. *Purisimeno Chumash Prehistory: Maritime Adaptations Along the Southern California Coast*. Fort Worth: Harcourt Brace.

Glennie, G.D. 1983. Replication of an A.D. 800 Anasazi Pithouse in Southwestern Colorado. Pullman: Washington State University Press.

Goble, P. 1992. *Crow Chief*. New York: Orchard Books.

Godwin, P. 2001. Bushmen: Last Stand for Southern Africa's First People. *National Geographic* 199 (February): 90–117.

Goodall, J. 2000. *Africa in My Blood: An Autobiography in Letters: The Early Years*. Boston: Houghton Mifflin.

Gopher, E. 1998. Early Pottery-Bearing Groups in Israel—The Pottery Neolithic. In *The Archaeology of Society in the Holy Land*, ed. T.E. Levy, 205–221. London: Leicester University Press.

Gordon, R.J. 1984. The !Kung in the Kalahari Exchange: An Ethnohistorical Perspective. In *Past and Present in Hunter Gatherer Studies*, ed. C. Schrire, 195–224. Orlando, Fla.: Academic Press.

Greenberg, J. 1987. *Language in the Americas*. Stanford: Stanford University Press.

Grove, J. 1990. *The Little Ice Age.* London: Routledge.

Hanley, S. B. 1977. Marriage and Fertility in Japanese Villages. In *Population Patterns in the Past,* ed. R. D. Lee. San Diego: Academic Press.

Hansen, E. d. R. 1979. "Overlaying" in Nineteenth-Century England: Infant Mortality or Infanticide? *Human Ecology* 7(4):333–352.

Harris, M. 1979. The Yanomamö and the Causes of War in Band and Village Societies. In *Brazil: Anthropological Perspectives,* ed. M. L. Margolis and W. E. Carter, 121–133. New York: Columbia University Press.

———. 1984. Animal Capture and Yanomamo Warfare: Retrospect and New Evidence. *Journal of Anthropological Research* 40:183–201.

———. 1984. A Cultural Materialist Theory of Band and Village Warfare: The Yanomamo Test. In *Warfare, Culture, and Environment,* ed. R. B. Ferguson, 111–140. New York: Academic Press.

Harris, M., and E. B. Ross. 1987. *Death, Sex, and Fertility: Population Regulation in Preindustrial and Developing Societies.* New York: Columbia University Press.

Harrold, F. B. 1980. A Comparative Analysis of Eurasian Paleolithic Burials. *World Archaeology* 12(2):195–211.

Hart, C. W. M., and A. R. Pilling. 1960. *The Tiwi of North Australia.* New York: Holt, Rinehart and Winston.

Hassan, F. 1975. Determination of the Size, Density, and Growth Rate of Hunting-Gathering Populations. In *Population, Ecology, and Social Evolution,* ed. S. Polgar, 27–52. The Hague: Mouton.

Hausfater, G., and S. Blaffer Hrdy, eds. 1984. *Infanticide: Comparative and Evolutionary Perspectives.* Hawthorne, N.Y.: Aldine de Gruyter.

Haviland, W. 1967. Stature at Tikal: Implications for Ancient Maya Demography and Social Organization. *American Antiquity* 32:316–325.

Headland, T. N., and L. A. Reid. 1989. Holocene Foragers and Interethnic Trade: A Critique of the Myths of Isolated Independent Hunter-Gatherers. In *Between Lands and State: Interaction in Small-Scale Societies,* ed. S. Gregg, 333–340. Carbondale: Southern Illinois Press.

Heidenreich, C. E. 1978. Huron. In *Handbook of North American Indians,* ed. B. G. Trigger, 15:368–388. Washington, D.C.: Smithsonian Press.

Hill, K., C. Boesch, et al. 2001. Mortality Rates Among Wild Chimpanzees. *Journal of Human Evolution* 40:437–450.

Hill, K., and A. M. Hurtado. 1995. *Ache Life History: The Ecology and Demography of a Foraging People.* Hawthorne, N.Y.: Aldine de Gruyter.

Hill, K., and H. Kaplan. 1999. Life History Traits in Humans: Theory and Empirical Studies. *Annual Review of Anthropology* 28:397–430.

Hodell, D. A., J. H. Curtis, et al. 1995. Possible Role of Climate in the Collapse of the Classic Maya Civilization. *Nature* 375:391–394.

Hollimon, S. E., and D. W. Owsley. 1994. Osteology of the Fay Tolton Site: Implications for Warfare During the Initial Middle Missouri Variant. In *Skeletal Biology in the Great Plains: Migration, Warfare, Health, and Subsistence*, ed. D. W. Owsley and R. L. Jantz, 345–353. Washington, D.C.: Smithsonian Institution Press.

Holmberg, A. R. 1950. *Nomads of the Long Bow: The Siriono of Eastern Bolivia*. Washington, D.C.: U.S. Government Printing Office.

Horowitz, A. 1987. *Rousseau, Nature, and History*. Toronto: University of Toronto Press.

Howard, J., and J. C. Janetski. 1992. Human Scalps from Eastern Utah. *Utah Archaeology* 5(1):125–132.

Hrdy, S. B., C. Janson, et al. 1995. Infanticide: Let's Not Throw Out the Baby with the Bathwater. *Evolutionary Anthropology* 3:151–154.

Hurst, W. B., and C. G. Turner II. 1993. Rediscovering the "Great Discovery": Wetherill's First Cave 7 and Its Record of Basketmaker Violence. In *Anasazi Basketmaker: Papers from the 1990 Wetherill–Grand Gulch Symposium*, ed. V. M. Atkins, 143–191. Salt Lake City: Bureau of Land Management.

Ingram, M. J., G. Farmer, et al. 1981. Past Climates and Their Impact on Man: A Review. In *Climate and History: Studies in Past Climates and Their Impact on Man*, ed. T. M. L. Wigley, M. J. Ingram, and G. Farmer, 3–50. Cambridge: Cambridge University Press.

Isaac, B. 1977. The Sirionó of Eastern Bolivia: A Reexamination. *Human Ecology* 5:137–154.

———. 1987. Throwing and Human Evolution. *The African Archaeological Review* 5(3–17).

Jantz, R. L., and D. W. Owsley. 1997. Pathology, Taphonomy, and Cranial Morphometrics of the Spirit Cave Mummy. *Nevada Historical Society Quarterly* 40:62–84.

Johnson, A. W., and T. K. Earle. 1987. *The Evolution of Human Societies from Foraging Group to Agrarian State*. Stanford: Stanford University Press.

Keeley, L. H. 1996. *War Before Civilization*. New York and Oxford: Oxford University Press.

Kelly, R. C. 2000. *Warless Societies and the Origin of War*. Ann Arbor: University of Michigan Press.

Kelly, R. L. 1995. *The Foraging Spectrum: Diversity in Hunter-Gatherer Lifeways*. Washington, D.C.: Smithsonian Institution Press.

Kemp, B. 1989. *Ancient Egypt: Anatomy of a Civilization*. London and New York: Routledge.

Keys, D. 1999. *Catastrophe: An Investigation into the Origins of the Modern World*. London: Century.

Kidder, A. V., and S. J. Guernsey. 1919. *Archaeological Explorations in North-eastern Arizona.* Washington, D.C.: Government Printing Office.

Kirch, P. V. 1984. *The Evolution of Polynesian Chiefdoms.* Cambridge: Cambridge University Press.

Kirchoff, P. 1948. The Warrau. In *Handbook of South American Indians: The Tropical Forest Tribes,* ed. J. H. Steward, 3: 869–881. Washington, D.C.: United States Printing Office.

Kirkbride, D. 1982. Umm Dabaghiyah. In *Fifty Years of Mesopotamian Discovery,* 11–21. London: British School of Archaeology in Iraq.

Klein, R. G. 1992. The Impact of Early People on the Environment: The Case of Large Mammal Extinctions. In *Human Impact on the Environment: Ancient Roots, Current Challenges,* ed. J. E. Jacobsen and J. Firor, 13–34. Boulder, Colo.: Westview Press.

Klima, B. 1997. *Pavlov I—Northwest: The Upper Paleolithic Burial and Its Settlement Context.* Brno: Academy of Sciences of the Czech Republic, Institute of Archaeology.

Knauft, B. M. 1990. Melanesian Warfare: A Theoretical History. *Oceania* 60(4):250–311.

———. 1991. Violence and Sociality in Human Evolution. *Current Anthropology* 32:391–428.

Knuckey, G. 1992. Patterns of Fracture upon Aboriginal Crania from the Recent Past. *Proceedings of the Australasian Society for Human Biology* 5:47–58.

Kraft, J. C., I. Kayani, and O. Erol. 1980. Geomorphic Reconstructions in the Environs of Ancient Troy. *Science* 209:776–782.

Krech, S. I. 1999. *The Ecological Indian: Myth and History.* New York: W. W. Norton.

Kroeber, C. B., and B. L. Fontana. 1986. *Massacre on the Gila: An Account of the Last Major Battle Between American Indians, with Reflections on the Origin of War.* Tucson: University of Arizona Press.

Lamb, H. H. 1988. *Weather, Climate and Human Affairs.* London: Routledge.

———. 1995. *Climate, History and the Modern World.* London: Routledge.

Lambert, P. M. 1997. Patterns of Violence in Prehistoric Hunter-Gatherer Societies of Coastal Southern California. In *Troubled Times: Violence and Warfare in the Past,* ed. D. L. Martin and D. W. Frayer, 77–110. Amsterdam: Gordon and Breach.

Landcaster, J. B., H. S. Kaplan, et al. 1999. The Evolution of Life History, Intelligence, and Diet Among Chimpanzees and Human Foragers. In *Evolution, Culture, and Behavior: Perspectives in Ethnology,* ed. F. Tonneau and N. S. Thompson. Vol. 13. New York: Plenum.

Langer, W. L. 1972. Checks on Population Growth: 1750–1850. *Scientific American* Feb:92–99.

———. 1974. Infanticide: A Historical Survey. *History of Childhood Quarterly* 1:353–365.

Leahy, M. J. 1991. *Explorations into Highland New Guinea, 1930–1935*, ed. D. E. Jones. Tuscaloosa: University of Alabama Press.

LeBlanc, S. A. 1983. *The Mimbres People: Ancient Painters of the American Southwest*. London: Thames and Hudson.

———. 1999. *Prehistoric Warfare in the American Southwest*. Salt Lake City: University of Utah Press.

———. 2001. Warfare and Aggregation in the El Morro Valley, New Mexico. In *Deadly Landscapes: Case Studies in Prehistoric Southwestern Warfare*, ed. G. E. Rice and S. A. LeBlanc, 19–49. Salt Lake City: University of Utah Press.

Lee, R. B. 1965. *Subsistence Ecology of !Kung Bushmen*. Berkeley: Department of Anthropology, University of California, Berkeley.

Lee, R. B., and R. H. Daly, eds. 1999. *The Cambridge Encyclopedia of Hunters and Gatherers*. Cambridge: Cambridge University Press.

Lee, R. B., and I. DeVore. 1976. *Kalahari Hunter-Gatherers: Studies of the !Kung San and Their Neighbors*. Cambridge, Mass.: Harvard University Press.

Le Page du Pratz, A. S. 1758. *Histoire de la Louisiane*. Paris.

Leroi-Gourhan, A. 1968. *The Art of Prehistoric Man in Western Europe*. London: Thames and Hudson.

Le Roy Ladurie, E. 1971. *Times of Feast, Times of Famine: A History of Climate Since the Year 1000*. New York: Noonday Press.

Lourandos, H. 1985. Intensification and Australian Prehistory. In *Prehistoric Hunter-Gatherers: The Emergence of Cultural Complexity*, ed. T. D. Price and J. A. Brown, 385–423. Orlando, Fla.: Academic Press.

McNeil, W. H. 1976. *Plagues and Peoples*. Garden City, N.Y.: Anchor Press/Doubleday.

Malotki, E. 1993. The Destruction of Awat'ovi. In *Hopi Ruin Legends*, ed. M. Lomatuway'ma, L. Lomatuway'ma, and S. Namingha, Jr., 275–297. Lincoln: University of Nebraska Press.

Malouf, C., and S. Conner. 1962. *Symposium on Buffalo Jumps*. Missoula: Montana Archaeological Society.

Malthus, T. R. 1959. *Population: The First Essay*. Ann Arbor: University of Michigan Press.

Manson, J., and R. Wrangham. 1991. Intergroup Aggression in Chimpanzees and Humans. *Current Anthropology* 32:369–390.

Marcus, J., and K. V. Flannery. 1996. *Zapotec Civilization: How Urban Society Evolved in Mexico's Oaxaca Valley.* New York: Thames and Hudson.

Martin, P. S., and R. G. Klein, eds. 1984. *Quaternary Extinctions: A Prehistoric Revolution.* Tucson: University of Arizona Press.

Maschner, H. D. G., and K. L. Reedy-Maschner. 1997. Raid, Retreat, Defend (Repeat): The Archaeology and Ethnohistory of Warfare on the North Pacific Rim. *Journal of Anthropological Archaeology* 17:19–51.

Meggitt, M. J. 1977. *Blood Is Their Argument.* Palo Alto, Calif.: Mayfield.

Melbye, J., and S. I. Fairgreive. 1994. A Massacre and Possible Cannibalism in the Canadian Arctic: New Evidence from the Saunaktuk Site (NgTn-1). *Arctic Anthropology* 31(2):57–77.

Mesquia, C. G., and N. I. Wiener. 1996. Human Collective Aggression: A Behavioral Ecology Perspective. *Ethnology and Sociobiology* 17:247–262.

———. 1999. Male Age Composition and Severity of Conflicts. *Politics and the Life Sciences* 18(2):181–189.

Miller, J. 1998. Middle Columbia River Salishans. *Handbook of North American Indians: Plateau,* ed. D. E. Walker, Jr., 12:253–270. Washington, D.C.: Smithsonian Institution.

Minnis, P. E. 1985. *Social Adaptation to Food Stress: A Prehistoric Southwestern Example.* Chicago: University of Chicago Press.

Moratto, M. J. 1984. *California Archaeology.* Orlando, Fla.: Academic Press.

Morgan, J. 1979 [1852]. *The Life and Adventures of William Buckley: Thirty-two Years a Wanderer Amongst the Aborigines.* Canberra: Australia National University Press.

Moss, M. L., and J. M. Erlandson. 1992. Forts, Refuge Rocks, and Defensive Sites: The Antiquity of Warfare Along the North Pacific Coast of North America. *Arctic Anthropology* 29(2):73–90.

Nelson, B. A. 1994. Outposts of Mesoamerican Empire and Architectural Patterning at La Quemada, Zacatecas. In *Culture and Contact: Charles C. Di Peso's Gran Chichimeca,* ed. A. I. Woosley and J. C. Ravesloot, 173–190. Albuquerque: University of New Mexico Press.

Nishida, T. 1994. Review of Recent Findings on Mahale Chimpanzees: Implications and Future Research Directions. In *Chimpanzee Cultures,* ed. R. Wrangham, W. C. McGrew, F. B. M. de Waal, and P. G. Heltne. Cambridge, Mass.: Harvard University Press.

Owsley, D. W., and R. L. Jantz. 2000. Biography in the Bones. *Discovering Archaeology* 2(1):56–58.

Owsley, D. W., R. W. Mann, et al. 1994. Culturally Modified Human Bones from the Edwards I Site. In *Skeletal Biology in the Great Plains: Migration, Warfare, Health, and Subsistence,* ed. D. W. Owsley and R. L. Jantz, 363–375. Washington, D.C.: Smithsonian Institution Press.

Palter, J. 1999. Slinging Spears: Recent Evidence on Flexible Shaft Spear Throwers. *Society for American Archaeology Newsletter* 17(2):2, 3, 16.

Parkington, J. E. 1984. Soaqua and Bushmen: Hunters and Robbers. In *Past and Present in Hunter Gatherer Studies*, ed. C. Schrire, 151–174. Orlando, Fla.: Academic Press.

Peters, J. F. 1998. *Life Among the Yanomami*. Peterborough, Ont.: Broadview Press.

Pijoan, C. M., and J. M. Lory. 1997. Evidence for Human Sacrifice, Bone Modification, and Cannibalism in Ancient Mexico. In *Troubled Times: Violence and Warfare in the Past*, ed. D. L. Martin and D. W. Frayer, 217–239. Amsterdam: Gordon and Breach.

Polgar, S. 1972. Population History and Population Policies from an Anthropological Perspective. *Current Anthropology* 13:203–209.

Price, T. D., and J. A. Brown, eds. 1985. *Prehistoric Hunter-Gatherers: The Emergence of Cultural Complexity*. New York: Academic Press.

Price, T. D., A. B. Gebrauer, et al. 1995. The Spread of Farming into Europe North of the Alps. In *Last Hunters—First Farmers: New Perspectives on the Prehistoric Transition to Agriculture*, ed. T. D. Price and A. B. Gebrauer, 95–126. Santa Fe: School of American Research Press.

Pringle, H. 1998. Crow Creek's Revenge. *Science* 279:2039.

Proulix, D. A. 1989. Nasca Trophy Heads: Victims of Warfare or Ritual Sacrifice? In *Cultures in Conflict: Current Archaeological Perspectives*, ed. D. C. Tkaczuk and B. C. Vivian, 73–85. Proceedings of the Twentieth Annual Conference of the Archaeological Association of the University of Calgary.

Ramenofsky, A. F. 1987. *Vectors of Death: The Archaeology of European Contact*. Albuquerque: University of New Mexico Press.

Rappaport, R. 1967. *Pigs for Ancestors*. New Haven, Conn.: Yale University Press.

———. 1977. Ecology, Adaptation, and the Ills of Functionalism. *Michigan Discussions in Anthropology* 2:161.

Ray, V. F. 1933. *The Sanpoil and Nespelem: Salishan Peoples of Northeastern Washington*. Seattle: University of Washington Press.

Read, D., and S. A. LeBlanc. n.d. Population Growth, Carrying Capacity, and Conflict. Paper submitted to *Current Anthropology*.

Redman, C. L. 1999. *Human Impact on Ancient Environments*. Tucson: University of Arizona Press.

Redmond, E. M. 1994. *Tribal and Chiefly Warfare in South America*. Studies in Latin American Ethnohistory and Archaeology, vol. 5. Ann Arbor: Museum of Anthropology, University of Michigan.

Renfrew, C. 1996. Language Families and the Spread of Farming. In *The*

Origins and Spread of Agriculture and Pastoralism in Eurasia, ed. D. Harris, 70–92. London: UCL Press, 70–92.

Ritchie, M. A. 1996. *Spirit of the Rainforest: A Yanomamo Shaman's Story*. Chicago: Island Lake Press.

Roper, M. A. 1996. A Survey of the Evidence for Intrahuman Killing in the Pleistocene. *Current Anthropology* 10:427–459.

Rose, L. 1986. *The Massacre of the Innocents: Infanticide in Britain 1800–1939*. London: Routledge and Kegan Paul.

Ross, A. 1904. *Adventures of the First Settlers on the Oregon or Columbia River, 1810–1813*. Cleveland: Arthur H. Clark.

Rotha, P. 1980. Nanook and the North. *Studies in Visual Communication* 6(2):34–60.

Rushforth, S., and S. Upham. 1992. *A Hopi Social History*. Austin: University of Texas Press.

Sandars, N. K. 1985. *Prehistoric Art in Europe*. Harmondsworth, England: Penguin Books.

Scarre, C. 1999. *The Seventy Wonders of the Ancient World: The Great Monuments and How They Were Built*. London, New York: Thames and Hudson.

Scarre, C., and B. M. Fagan. 1997. *Ancient Civilizations*. New York: Longman.

Schapera, I. 1930. *The Khoisan Peoples of South Africa: Bushmen and Hottentots*. London: George Routledge and Sons.

Schele, L., and M. E. Miller. 1986. *The Blood of Kings: Dynasty and Ritual in Maya Art*. New York: G. Braziller.

Schrire, C. 1980. An Inquiry into the Evolutionary Status and Apparent Identity of San Hunter-Gatherers. *Human Ecology* 8:9–32.

Service, E. R. 1962. *Primitive Social Organization: An Evolutionary Perspective*. New York: Random House.

Shafer, H. J. 1995. Architecture and Symbolism in Transitional Pueblo Development in the Mimbres Valley, SW New Mexico. *Journal of Field Archaeology* 22(1):23–47.

Shreeve, J. 1995. *The Neandertal Enigma: Solving the Mystery of Modern Human Origins*. New York: William Morrow.

Sladek, V. 2000. *The People of the Pavlovian: Skeletal Catalogue and Osteometrics of the Gravettian Fossil Hominids from Dolni Vestonice and Pavlov*. Brno: Academy of Sciences of the Czech Republic, Institute of Archaeology.

Soltis, J., R. Boyd, et al. 1995. Can Group-Functional Behaviors Evolve by Cultural Group Selection? An Empirical Test. *Current Anthropology* 36:473–494.

Sothers, R. B. 1984. The Great Tambora Eruption of 1815 and Its Aftermath. *Science* 224:1191–1198.

Sponsel, L. E. 1998. Yanomami: An Arena of Conflict and Aggression in the Amazon. *Aggressive Behavior* 24:97–122.

Stern, J. T., and R. L. Susman. 1983. The Locomotor Anatomy of Australopithecus Afarensis. *American Journal of Physical Anthropology* 60(3):279–317.

Steward, J. H., ed. 1948. *Handbook of South American Indians.* Vol. 3. Bureau of American Ethnology, Smithsonian Institution. Washington, D.C.: United States Government Printing Office.

Stiner, M. C., N. D. Munro, et al. 2000. The Tortoise and the Hare: Small-Game Use, Broad-Spectrum Revolution, and Paleolithic Demography. *Current Anthropology* 41(1):39–74.

Stone, L. 1966. Social Mobility in England, 1500–1700. *Past and Present* 33:16–55.

Storey, R. 1985. Estimates of Mortality in a Pre-Columbian Urban Population. *American Anthropologist* 87:519–535.

Strangeland, C. 1966 [1904]. *Pre-Malthusian Doctrine of Population: A Study in the History of Economic Theory.* New York: Augustus M. Kelley.

Sugiyama, S. 1989. Burials Dedicated to the Old Temple of Quetzalcoatl at Teotihuacan, Mexico. *American Antiquity* 54(1):85–106.

———. 1993. Worldview Materialized in Teotihuacan, Mexico. *Latin American Antiquity* 4(2):103–129.

Surovell, T. A. 2000. Early Paleoindian Women, Children, Mobility, and Fertility. *American Antiquity* 65:493–508.

Tacon, P. S. C., and C. Chipppendale. 1994. Australia's Ancient Warriors: Changing Depictions of Fighting in the Rock Art of Arnhem Land, N.T. *Cambridge Archaeological Journal* 4(2):221–248.

Tannahill, R. 1975. *Flesh and Blood: A History of the Cannibal Complex.* New York: Stein and Day.

Tattersall, I. 1993. Madagascar's Lemurs. In *Scientific American* 268 (January):110–117.

Taylour, L. W. 1983. *The Mycenaeans.* London: Thames and Hudson.

Teit, J. A. 1928. *The Middle Columbia Salish.* Seattle: University of Washington Press.

———. 1930. The Salishan Tribes of the Western Plateaus. In *45th Annual Report of the Bureau of American Ethnology for 1927–1928*, ed. F. Boas, 23–396. Washington, D.C.: Government Printing Office.

Thieme, H. 1997. Lower Paleolithic Hunting Spears from Germany. *Nature* 385:807.

Thomas, W. L., ed. 1956. *Man's Role in Changing the Face of the Earth.* Chicago: University of Chicago Press.

Tierney, P. 2000. *Darkness in El Dorado*. New York: W. W. Norton.

Titiev, M. 1944. *Old Orabi: A Study of the Hopi Indians of Third Mesa*. Cambridge, Mass.: Harvard University Press.

Topic, J. R. 1989. The Ostra Site: The Earliest Fortified Site in the New World? In *Cultures in Conflict: Archaeological Perspectives*, ed. D. C. Tkaczuk and B. C. Vivian, 215–228. Proceedings of the Twentieth Annual Chacmool Conference, Archaeological Association of the University of Calgary.

Trubitt, M. B. D. 2000. Mound Building and Prestige Goods Exchange: Changing Strategies in the Cahokia Chiefdom. *American Antiquity* 65(4):669–690.

Turnbull, C. M. 1961. *The Forest People*. New York: Simon and Schuster.

United Nations Population Fund. 2001. *The State of World Population 2001*. New York: United Nations Publications.

Vayda, A. P. 1960. *Maori Warfare*. Wellington, New Zealand: The Polynesian Society.

Vencl, S. 1991. Interpretation des Blessures Causée par les Armes au Mésolithique. *L'Anthropologie* 95(1):219–228.

Verbicky-Todd, E. 1984. *Communal Buffalo Hunting Among the Plains Indians: An Ethnographic and Historic Review*. Edmonton: Alberta Culture, Historical Resources Division.

Villa, P. 1992. Cannibalism in Prehistoric Europe. *Evolutionary Anthropology* 1(3):93–104.

Wagley, C. 1969. Cultural Influences on Population: A Comparison of Two Tupi Tribes. In *Environment and Cultural Behavior: Ecological Studies in Cultural Anthropology*, ed. A. P. Vayda, 268–280. Garden City, N.Y.: Natural History Press.

Walker, P. L. 1990. *Appendix 5: Tool Marks on Human Bone from Saunaktuk*. Yellowknife, NWT: Prince of Wales Northern Heritage Center.

Walker, P. L., and B. S. Hewlett. 1990. Dental Health, Diet, and Social Status Among Central African Foragers and Farmers. *American Anthropologist* 92:383–398.

Warner, W. L. 1931. Murngin Warfare. *Oceania* 1:457–494.

Washburn, W. E. 1978. Seventeenth-Century Indian Wars. In *Handbook of North American Indians: Northeast*, ed. B. G. Trigger, 15: 89–100. Washington, D.C.: Smithsonian Institution.

Watson, P. J., and S. A. LeBlanc. 1990. *Girikihaciyan: A Halaf Site in Southeastern Turkey*. Los Angeles: Institute of Archaeology, University of California.

Watson, P. J., S. A. LeBlanc, et al. 1980. Aspects of Zuni Prehistory: Preliminary Report on Excavations and Survey in the El Morro Valley of New Mexico. *Journal of Field Archaeology* 7:201–218.

Webster, D. 1975. Warfare and the Evolution of the State: A Reconsideration. *American Antiquity* 40:464–470.

———. 1977. Warfare and the Evolution of Maya Civilization. In *The Origins of Maya Civilization*, ed. R. E. W. Adams, 335–371. Albuquerque: University of New Mexico Press.

———. 1993. The Study of Maya Warfare: What It Tells Us About the Maya and What It Tells Us About Maya Archaeology. In *Lowland Maya Civilization in the Eighth Century A.D.*, ed. J. A. Sabloff and J. S. Henderson, 415–444. Washington, D.C.: Dumbarton Oaks.

———. 1998. Warfare and Status Rivalry: Lowland Maya and Polynesian Comparisons. In *Archaic States*, ed. G. M. Feinman and J. Marcus, 311–351. Santa Fe: School of American Research.

Wendorf, F. 1968. Site 117: A Nubian Final Paleolithic Graveyard Near Jebel Sahaba, Sudan. In *Prehistory of Nubia*, ed. F. Wendorf. Vol. 2, 954–995. Dallas: Southern Methodist University Press.

Wendorf, F., and R. Schild. 1986. The Wadi Kubbaniya Skeleton: A Late Paleolithic Burial from Southern Egypt. In *The Prehistory of Wadi Kubbaniya*, ed. A. Close. Dallas: Southern Methodist University Press.

Wenke, R. J. 1989. Egypt: Origins of Complex Societies. *Annual Review of Anthropology* 18:129–155.

———. 1991. The Evolution of Early Egyptian Civilization: Issues and Evidence. *Journal of World Prehistory* 5:279–329.

Wheat, J. B. 1972. The Olsen-Chubbuck Site: A Paleo-Indian Bison Kill. *American Antiquity* 37(1, part 2).

Wheeler, S. M. 1968. *The Indus Civilization.* Supplementary volume to *The Cambridge History of India.* Cambridge: Cambridge University Press.

White, T. D. 1968. Cut Marks on the Bodo Cranium: A Case of Prehistoric Defleshing. *American Journal of Physical Anthropology* 69:503–511.

White, T. D., and N. Toth. 1991. The Question of Ritual Cannibalism at Grotta Guattari. *Current Anthropology* 32:118–138.

Whiteley, P. M. 1988. *Deliberate Acts: Changing Hopi Culture Through the Oraibi Split.* Tucson: University of Arizona Press.

Wigley, T. M. L., M. J. Ingram, et al., eds. 1981. *Climate and History: Studies in Past Climates and Their Impact on Man.* Cambridge: Cambridge University Press.

Wilbert, J. 1972. *Survivors of Eldorado: Four Indian Cultures of South America.* New York: Praeger.

Wilcox, D. R., and J. Haas. 1994. The Scream of the Butterfly: Competition and Conflict in the Prehistoric Southwest. In *Themes in Southwest Prehistory*, ed. G. J. Gumerman, 211–238. Santa Fe: School of American Press.

Wilkie, D. S., and B. Curran. 1993. Historical Trends in Forager and Farmer Exchange in the Ituri Rain Forest of Northeastern Zaire. *Human Ecology* 21(4):389–417.

Wilkinson, L. P. 1979. *Classical Attitudes to Modern Issues.* London: William Kimber.

Willey, P. 1990. *Prehistoric Warfare on the Great Plains: Skeletal Analysis of the Crow Creek Massacre Victims.* New York: Garland Publishing.

Williams, E. 1987. Complex Hunter-Gatherers: A View from Australia. *Antiquity* 61:310–321.

Wilson, D. 1987. Reconstructing Patterns of Early Warfare in the Lower Santa Valley: New Data on the Role of Conflict in the Origins of Complex North Coast Society. In *The Origins and Development of the Andean State,* ed. J. Haas, S. Pozorski, and T. Pozorski, 56–69. Cambridge: Cambridge University Press.

Wood, J. W. 1994. *Dynamics of Human Reproduction: Biology, Biometry, Demography.* New York: Aldine de Gruyer.

Woodburn, J. 1968. An Introduction to Hadza Ecology. In *Man the Hunter,* ed. R. B. Lee and I. De Vore, 49–55. Chicago: Aldine.

Wrangham, R. W., 1996. The Evolution of Coalitionary Killing. *Yearbook of Physical Anthropology* 42:1–30.

Wrangham, R. W., W. C. McGrew, et al., eds. 1994. *Chimpanzee Cultures.* Cambridge, Mass.: Harvard University Press.

Wrangham, R. W., and D. Peterson. 1996. *Demonic Males: Apes and the Origins of Human Violence.* Boston: Houghton Mifflin.

Wrangham, R. W., and D. Pilbeam. 2002. Apes as Time Machines. In *African Apes.* Vol. I of *All Apes Great and Small,* ed. B. M. F. Galdikas, N. Briggs, L. K. Sheeran, G. L. Shapiro, and J. Goodall, 5–18. New York: Kluwer Academic/Plenum Publishers.

Wrigley, E. A. 1969. *Population and History.* New York: McGraw-Hill.

Wrigley, E. A., and R. S. Schofield. 1981. *The Population History of England 1541–1871: A Reconstruction.* London: Edward Arnold.

INDEX

Aborigines
  Buckley on, 114–15, 122–23
  and climate, 8
  as foragers, 104, 105, 108
  infanticide, 49
  myth of peacefulness, 58, 120–21
  as noble savages, 13
  tools, 119–20, 121
  warfare among, 119–23
  weapons, 63, 121
abortion, 53
Acropolis (Greece), 5, 173–74
Aegean region, 10–11, 12, 172–74
Afghanistan, 215–16
Africa, 212, 217, 222
aggression, 73, 78, 220–22
agriculture. *See* farming
Alexander the Great, 67, 214
Al Qaeda, 215
altruistic behavior, 221
Amazonia, 203
ambush, 57, 67, 127, 224
American Indians. *See* Native Americans
Anasazi people, 1–2
Anatolia, 142, 143
ancient states, 161–62, 174, 192
Andes mountains, 157
animals, 41, 104, 129, 138, 172
anthropology, 7, 19, 20
archaeology, 1, 4, 7–8, 10, 19, 20, 56, 58, 106
Arctic regions, 28, 117–19
armor, 63, 70, 117
Athapaskan Indians, 118
Australia, 119, 120, 122
  See also Aborigines
Australopithecines, 79, 87, 94

Austronesian language family, 146
Awatovi (prehistoric town), 199–201

Bali, 39, 40
Balkan region, 212, 213, 222
bands, 103–4, 164, 181, 186
Bantu speakers, 106–7, 115–16, 145, 146
bastions, 61–62, 178, 190
battleaxe, 4
bin Laden, Osama, 215
biology, 19, 42
bipedalism, 78
birth rate, 177, 227
birth spacing, 45, 102, 109, 113
blood chemistry, 220–21
bones, 17, 60, 65, 95
bonobos, 80, 84, 86, 91
boomerangs, 121
boreholes, 110
brain, 95
breadfruit, 38
breast-feeding, 48
Buckley, William, 114, 122–23
buffalo, 14, 18, 19, 29–30, 32, 63
buffer zones, 140, 155, 169, 210–11, 217
Burch, Ernest, 67, 117–18
bureaucracy, 162
burial, 63–64, 96, 115, 124, 125, 204
burning, 62
Bushmen, 35, 58, 103–5, 107, 114–16, 201, 207

Cahokia (Ill.), 178, 189–90
California, 58, 136–37, 145, 153, 154
camels, 140
cannibalism, 34, 53, 60–61, 65, 95, 97
canoes, 168, 188

Caribbean islands, 34
carrying capacity
    and climate in prehistoric Southwest, 148
    and environment, 38–45, 47, 50, 51,
        53–54, 69, 74
    and myth of peaceful past, 76
    and neighbors, 72
    and population growth, 166–67, 227
    and warfare, 147
Casas Grandes (Mex.), 148
catastrophes. *See* natural disasters
Cauca people, 189
cave art. *See* rock art
caves, 100–101
Cave 7 (Utah), 64
Cerro Carapo (Peru), 59
Cerro Sechín (Peru), 195
Chaco Canyon (Mex.), 148
Chagnon, Napoleon, 68, 151–52
change, 42, 207, 232n.13
chiefdoms
    earliest, 160
    elites in, 166, 184, 226
    food transport in, 170
    hilltop fortresses, 163
    infanticide in, 175
    leaders in, 159, 160
    modern, 216–17, 218
    Nile River, 182
    population growth in, 197
    social structure, 158, 184
    warfare in, 161, 167, 185, 187–91, 195
children, 46, 72, 102, 132, 133, 156, 177,
    178
chimpanzees, 77–86
    field studies, 80–81, 108
    food, 80–81, 85
    human parallels, 82–83, 99
    hunting, 81, 84, 90
    infanticide, 82
    intelligence, 83, 85–86
    killings, 78
    population, 82, 85
    sexual dimorphism, 92
    warfare, 7, 81–83, 85–86, 88, 94, 220,
        222
    See also bonobos
China, 32, 50, 62, 129, 133, 176, 191–92,
    194, 219
cholera, 50
Churchill, Winston, 67
cities, 177–78, 191, 197, 227
civilization, 6–7, 14
climate, 26, 42–43, 53, 69, 73, 135, 141,
    148–49, 153–54, 232n.14
coevolution, 78–80, 94, 97

Cold War, 196
Comanche Indians, 57
common chimps. *See* chimpanzees
competition, 19, 73, 92, 98, 160, 212, 223
complex societies, 157–98, 213–15, 223,
    224, 226
conflict, 55–76
conservation
    and ecological balance, 25–26, 29–31, 37
    impact of world economies, 32–33
    inherent, 9–10, 25–26, 28, 69, 85
    lack of, 33–34, 36–37
    and technology, 138
cooperation, 73, 131
Copper Eskimos, 201, 202, 241n.3
copper tools, 4
corn, 129, 139
Cro-Magnon man, 124, 225
crops, 39–40, 149, 170
Crow Creek burial site, 64
crying, 221

Daily, Gretchen, 109
Dani people, 6, 155
Darwin, Charles, 45
Dead Birds (film), 205
decapitation, 59, 125, 130
defensive sites, 1–2, 56, 61–62, 124, 142,
    178, 204
    See also forts and fortresses; *specific sites*
demographic change, 23–24
De Soto, Hernando, 188–89, 190
DeVore, Irven, 36, 107, 110
Diamond, Jared, 6
diet. *See* food
disease, 50, 70, 71, 72, 85
dogs, 93–94, 118
Dolní Vestonice (Czech.), 124
Dust Bowl (U.S.), 42

Earle, Tim, 190
Easter Island, 170–71
East Timor, 217
ecological balance, 24, 74
    in Aegean, 174
    in complex societies, 164, 175
    and conservationist behavior, 25–26,
        29–31, 37
    as elusive, 225
    from external factors, 207
    among foragers, 113
    requirements for, 53
ecological imbalance, 69, 73
ecological stress, 31, 69, 212
ecology, 27, 229
    of chimpanzees, 84

human, 24–25
island situations, 34–35
and warfare, 9–22
See also ecological balance
egalitarian societies, 102–3, 131, 163–64
Egypt, 162, 166, 174, 182–83, 186, 194, 223
Ehrlich, Paul and Anne, 109
elephants, 27, 31–32, 45, 46, 172
elites, 158–59, 166, 176, 180, 184, 187, 194, 226
El Morro Valley (N.M.), 1–3, 11, 58, 69
El Niño, 153–54, 174–75
empathy, 3–4
empty zones, 62
England, 42, 43, 47, 48, 61, 175
environment
carrying capacity, 38–45, 47, 50, 51, 53–54, 69, 74
changes in, 54, 73, 74, 112, 129
in complex societies, 169–70, 174
degradation of, 12, 25–26, 28, 48, 53, 129, 171, 192, 197, 226–28
difficult, 105–6
and farming, 224, 225–26
humans' impact on, 32–34, 138
humans' relation to, 24–25
and Native Americans, 15–16
"natural," 26–28
pristine, 228, 229
See also ecological balance; ecology
epidemics, 50–51
Eric the Red, 33
Eskimos, 8, 17, 49, 63, 67, 71, 104, 105, 113, 117–19, 201, 202
ethnography, 7, 8, 10, 66, 105
extinction, 18–19, 26, 28, 30, 34, 52, 172

Fagan, Brian, 174
family size, 132
famine, 43, 149, 166, 178–79
farmers of wilds, 104
farmer warfare, 6, 150–56
farming, 109, 127, 238n.3
and carrying capacity, 39–40
English, 47
and environment, 224, 225–26
in Middle East, 209
and natural resources, 212
optimal method of, 169–70
overexploitation in, 41
as recent human invention, 103
tribal, 127–56, 207
Fertile Crescent (Turkey), 128
feuding, 57, 122, 197
field studies, 80–81, 105, 108

"fierce people," 57–58, 205
Fiji, 188, 190
fire, 27, 89, 93
First World War, 15, 67, 196, 213
fishing, 31, 40, 91, 153
fish traps, 165
fish weirs, 122
Flaherty, Robert, 17
Flannery, Kent, 183
food, 13, 14, 53
of chimpanzees, 80–81, 85
and climate, 43
in complex societies, 166–67
distribution, 112
in foraging societies, 102, 108, 110, 112
hunting for, 90
and population growth, 46–47
processing, 110
as scarce resource, 9, 19
sharing, 91, 221
shortage, 37–38, 41, 44–47, 69, 110, 208
storage, 129–30
stress, 69–70, 73, 110
transport, 170
foragers and foraging, 29, 80, 100–127, 204, 215
Fore people, 60
forts and fortresses, 2, 11, 56, 61, 136, 157, 163, 174, 184–85, 190–91
fossils, 65, 95
foundling hospitals, 49
France, 166, 180
friend-enemy relationships, 68
fur seals, 136–37
fur trade, 31

Gebusi people, 201, 202
gender, 220–21
genetic selection, 220–21
geology, 42
Germany, 146, 213
glaciers, 43
global warming, 42
Goodall, Jane, 7, 77, 80, 81, 83, 85, 108
grain, 47, 129–30
Grand Valley Dani: Peaceful Warriors (Heider), 151
gray whale, 45–46, 172
great auk, 172
Great Wall of China, 5, 61, 167
Greenland, 33, 149
group size, 98
guerrilla warfare, 167–68, 212
Guns, Germs, and Steel (Diamond), 6

Hadrian's Wall, 61, 167
Hadza people, 35–36, 104

Harappan civilization, 192–93
Harris, Marvin, 177
Hatunmarca site (Peru), 157, 158
Hawaii, 34, 165, 173, 188, 190
health, 72, 149
Heider, Carl, 150–51
Herero people, 115–16
Herodotus, 60
hilltop sites. *See* defensive sites; forts and
　　fortresses; *specific sites*
Hitler, Adolf, 215
Homberg, Allan, 203
Homer, 10, 48, 162
homicide, 57, 202
Homo erectus, 79, 93, 95
Hopi Indians, 54, 65, 158, 199–201, 206,
　　207, 222
horses, 40
human ecology, 24–25
Human Ecology (journal), 36
human sacrifice, 64
hunger, 71
hunter-gatherers. *See* foragers and foraging
hunting, 98, 132
　　chimpanzee, 81, 84, 90
　　large game, 90–91
　　net, 112
　　and optimal-foraging model, 29
　　and warfare, 90–91
　　Yanomama, 33
Huron Indians, 61
hurricanes, 24, 38
Hussein, Saddam, 215
Hutterites, 45, 46, 133

Ice Age, 42
Iceland, 33, 149
Ice Man. *See* Ötzi
ideology, 219
India, 164, 217, 219
Indians, American. *See* Native Americans
Indonesia, 217
Industrial Revolution, 159, 178, 198,
　　227–29
infanticide, 48–49, 53, 82, 113, 117, 175–76
infant mortality, 46, 110
information, 215
ingenuity, 41
inherent conservation, 9–10, 25–26, 28, 69,
　　85
intelligence, 79, 83–86, 89, 97–99, 127, 225
intergroup conflict, 98, 127, 208, 222, 224
Ireland, 178–79
iron, 220
Iron Age, 17, 61, 191
islands, 34–35, 172, 173

isolation, 72, 173, 203
ivory trade, 31

Japan, 49, 134, 176, 179–80, 213

kachinas, 200
Kadesh, battle of, 223
Kalahari Desert, 107, 108, 110, 241–42n.3
Keeley, Lawrence, 8, 154
Kennewick Man, 126
Khoisan speakers, 107
"killed man" motif, 125
Kinboko Canyon (Ariz.), 59
King Philip's War, 18
Knossos, palace of (Crete), 162, 173
Krapina site (Yugo.), 97
!Kung people, 35, 36, 103–16, 201, 222
Kuwait, 215

land, 19, 154, 213
language, 58, 89, 145–46
Laws of Hammurabi, 162
leadership, 161–62, 164, 180–82, 214, 215
Leakey, Louis, 79, 80
Lee, Richard, 107, 110
Levant, 40, 141
lions, 92
Little Ice Age, 43, 149, 154, 206, 228
London (England), 177
Lucy (Australopithecine), 79, 87

maces, 142
Madagascar, 34
Maiden Castle (England), 163, 191
male dominance, 85–86, 220
malnutrition, 226
Malthus, Thomas, 233–34n.28
manioc root, 44
manuports, 87–89
Maori people, 52, 61, 136, 172, 187
Marcus, Joyce, 183
Maricopa people, 210–11, 213, 215
Maring people, 25
marriage, 48, 110, 165, 176–77
massacre, 67–68, 125, 127, 148
Maya civilization, 30, 31, 64, 163, 166, 174,
　　192
Mead, Margaret, 66
Medieval Warm Period, 43, 148–49, 154
Melanesia, 49, 53
Merriam's elk, 172
Mesa Verde cliff dwellings, 148
Mesoamerica, 129, 139, 183–84, 192
Mesolithic period, 125–26
Mesopotamia, 162, 163, 194, 213
Mesquida, Christian, 211

Mexico, 129, 139, 219, 223
Middle East, 139, 142, 143, 160, 192, 194, 196, 209, 213, 222, 223
Mimbres Valley (N.M.), 55, 69, 130, 134–37, 141, 147
Minoan culture, 162, 173
miscalculation, 215, 216
Mississippian Culture, 189
moa, 52, 172
Moche people, 64, 175
Mohenjo-Daro, 192
monkeys, 81, 84
Monte Alban (Mex.), 184–85
Murngin people, 123, 127
Mycenaean culture, 162, 173–74

Nanook of the North (film), 17
Napoleonic wars, 193–94
nation-states, 216–19
Native Americans
    and buffalo, 14, 18–19, 29–30
    chiefdom warfare, 188–89
    and environment, 15–16
    guerrilla warfare, 167
    horses, 40
    impact of European politics, 32
    as noble savages, 13–14, 16, 18
    of Plateau region, 203–5
    shellfish, 153
    See also specific tribes
natural disasters, 24, 38, 51, 70, 71
natural resources, 13, 14–15, 212
Neandertals, 79–80, 95–98, 124
neighbors, 72, 73
Neolithic revolution, 129
net hunting, 112
New England, 18, 139, 238–39n.6
New Guinea
    alliances in, 213
    armor in, 63
    boom-and-bust cycle, 76
    cannibalism in, 60
    ecology of valleys, 33
    languages, 145
    lookout towers, 21
    Maring people, 25
    "peaceful society," 202, 205
    raids in, 68
    sweet potato, 40
    tribal farmers, 6, 207
    warfare in, 6, 57, 72, 150–51
New Zealand, 52, 61, 136, 172
Nile River, 182–83
noble savage, 12–13, 16, 18, 74, 76, 104, 113, 229, 231n.11
no-man's-land, 140, 154, 210

North America, 126, 139, 149, 164, 188–89
nutrition, 31, 60

Oaxaca (Mex.), 184–85
Ofnet site (Bavaria), 125
one-child policy, 50
optimal foraging, 29
oral traditions, 65–66, 201
Ostra site (Peru), 88–89
Ötzi (Ice Man), 3, 4
overexploitation, 30–33, 35–36, 41, 112, 211
overgrazing, 10–11, 12, 26, 41, 137, 163, 169
overlaying, 49, 176

Pacific islands, 51
Paiute people, 36, 104
parry fractures, 60
peaceful societies, 199–207, 222, 224–25, 241nn.2–3
Peru, 61, 64, 94, 157, 159, 190, 192, 219, 223
Pilgrims, 17–18
Pima Indians, 210, 213
pitched battles, 67, 123
plague, 50, 206
Plains Indians, 14, 29–30, 40
plants, 13, 14, 41, 104
plasticity, 41
Plateau region (N. Amer.), 203–5, 207
Poland, 194
Polynesia, 38, 49, 176, 187–88, 207, 222
population
    chimpanzee, 82, 84
    control, 53, 71, 87, 109, 119, 134, 167
    of farmers, 132
    in Mimbres Valley, 135–36
    and natural disasters, 51
    size, 26, 51, 73–74
    of Southwest, 148, 149
    stable, 49, 51, 112
    See also population growth
population growth, 10, 23–24, 25
    by rapid reproduction, 45, 46, 133–34
    and carrying capacity, 166–67, 227
    in chiefdoms and states, 197
    and climate, 149
    and Irish potato famine, 178–79
    Malthus on, 233–34n.29
    outgrowing environment, 37
    regulation of, 47, 50
    and resources, 38, 42, 148, 169
    in Tikopia, 53
potatoes, 178–79
pottery, 55, 64
poverty, 211, 212

predators, 84, 87, 89, 93, 97–98
pristine states, 161
protohumans, 77–99, 225
pseudo-conservationist behaviors, 28
psychological warfare, 223–24
public works, 165, 169
Pueblo Indians, 148, 222
pueblos, 62
Pygmies, 112, 201
pyramids, 178, 189

rabbits, 135
raids, 67, 68, 81, 118, 127
Ramses II, 223
religion, 131, 160
reproductive rate, 45–47, 112–13, 133–34
resource stress, 69, 71, 116, 169
rock art, 5, 64, 116, 121–22, 124–25, 127, 148
rock throwing, 77, 87–89
Roggeveen, Jacob, 171
Ross, Eric, 177
Rousseau, Jean-Jacques, 12
Russia, 194, 213, 215

Samoa, 23, 27, 38, 66–67, 160, 161, 165, 188, 191, 218
San speakers, 106–7, 114, 115, 116
savanna, 86–87
scalping, 59, 60
Scandinavia, 206
seals, 136–37
Second World War, 15, 67, 68, 186, 194, 196, 213
sedentary-egalitarian societies, 131
sexual dimorphism, 92–93
sexual specialization, 92
Shanidar Cave (Iraq), 59, 96
shellfish, 153
shields, 63, 115, 120, 121
Sioux Indians, 40
Siriono people, 201, 202–3
site clusters, 62
skeletons, 59, 95, 122, 126, 154
Skhul IX, 59, 96
sling missiles, 61, 63, 142
social classes, 158–59
social practices/mechanisms, 25, 180
Somalia, 216
South America, 33, 44, 113, 129, 189
Southwest (U.S.), 1, 3, 8, 30, 31, 56, 60, 62, 69, 72, 134, 147–49, 199
spears, 89, 126, 144, 238n.43
spear-throwers, 121
spices, 32
Stalin, Josef, 214

starvation, 38, 69–70, 72, 73, 85, 166–67, 176, 226
states, 158, 159, 161–62, 166, 170, 186, 191–93, 197
Sudan, 125, 127
survival of fittest, 75
sustainability, 26, 149
sweet potato, 40

tactics, 67
Taliban, 215–16
Tambora volcano, 42
taxation, 162
technology, 26, 41, 53, 110, 138, 164, 203, 226, 227
Teotihuacán (Mex.), 64, 189, 194
terraces, 39, 40, 165
territoriality, 82
terrorism, 212, 224
throwing-stones, 87–89
Tierney, Patrick, 151
Tikopia island, 51–53, 68
Tongans, 168, 188
tools
    Aborigines,' 119–20, 121
    coevolution of use with intelligence, 79, 89, 97
    copper, 4
    farming, 130
    of foragers, 101–2
    for hunting, 90, 91
    of protohumans, 79, 89, 90, 91, 95
    Warraus,' 203
traits, 79, 89, 221
trees, 128–29, 137–38, 140
tribal farmers, 6, 128–56, 207, 215, 218
tribal warfare, 6, 147–56, 186, 195–96
tribes, 130–31, 164, 181
trophy heads, 59–60, 127
tropical foraging, 106
Troy (Hisarlik), 10–11, 48
Turkey, 62, 128, 140, 141–42, 143
turtle shells, 112
typhoons. *See* hurricanes

Upper Paleolithic period, 124–25

Victoria (Australia), 122
Vikings, 33, 149, 163, 174, 175, 206, 207, 222

walled cities, 191
Wampanoag Indian village, 18
Wanka people, 157, 158
warfare
    and carrying capacity, 147
    in chiefdoms, 161, 167, 185, 187–91, 195

chimpanzee, 7, 81–83, 85–86, 88, 94, 220, 222
in complex societies, 157–98, 213–15, 223, 224
definition of, 56–57
and ecology, 1–22
as emotionally charged, 212
evidence of, 7–8, 58–61, 63, 69, 205
farmer, 6, 150–56
among foragers, 113–27
guerrilla, 167–68
Hopi, 201
and hunting, 90–91
ideological, 219
and leadership, 181
miscalculation in, 215, 216
"modern," 194–96, 199, 212–16
motivation for, 207–10
Neandertal, 96–97
in New Guinea, 6, 57, 72, 150–51
and population control, 71, 119
prehistoric and protohuman, 56, 77–99, 157, 205
psychological, 223–24
as result of imbalance with nature, 24
return of enemy after, 186–87
sanitizing of, 5
scarce resources as cause of, 9, 12, 71
"senseless," 209, 211

state-level, 186, 191–93
throughout history, 3, 8–9, 78, 219–20
in Tikopia, 68
tribal, 6, 147–56, 186, 195–96
Yanomama, 151–53
warlords, 216–17
Warner, Lloyd, 123
Warrau (Warao) people, 202, 203, 207
warriors, 181, 201
water control systems, 40
weapons, 62–63, 91
Western Samoa. *See* Samoa
Wiener, Neil, 211
Wilson, David, 191
witchcraft, 177
women, 71, 110, 176–77, 208, 220
World War I. *See* First World War
World War II. *See* Second World War
Wrangham, Richard, 77, 78, 85–86, 220
writing, 7, 191

Yanomama people, 33, 44, 57, 58, 68, 144, 151–53, 155, 205–6
Yugoslavia, 217
Yuman people, 210–11, 213

Zapotec civilization, 185
Zulu people, 115, 168, 187
Zuni Indians, 54, 200